CREATIVE RE-USE OF BUILDINGS

VOLUME ONE

Principles and Practice

CREATIVE RE-USE OF BUILDINGS

VOLUME ONE

Principles and Practice

DEREK LATHAM

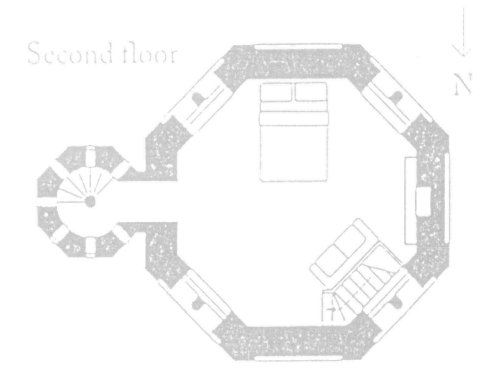

DONHEAD

First published in the United Kingdom in 2000 by
Donhead Publishing Ltd
Lower Coombe
Donhead St Mary
Shaftesbury
Dorset SP7 9LY
Tel. 01747 828422

ISBN 1 873394 36 5

A CIP catalogue record for this book is available from the British Library

Composition by Scribe Design, Gillingham, Kent
Printed by The Bath Press, Bath

General caveat
The details illustrated in this book were designed for a specific location and the author can take no
responsibility for these details if copied and applied elsewhere.

Contents

VOLUME TWO BUILDING TYPES: SELECTED EXAMPLES

Case Studies

Colour Plates

Preface

'Creative Re-use' is more than just the conversion or rehabilitation of a property for a new, or continued use. It is a process that harnesses the energy and quality of the original building, whether of special architectural or historic interest or simply a work-a-day redundant building, and combines this with the new energy and activity that the new use brings. The balance between the existing building and the new use is variable dependent upon character, condition and the needs of the user. The aim is to achieve a harmonious balance, celebrating both.

This book introduces 'Creative Re-use' as an active force, a worthwhile option, that is more likely to achieve a balance of user needs and wider community responsibility than demolition and redevelopment, or, in many cases development on a greenfield site.

The book brings together and examines the main elements of 'Creative Re-use' in order to encourage a greater understanding of the concept and promote its wider application. The reader is encouraged to develop a clear philosophy and to appreciate how to contribute towards a successful re-use scheme. The key is an understanding of the process. Creative Re-use is not a style or an 'ism' but a methodology imbued with both sensitivity and inspiration, with a very practical application.

During a period when town and city centres are intensifying, greenfield development is discouraged and the 'Green' conservation issues of Agenda 21 have begun to permeate the nation's psyche; when the nature of institutions is changing dramatically, with hospitals, sanatoriums, military camps, mills and even office blocks becoming redundant, the book is designed to equip the reader with the ability to react positively.

Volume One focuses on the overall process and the roles of the key participants. This should enable each of these key players to appreciate their ability to initiate action or contribute towards a successful outcome. Volume One also seeks to clarify the process of creative re-use in a new light. By consolidating current thinking and drawing upon practical experience, with selected case studies and examples, the book widens the information available, not only to the practitioner, and student, but also to a wider readership of clients, users, and decision makers.

Volume Two illustrates, with examples from different parts of Britain, the creative scope re-use offers by examining the conversion of buildings of different shape, size and type to a wide variety of uses.

Acknowledgements

Tim Abbot of De Montfort University for advising on the structure and initial stages of the book. Colin Redman of Grosvenor Estates for his analytical appreciation of the economics of re-use. Jason Boyle for assistance with early research. Leanne Belmore for her tenacity and dedication, organising and collating all the information. Maxine Dudley for draughting plans and elevations. Samantha Jackson for word-processing numerous drafts. Jill Pearce and her team at Donhead for their unstinting support. And my wife Pauline for her forbearance during holidays when I worked on manuscripts.

But mostly to the architects who have worked with me to realise the projects illustrated in the case studies.

Introduction

In the 1960s, in the name of progress, massive slum clearance programmes removed whole sectors of the inner city, one after the other, like spokes snapped from a wheel. These modern clearances replaced the familiar but condemned streets with a variety of new housing, from high-rise blocks to rows of identical terraces. Town centres were all but wiped out by Comprehensive Development Areas, which created concrete shopping precincts for a limited circle of high street retailers; precincts crowned by faceless office blocks.

Liverpool exemplified the process. 'For years [Liverpool] has dealt with its post-war housing shortage by tearing down inner slums and re-housing people in ugly new developments on its outskirts, leaving large tracts of valuable land unused. In 1966 the [city] corporation scheduled for demolition 78,000 houses – effectively most of the residential heart of the city – so condemning more large areas to blight and eventual butchery.'[1]

Councils seemed to vie with each other to complete the destruction of their built heritage, encouraged by government and supported by architects and planners, who presented watercolour images of a sunlit concrete world peopled with brightly painted figures living under a blue sky. The residents, the retailers and the office users had no choice but to occupy the buildings that resulted from this process, use them, and live with them.

But who takes the blame for this sad episode in our urban history? Was it genuinely the realisation of the Corbusian dream, or just an excuse to change the architectural order?

Developers blame the architects, forgetting the original arguments about plot ratios and cost indices. Architects blame rigid planning controls, which forced them to conform to dimensional master plans, complete with building lines and height restrictions (though at the time in question, most planners were also architects).

Town planners blame government legislation, which produced statutory land use plans that removed areas of industry, enlarged the commercial and retail zones, and joined together the various residential areas, supposedly to make living cleaner and easier (certainly they were easier to colour on the plan!). For administrative expediency, the larger the redevelopment area, the quicker the rubric-like pattern on the plan would be removed, so 'solving' problems with a simple geometry of organisation.

The wishes of the electorate were cited by contemporary ministers, in their rush to provide new housing, shops, offices and factories. 'Homes fit for Heroes' were needed in our 'brave new world'. However, the process of destruction and replacement didn't stop once the immediate shortage had been satisfied; instead, the process became a programme in which dirty old buildings were replaced by nice new ones. The bureaucrats didn't wait to see how age might weary the new, but pushed blindly ahead with commissioning more and more of the same developments, applying simple 'cost yardsticks' to achieve greater housing density. The people's lives became drearier as a result, as they accepted the grim blandness around them, and learnt – like characters in George Orwell's *1984* – to condemn those ornate, blackened vestiges of Victorian 'vulgarity' waiting under suspended sentence for their turn to come.

On the other hand, half-timbered coaching inns were a different matter. They were old and characterful, and thus worth keeping, even if jacked up to construct a car park underneath, moved sideways to avoid interrupting a vista, and left sandwiched between new multi-storey buildings as in Deangate, Manchester.

Some towns were saved in their entirety – but only just. It's difficult now to believe how much of Chester, for example, was threatened by redevelopment. And Chesterfield's medieval market place was saved, not by the vision of some shining knight, but by the much more mundane arrival of recession, in the 1970s. Not that there was a shortage of crusaders at the time; it's just that they tended to be considered 'nowt but crackpots' by 'progressive' government officials.

Wiser now, no one will admit to responsibility for the past. The conspiracy of blamelessness blankets reality. Was it really the architects that got it all wrong?

It has to be stated, in the profession's defence, that some skilled architects produced good developments, though their well-designed and humane housing estates were derided at the time for being too suburban. They also produced some good high density schemes. Sometimes artists worked with architects, new materials were found and used, and old materials used in fresh ways. New housing layouts were tried and accepted, new shopping patterns created, and working environments were improved, all culminating in a new concept, lifestyle. No longer did son blindly follow father: in the new 'permissive' society, people began to feel confident enough to put quality of life before security.

In that search for quality of life, the conservation movement was born – the movement as we now know it, as opposed to a perceived lunatic fringe. The Civic Trust was inaugurated in 1957 by Duncan Sandys: its birth a response to a growing understanding that the pace of change was obscuring that which was good with a muddle of mediocrity. Pressures were too diverse, controls too bureaucratic, and talent spread too thinly to achieve consistent results, so it is now difficult, looking back, to find individual examples of the brilliance which led the way.

It was about this time that I entered the profession, choosing to work for Clifford Wearden, an architect and planning consultant already critically acclaimed for his high density housing. Having joined his team, however, I soon became aware, working in North Kensington, that the brave new urban world we envisaged would not be made available to the existing community in their Rachman-owned, furnished tenancies. They were to be removed along with the property.

In the process of working with Shelter in London, and later on for the council in Derby, I came to develop a concept of gradual renewal.[2] This keeps the community in place, redeveloping only the very worst property, while turning its attention to repair, rehabilitation and improvement of the rest. The gradual renewal idea resulted in the abandonment of, not only the slum clearance area programme in Derby, but also the new housing schemes on the outskirts originally planned to replace the slums. Instead, Derby adopted a policy of selective renewal and general improvement.

As the 1970s unfolded, complete with love, peace and flower power, people began to see the future through the rose tinted spectacles of the past, and the desire to preserve buildings grew. The Civic Amenities Act of 1967 was the precursor, legitimising the concept of Conservation Areas, but the real catalyst was to come in 1975, when European Architectural Heritage Year (EAHY) used a mixture of education, subsidy and competitiveness to bring the movement to maturity.

Moving to lead the Design and Conservation Team at Derbyshire County Council, I compiled a Buildings At Risk register, established a materials bank, and promoted a repairs campaign that offered grants whilst not being afraid to threaten compulsory purchase. It was a phase of my career when I was able to wear two hats. Wearing the second, as the Chairman of the technical panel on the newly formed Derbyshire Historic Buildings Trust, I was well placed to create a successful working relationship: the Trust was able to acquire those derelict buildings under threat of compulsory purchase orders by the Council. Out of this experience in Derbyshire, working for the county and managing projects for the Trust, came the confidence that made possible the rescue of the Railway Cottages in Derby; an ideal opportunity to put my own philosophy into practice (1980).

Now, 20 years later, conservation has truly come of age, and in its maturing the very term *conservation* has acquired many subtle shades of meaning. The word heritage sprang into life and acquired for a time, an agency, a Ministry, even a lottery. Conservation in its widest sense has gone 'green' (at last!) and every right thinking person now acknowledges the need to conserve our built heritage (even if they do not fully understand what that means). Older organisations like the Society for the Protection of Ancient Buildings (SPAB), the National Trust and the Ancient Monument Society (AMS) are now the very model of respectability, while 'fringe' groups, formerly considered only of minority interest, concerned with 1930s architecture and the modern movement, are now represented by societies which public and government alike take increasingly seriously. The Architectural Heritage Fund, born of European Architectural Heritage Year, has grown from a mere fledgling into a bird of flight, able to support the funding of numerous projects on its still-growing wing span. Postgraduate (Diploma) and masters courses in architectural conservation have also thrived, and as an external examiner I have seen the steadily improving standards and relevance of such courses. I have also seen the Association of Conservation Officers (ACO) grow from a disparate order of self-appointed evangelists into an independent professional body, meeting, learning and lobbying for the cause. That the ACO has now become the Institute of Historic Building Conservation (IHBC) amply illustrates its maturity.

Public awareness of, and interest in architecture has also flourished, taking a complete U-turn from the revulsion and suspicion that the layman and woman harboured for the architectural profession not so very long ago. Aided by a little royal patronage (or was it, perhaps, the opposite?), the art of architecture has become, once again, a fashionable subject for discussion and debate among the chattering classes, and enjoys increasing media coverage. But even more importantly, architecture is now talked about in pubs.

It is in the light of this re-awakening of the art of architecture, coupled with the present cult status of conservation, that this book will define and explore a philosophy of Creative Re-use.

■ REFERENCES

1. Barnard, R., 'Community Action in a Twilight Zone', *RIBAJ*, October 1970, p 446.
2. Latham, D., 'Design for Community Living in Redevelopment Areas'. Thesis LCAT, 1970. Latham, D., 'Community Survival in the Renewal Process – An Integral Part of the Housing Problem', Thesis Nottingham Trent University, 1973.

Case Study 1.1

CREATIVE RE-USE AT ITS MOST BASIC LEVEL – 'STONE TENTS'

From: Field Barns, Derbyshire
To: 'Stone Tents'

While housing market pressures lead to a delicate, well-dressed quality in Cotswold villages, the robust field barns throughout the northern uplands are being stripped of their stone slate roofs. No longer with a viable use, these barns supply a rapacious (if illegal)

'Stone Tent' camping barn.

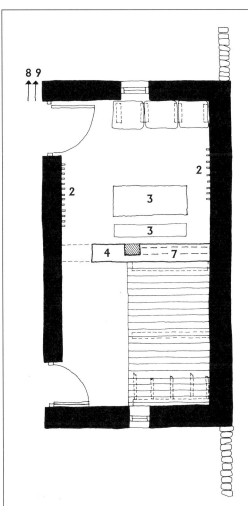

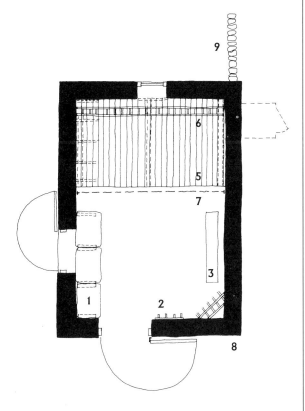

Plan of camping stable.

'Stone Tent' camping stable.

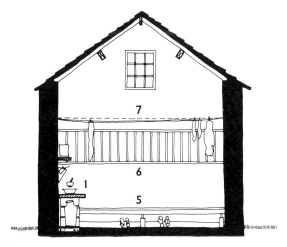

Section through camping stable.

Key
1. Stone worktop for cooking with shelf over
2. Coat hooks for drying and hanging storage
3. Bench and table
4. Existing post and low wall

5. Raised timber sleeping platform with boot rail under
6. Hay rack for storage
7. Washing line for drying
8. Water minimum 20 yards
9. External chemical latrine in timber shelter

market for second-hand materials generated by conservation zeal.

The Duchess of Devonshire had not reckoned on the stupidity of bureaucracy when she tried to solve this conundrum in 1982; proposing the use of field barns as simple shelters for hikers in the same manner as Scottish bothies. Bureaucracy dictated that if the barns were to be occupied, even for just one night at a time, then as buildings they would have to comply with the Building Regulations standards. Heating, sanitation, insulation, daylight and ventilation would all need to be considered. Compliance would not only have been prohibitively costly but would also have altered the structure beyond recognition.

The solution was an application for a licence to use the barns under legislation used for campsites, calling the buildings 'Stone Tents'.[a] Fortunately the Chief Executive of the district council had the wit to understand the plea and issued licences, subject to annual renewal, on the basis that the barns' statuses as tents would end if the licence was not renewed. The conceit was simple: once the 'camp was struck' the tents would be gone and all that would remain would be field barns. This apparent contradiction is now enshrined in official policy:[b] such is the coinage of creative re-use.

References

a. The Girl Guides Association agreed to act as the licensees on behalf of the Chatsworth Estate. The Peak Park now runs a whole series of camping barns managed by the YHA. Section 269 of the 1936 Public Health Act gives power to Local Authorities to issue licences to use land to erect or move moveable dwellings, i.e. 'any tent, any van, or other conveyance whether on wheels or not and . . . any shed or similar structure being a tent, conveyance or structure which is used either regularly, or at certain seasons only, or intermittently for human habitation, provided it does not include a structure to which Building Bylaws apply.'

b. *Camping Barns in England*, joint publication YHA (England and Wales Ltd/MAFF/ Countryside Commission, 1999. Also Countryside Information Leaflet *Accommodation Barns*, Countryside Commission, John Dower House, Cheltenham GL50 3RA.

PART ONE

THE CONTEXT FOR RE-USE

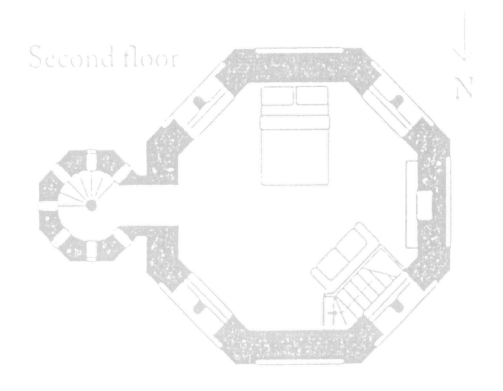

CHAPTER 1

The Appeal of Older Buildings

Old buildings generate popular appeal. Is this because people are consciously aware of the advantages of retaining them, and can see the benefits of characterful old architecture to their community? Or do they just feel comfortable with the familiar? Perhaps there is a more comprehensive answer. Professor Derek Linstrum, in his lecture series at the York Institute for Advanced Architectural Studies, suggested there are motives – deep-seated, interwoven, contradictory – which can be expressed in terms of five main categories. The headings Professor Linstrum suggests are these: archaeological, aesthetic, economic, functional, and psychological. The list isn't arbitrary in its order, but mirrors the evolution of the conservation arguments in favour of rescue and restoration. We will now go on to look at each of these five headings in detail.

■ ARCHAEOLOGICAL MOTIVES

Inspired by their love of everything gothic and medieval, the Victorians had their own characteristic approach to the 'repair' of the buildings they inherited. Their position was both romantic and perfectionist. They felt the need to correct the dogstooth ornamentation on a Norman arch by regularising the pattern, rather than allowing it to reflect the different stone sizes, as the Normans had intended. Ruins, however authentic, ran the risk of being reshaped into silhouettes that achieved, in Victorian eyes, a more 'pleasing appearance of decay'. But not all their efforts are so easy to dismiss. Some of the great restorers of the Victorian period had a great deal to offer; indeed some, like Pugin and Giles Gilbert Scott, have, through their particular interpretation of gothic architecture, created masterpieces of Gothic Revival which we are now at pains to repair and maintain. Their philosophy was strong, clear and well-presented to a learned and influential section of the public, who in turn provided the patronage that allowed them to fulfil their ideals. But what they did not do, what they never even aimed or pretended to do, was to safeguard the object of their restoration. Instead, that object was subjected to their own ideals and intentions. The world view of the original makers was secondary to the world view of the Victorians themselves.

This approach did not go unchallenged, and it was in answer to the misapplied scholarship of the early Victorians that William Morris and W. R. Lethaby, embracing the archaeological argument, founded the Society for the Protection of Ancient Buildings. The Society set out its Repair Not Restore philosophy in a manifesto, copies of which are still available and can be secured by making any sort of membership application to SPAB.

The archaeological approach, as formulated and practised by the newly formed SPAB, was so rigorously applied that, for example, if a stone was worn to the point of needing replacement or refacing, this wouldn't be done with new stone. Instead, they used a form of tile stitching, which would either be left exposed, or covered by a render based on washed ground stone. This allowed all repairs to be clearly identifiable, leaving those parts of the building presumed to be original to remain untainted. The remaining, unrepaired parts of the building were allowed their own integrity, and were merely overlaid by very obvious repairs. This was appropriate for the student of history, and entirely understandable as a reaction to the early restorers' excesses, but there was a price to pay in swinging away from a romantic approach to an uncompromisingly archaeological position. Nothing is permanent, and if the tile stitching process were to be continued rigorously over the years it would only be a matter of time before the whole building was faced in tile and render.

Nevertheless, the archaeological approach has an integrity all its own. As endorsed by the Council of British Archaeology, it is primarily concerned with buildings as pieces of historic evidence, and the intrinsic value of that architectural evidence to our own and future generations. Despite the undoubted integrity of the position, though, there are three immediately obvious problems with it. Firstly, that we are sometimes too close in time to a building to assess it objectively. Secondly, that it is not really for us to say what future generations will or should value. Are we to preserve absolutely everything without discrimination, or allow a process of selection by survival of the fittest? Finally, following on from that thought, the archaeological approach may involve the preservation of buildings whose style is unpopular or whose very presence reminds us of a past we'd rather forget (such as pottery banks, textile mills, early housing estates and colliery pit-heads).

Ultimately there is no single 'right' solution to the problem of what we preserve, and what we allow to be altered. The decision is easier when the building is special, well-documented and widely appreciated. In more difficult cases, a process of research and analysis can lead the way; perhaps, given the priorities of the local population, and the possibly dark alternatives for the building, creative re-use will emerge as the best way forward. Reviving buildings in this particular way, and thus ensuring their ultimate survival, albeit in a slightly altered form, does, after all, retain more architectural archaeology for the future, overall. The process can even embrace apparently unwelcome reminders of the past, and by turning them to good use, enable them to offer compensation to society by contributing in a new role. Not all old buildings can justify substantial public subsidy merely to be preserved for the nation in the future. Important buildings aside, creative re-use allows for a whole second level of architectural heritage to survive; buildings that have found a new lease of life, and work for a living, but which might otherwise (having failed the public subsidy test) have disappeared entirely.

■ AESTHETIC APPRECIATION

A common emotional view evoking popular support, aesthetics can be split into two strands: visual amenity, and cultural value.

■ Visual amenity

Visual amenity is concerned with the subjective enjoyment society experiences from its visual environment. It responds to popular taste, and is not inhibited by fixed criteria dictating what should or shouldn't be preserved. It encourages positive improvement and exploitation of the amenity for our own benefit and for future generations. It is a planning-based approach to conservation, associated with local civic societies and conservation area designations. The problem in trying to cater for the future is, of course, that popular aesthetic taste is constantly changing, and at any one time is likely to have its own blind spots and prejudices. It seems incredible to us now that the Georgian Group had to be formed in 1938 in order to challenge the then popular antipathy to Georgian architecture, and that the Victorian Society was founded as late as 1950 to help overcome a similar distaste for Victorian design. The recent formation of DoCoMoMo to protect early modern architecture illustrates that such prejudices continue, even in our own enlightened age.

The standards that visual amenity demands can be met by developing a brief for creative re-use that responds: to the building's users' needs (see Chapter 6), to the requests of amenity bodies, and to the requirements laid down by planning author-ities (Chapter 9). Visually, the concept of creative re-use has much to commend it. So many new buildings today are designed without reference to their location – in other words, they have no sense of context. Even if not designed in the international style, few new buildings carry a sense of place, a response to their genus loci. Those that do, that have been designed in a vernacular style using local materials and details, all too often lapse into a Disneyland pastiche. Creative re-use uses existing buildings, buildings that fit, and so the character of the locale is maintained.

■ Regional and particular character

Mills in Lancashire and Yorkshire, and even in the valleys south of Stroud; the warehouses around the docks in Gloucester; the Agricultural Hall in Islington; the dour Georgian crescents and squares of Newcastle; the tumble of chapels and mills on the steep hillside of Hebden Bridge; the dome of the Royal Hospital in Buxton; the streets of converted early Victorian terraced houses in the Jewellery Quarter, Birmingham; the gaggle of fisherman's buildings and harbour houses along the sound at Lerwick, Shetland; the refined rhythm of polite Georgian townscape in Cheltenham, and the crush of bold, but ornate commercial Victorian buildings that celebrate success in the heart of Leeds, Glasgow, Manchester and Birmingham. All have their own style. (See Chapter 16, Volume Two.)

■ Cultural value

Conrad Smigielski, a past planning officer at Leicester said in the Leicester City Plan 1968, that 'a city without old buildings is like a man without a memory'. Coming from central Europe, he was only too aware of the cultural loss involved in the loss of old buildings and was amazed to see how we took our old building stock so much for granted. He understood only too well the cultural argument, which is concerned with the speed and scale of modern redevelopment, and how that redevelopment can destroy the fragile sense of time and place historic towns possess. The cultural argument challenges the application of a universally applied aesthetic and the resulting loss of local, regional or even national identity. It supports the policy of keeping all that we have that has the potential to be re-used, and recognises the important contribution this sense of continuity makes to the psychological well-being of a community.

Most existing, old-established buildings have a past firmly rooted in the community, whether as a place of worship, work, learning or rest. Civic buildings, in particular, carry forward an enduring message of pride in that community. The identity of those buildings becomes very closely associated with the identity of the local population, not only in the minds of long-established residents, but also in those of newcomers. Their use need not remain static, though a fine old banking hall might become a pub, a church a studio, a house an office, a redundant town hall a community centre, or a railway station an exhibition hall, while still maintaining that sense of identity for local people.

In the words of Sir James Richards in his *Introduction to Modern Architecture*,[1] 'excessive demands for the preservation of everything old are caused not only by love of old buildings but by mistrust of what present-day architects are likely to put in their place, so the best answer to unreasonable preservation is better quality architecture'. Which provokes the fascinating question: if we do, eventually, succeed in attuning modern design to its context, picking up the threads of tradition where they were broken off, to what extent will this diminish our drive to preserve the old?

So the cultural case is complex. On the one hand it may seem to be demanding the retention of everything old; on the other it seeks to develop contextual design, picking up the threads of tradition but maybe also looking to use new technology to reflect the cultural life of the present day. These demands aren't necessarily pulling in different directions. The need to preserve everything old can be subtly amended into an attempt to preserve – or creatively re-use – everything possible. The drive towards contextual design can succeed by creating serendipity – a sort of pleasant surprise arising from contrasting new elements that emanate from our own culture with those valued from the past, with sensitivity, wit and ingenuity. The result should be streets that are alive with cultural cross-referencing, mutual architectural respect and a shared sense of the narrative of the history of the place. In this way not only can the aesthetic needs of the population be satisfied, but their psychological needs can also be addressed.

■ ECONOMIC

■ Tourism and leisure

The argument for economic benefit from improving the visual amenity of a location is self-justifying and circular. That circle can quickly become a downward spiral if the competitive jostling between places to attract tourism is allowed to justify 'improvements' to the historic appearance of a place. The theatrical creation of historic (pastiche) street scenes sets a dangerous precedent. This is all very well if done openly, like Disney at Epcot – there's no possibility of any confusion between fantasy and reality there. But the Disney approach when used at historic sites with the sole intention of boosting revenue not only confuses the visitor, but ultimately devalues the site itself. That isn't to say that our historic towns and buildings can't be used as a resource for leisure and tourism. Indeed, leisure and tourism can be key generators for a programme of creative re-use – of all sorts of buildings, both ancient and not so old – and are central to the argument. These are considered further in Chapters 3 and 6.

■ Re-use is cheaper, quicker, and a good investment

The general trend is moving increasingly towards refurbishment, rather than new build. Consider the case of London's Design Museum on the south bank of the Thames, which re-used a (non-listed) factory, rather than demolishing and replacing it, even though a new building might have been perceived to promote a more modern image.

Old buildings are often cheaper to convert to new uses than new buildings cost to build, so the decision to re-use can be made on sound economic grounds. This decision is dependent upon a range of criteria affecting valuation and investment and these are analysed more fully in Chapter 7. In general there is much to be said in favour of re-use on economic grounds. Saving buildings, in much the same way that we might save any other hard-earned resource against an uncertain and unpredictable future is a way of banking our built investment, and husbanding the resources, labour and energy that they comprise. The economic asset represented by our existing building stock will only keep its value if it is maintained. Naturally enough, owners resent paying out money to maintain empty buildings unless they have some realistic expectation of them retaining or increasing their monetary value.

■ Old buildings are valuable energy resources

An environmental argument can be made for creative re-use. Accepting that the Earth's material and energy resources are finite, and in some cases fast depleting, it makes sense to slow down our consumption and make the best use of what we already have. Looked at this way, conservation of the effort, skill and dedication of the original builders is as much energy conservation as it is heritage conservation. Whether buildings are made of low energy consuming materials like stone, or high energy like steel and glass, the constructed building encapsulates that used energy. Demolition dissipates it, mostly to waste, though the re-use of reclaimed materials can go some way to compensating for it. The real cost of the energy lost by demolition is greater still as it ought to account for the additional bottom-to-top cost of replacing a building rather than re-using it.

Partial demolition, if carefully planned and handled, can result in the redundant fabric being dismantled in such a way as to make salvage and re-use of the materials part of the economic plan for the building. Salvaged materials can act as a quarry, or material bank, perhaps for the stitching of repairs into the remaining fabric, or, more dramatically, for the construction of extensions or new buildings on the same site. New buildings made of reclaimed materials can rapidly integrate themselves with the original building and with the environment in which they are constructed (see Jewellery Business Centre, 6.4).

In the process of conversion much of an interior may be stripped out because internal components have reached the end of their useful life. There is an opportunity to transform 'uneconomic' buildings using green materials to improve both comfort and energy efficiency. The lifespan of various elements within a building vary. Modern structures are often quoted as having a life expectancy of 60 years, and although a building may appear jaded by this stage, it need not have reached the end of its useful life. Investment in new windows, roof coverings, insulation and safety features might be needed, but the basic fabric of the structure should be capable of many more years of service. Even problems of decay or fatigue in the fabric itself can be arrested by intervention, thus retaining the embodied energy within the shell of the building. This long-life, loose-fit, low energy approach is fundamental. It asks us to forego certain present-day benefits in preference to an assumed long-term benefit to society as a whole.

This energy resource argument runs deep and is fundamental to creative re-use philosophy. By addressing the 'green' issues of embodied energy, retained skills, and intensity of use, we are also adding benefit to society in the long term. In the process we promote the retention and renewal of the older areas of our towns and cities, encouraging higher density and greater mixed use, discouraging the car and assisting public transport. Pollution issues may also be addressed. Where toxic industrial processes have occurred over several generations, re-using the remaining buildings may well seal in the accrued pollutants.

There is also a more mundane green issue here: by revitalising our existing high density urban townscape – people will forgive high density features like the lack of a car park if the building is interesting – the inner city is kept alive avoiding yet more urban sprawl in the green belt.

■ Re-use creates jobs

In addition to the saving of non-renewable resources, the creative re-use of buildings makes use of workers who need jobs: it is a labour intensive, rather than an energy resource intensive approach in a period of declining job opportunities. The money in tradesmen's pockets is therefore more likely to benefit the local economy.

■ FUNCTIONAL VALUE

Historic buildings, creatively re-used, can act as a catalyst and lubricator to the process of introducing alternative functions into areas otherwise swamped by market competition. In the centrally planned state, and the British New Town, the provision of community spaces is integrated into the urban centre, cheek by jowl with prime shop fronts. But in a market led economy it is difficult for authorities to find and afford such sites. The need to keep historic buildings, both for archaeological and aesthetic reasons, coupled with the economic imperative to put the building to some use, can easily lead to a community function for previously obsolete old structures. St Sampson's Church, in the heart of York's high rent shopping district, has been converted into an over-60s coffee shop and drop-in centre. A large and airy space complete with its own charming garden, St Sampson's provides a real oasis in the middle of the city. The costs of such conversions are likely to be shared by several interested agencies, and because the space is fulfilling more than one function, the public perception is likely to be that this is taxpayers' money well spent.

Sometimes a potential user goes out in search of the right building, rather than the other way round. Liverpool managed to secure the first out of London base for the Tate Gallery by virtue of having just the sort of space the gallery needed in the

Example   **1.1**

USE: **St Sampson's Church, York**
1848, incorporating fifteenth century elements, stone, aisled church with chapel and adjacent parish room. Disused 1962–8.

TO: **Social centre for old people**
An early example of church conversion (1968). Used as a day centre, for meals and dances with a reading room/library. Weekday services are held in the chapel and the churchyard has become a semi-public garden. Since imitated throughout the country, another church, the medieval St Michael's, Spurriergate, York has been converted (1989) with an introduced floor to provide café, shop and solace to people of all ages.[2]

Inside St Sampson's Centre, York.

old Albert Dock. By the same token, it's unlikely that the G Mex Centre would have been located in the centre of Manchester, had it not been for the availability of the old Grand Central Station.

When new uses are found for old buildings, this can act as a catalyst to the regeneration of the surrounding area, demonstrating that obsolete old structures can be forces for renewal and hope. New and established companies might make new offices in them, or managed business centres might be created, acting as incubators to an array of small businesses. Creative re-use has impact on the wider economy, far beyond the transformation of a single building. (This cause is now being championed by REVIVE – a campaign lobbying on behalf of all non-governmental conservation bodies.)[3]

Regeneration of whole areas, previously derelict, might be on offer too. Unless we understand how the economy of our streets interrelates with that of their surroundings, we will fail to do more than the early enhancement schemes achieved – merely beautifying the face, while the body continues to die. Conservation is about more than simply preserving our past history. More fundamentally, it is about maintaining the health of our towns and villages. Environmental streetscape improvements are all very well, but they must work in cohesion with a planned programme of revival, as well as the re-use of key buildings in the area, if the community is genuinely to benefit.

The functional value of conservation is given real meaning when buildings are found a new role; simply preserving them, intact but literally useless, is not enough. The argument for creative re-use doesn't need to be building-led, it can be use-led, the tangible benefits of using an old building can speak for themselves. Positive discrimination for old buildings isn't needed when it's apparent that conversion

Example   1.2

USE: **Railway station, Manchester Central**
1880, Sir John Fowler, Grade II, brick with
18 no. 64 m clear span iron arches. Large
vaulted undercroft. Closed 1968.

TO: **Exhibition centre (G Mex)**
10,000 m sq of clear space up to 26 m high
would be uneconomic to construct today.
Divisible into 1/4 : 3/4 by means of a
retractable vertical 'sail', a 5,500 seat arena
or 8,000 seat concert hall, plus 400 seat
restaurant and parking for 800 cars. Air
conditioning in eight sectors is controlled by
four plant areas in the undercroft. All
exhibitors are serviced from a duct under the
full length of the hall, including TV, gas and
compressed air. The glazed south wall has
been infilled with translucent polystyrene to
reduce heat gain.

A: **Arup and Partners**[4]

Exhibition Hall – roof and end glazing allows a mixture of natural
and artificial light. Air conditioning is inconspicuous and does
not interfere with the structure visually.

Restored ironwork.

Ground floor plan.

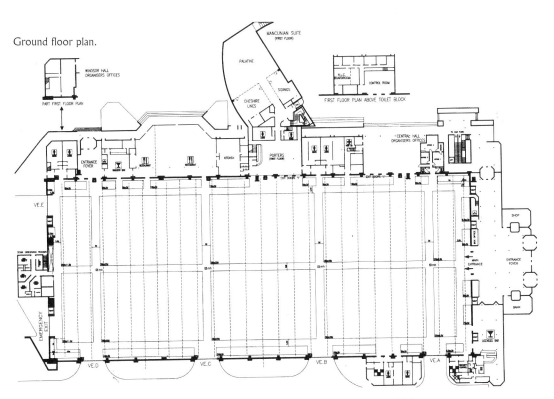

offers flexible and comfortable working space, for business, for health and education, for living and playing. The buildings are merely a facilitator of the new use. This functional approach is essentially a pragmatic one, ignoring the difference between new build and re-use; the brief is to analyse the prospective use in order to generate solutions that work with the building rather than against it (see Chapter 8).

■ PSYCHOLOGICAL NEED

There is undoubtedly a core preservation reflex in human nature; we cling to the security of the familiar, and perhaps we cling more in the late twentieth century, when the sheer pace of change might make us long for stability and for the past. We are learning to forgive ourselves for lacking confidence in current society, and feeling uncertain about what the future holds.

We deal, in part, with these feelings by designing 'historic' features into public, commercial, even residential building projects. A whole interior design industry has developed around the concept of historic theming in museums, shopping centres, restaurants, pubs, night-clubs and hotels. Speculative housing developments apparently have more 'kerbside' appeal (and thus greater sales potential) if they have a traditional look – perhaps featuring half-timbered gablets, or Victorian-style bargeboards – than if they have a modern design, which risks complete rejection.

In an era with such preferences (and prejudices), creative re-use obviously has popular appeal. Engaging both design ability and current technology to utilise our old buildings rather than replacing them, whether or not they are deemed to be special in themselves, is a process in keeping with the mood of the times. Creative re-use allows us to save and protect our heritage, while exploring its value as a resource; it prompts us to re-interpret our architectural needs and cultural aspirations, and sparks originality of mind through the process of turning constraints into advantages. Some interventions might be made on a small scale, allowing the new to grow out of the old, as in the case of the Sackler Gallery at the Royal Academy in London. Others might demand a larger scale, such as in the case of the new stand at Lord's Cricket Ground; and some demand major intervention, like the new Tate Gallery at Bankside Power Station, and the creative re-use of the British Museum. These are all projects that speak of a growing confidence in the process of re-use.

Whichever way the issue is considered, it appears that the popular appeal of older buildings is satisfied by creative re-use, and the advantages to the community of retaining existing structures and areas of character are clear. Even buildings of little or no intrinsic historic or architectural interest can be saved. So often demolished because they are thought useless, unlisted buildings offer great opportunities for creative re-use. Because they are unlisted, they can be materially altered, adapted to a wide variety of uses, and re-presented to the community, re-modelled and with a new image in keeping with their new role. The real limitations are not archaeological, aesthetic, economic or functional, but psychological: the limits created by preconceptions, and by lack of imagination. Once the will is there, the skills and ingenuity will follow.

REFERENCES

1. Richards, J., *Introduction to Modern Architecture*, Penguin, 1982.
2. Diocese of York.
3. Rose, V., *Catalytic Conversion: REVIVE Historic Buildings to Regenerate Communities*, SAVE, AHF, IHBC, and UK ABPT, London, 1995.
4. *Architects Journal*, Vol 23, No 1, September 1987, pp 22–33, also *Building*, Vol 253, No 26, 26 June 1988, pp 64–6.

Case Study   1.3

From: **St Michael's Church, Derby**
To: **Offices**

The conference room, once the ringing chamber, is a space that was probably visited by few of the former congregation. But it gives a sense of occasion to any meeting, and the specially made circular table of richly coloured cherrywood softens the severity of the bare stone walls. This room exemplifies the rewards of converting old buildings: the satisfaction of discovering that a redundant space is ideal for an entirely novel use. It is ironic that the closure of a church can lead to a new appreciation of its qualities. It was easy enough to dismiss St Michael's, when in use, as a conventional and even commonplace building. But the conversion encourages one to look at it afresh. The fine timber roof, once sunk in darkness, has become a huge feature. It has been cleaned and picked out in red in a thoroughly Victorian fashion.

The generous use of timber in the conversion, in the form of hardwood screens and balustrades, echoes its character and adds warmth. . .[a]

There is no such thing as a typical creative re-use project, as the process is by definition a tailor-made and not a standardised one. Nevertheless, the conversion of St Michael's Church, Derby to offices serves to illustrate some general points about creative re-use.

St Michael's with Derby Cathedral in the background.

During conversion showing floors introduced below clerestorey and above capitals.

■ Abandoned to demolition, re-use proposals having failed

Dating from 1858, St Michael's is a solid and serious building, made of local stone, and designed in a thirteenth-century style by Henry Isaac Stevens. The interior is laid out along the approved Puginian lines, with a separate chancel and proper side aisles. By the 1960s, a new ring road had left St Michael's stranded on the fringe of the town centre, with virtually no resident population in its parish. The church was declared redundant in December 1976, and for six years, despite various re-use proposals, the building stood empty and decaying.

■ Needed to change hands

Desirous of a permanent solution, the diocese offered a long lease on a peppercorn rent as a factor to be set against the cost of repair and conversion.

■ Additional internal space needed

Aside from providing two upper floors of drawing offices to house 25 architectural practice employees, the conversion had to create extra, lettable space. The ground floor has been divided into eight workspace units, housing a variety of businesses. The ringing chamber in the tower has become a spacious conference room; below it, in what was the church porch there is

First floor interior from the chancel.

now a reception area, and above it, the boiler room and archive. The lavatories were placed at the west end with a new meeting gallery above, and the kitchen/store has been neatly located in the old choir vestry.

■ Procurement method reduced costs

A series of trades contracts were run in parallel to retain flexibility, maintain control and reduce overheads at a cost of £140,000. The equivalent full contract cost would have been £200,000.

■ Analysis of the fabric

Many original fittings, including the altar and font, were removed by the diocese for use elsewhere, and the west window was donated to the Ely Stained Glass Museum (its removal prompting a welcome increase in the amount of natural light). Most of the other glass, including the Lavers east window, remains. Some memorials were also removed, but the unusual series of ceramic tile tablets survives, most of them rehoused in the reception area, where they can be clearly seen and read. Fine Minton tiles, recovered from the chancel, partly cover the floor here, and choir stalls have been brought in to provide seating for visitors. The screen which forms the entrance to the main part of the building is also a survivor, its panels cut out and replaced by glass. Thanks to the wealth of such detail, the reception area establishes at once the character of the building; it is still recognisably a church, albeit one re-used.

■ Ingenuity resolves building and fire regulations

Pass through the screen into the main body of the building, and the original scale is immediately obvious: the west end space extends right up into the open timber roof. The new offices rise as a simple glazed wall to the east, a frankly modern spiral staircase connecting the floors. Fire officers would not have passed the design if it hadn't been for the insertion of a powerful smoke fan high in the north wall, which allows the west end to be kept clear of smoke in case of a fire in the building. As a result of the fan, smoke lobbies weren't needed; they would have cluttered the glazed screen and reduced the usable floor space. This solution was taken from tower block technology.

■ Sense of original space retained, at worthwhile cost

It was the intention from the beginning to make the new visually distinct from the original, and to maintain views through the internal space. Added to this was the desire to support the new floor loads on the old structure and so avoid a heavy supporting concrete frame.

Ground floor interior.

Both new floors have been kept back from the walls of the building, thus avoiding the distressing effect of new floors cutting across existing window openings (a disastrous feature of some other schemes). The first floor runs along the level of the nave capitals, and the second just above the clerestory. The resultant floor heights are ideal, generous but not overawingly so. Heating the large spaces has proved less costly than it might have, due to recirculating fans at roof level. Both floors are intended to 'float' in the larger space of the nave. Additionally, the first floor is cut back at the east end, in order to preserve the chancel as a distinct space – this is still the climax of the building. A bridge links into the library, which has been placed at first floor chancel level. The second floor is really a platform, across just two bays of the nave. The views into and from this level are dramatic. Some working space had to be sacrificed to achieve this quality, but the effort has been worthwhile. St Michael's still gives the impression of being one building.

■ Maximising light, and giving some up

Lighting the middle floor of the building, which had no existing openings, could have been a problem. Instead of installing a profusion of opening roof lights, it was decided to replace whole sections of roof with glazed panels. An additional benefit of this strategy is that due to the way the first floor is recessed, light from the panels also filters down to the ground floor. Some opening lights were still needed, for ventilation purposes. The retention of a stained glass window – the Lavers east window – does reduce the potential natural light levels, but this loss is acceptable as it is a feature which gives a focus to the whole interior. The glass can now be seen at close range, and the quality of the figure drawing appreciated in a way that was not previously possible.[b]
Also see colour plate 1.

■ References

a. Powell, Kenneth, *Country Life*, 1985.
b. Project Architect: Martin Sutcliffe, Latham Architects.

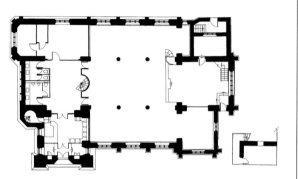

Ground floor plan.

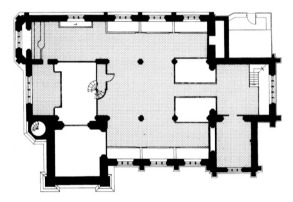

First floor plan.

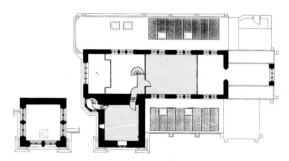

Belfry.   Second floor plan.

CHAPTER 2

Opportunities for Re-use

Opportunities for re-use come from various sources. They may reflect the personal requirements of an existing user, or the needs of an individual or organisation seeking a home. They may be financially driven: through an owner's desire to maintain or improve returns, or the interests of a developer. It may simply occur as a result of the availability of an empty building for re-use, or reflect some broader change in trends of usage.

■ PEOPLE-LED RE-USE

People may have a particular use in mind for a building. Established users with a clear brief – such as the expansion of a museum or art gallery – dictate both the location and the conversion activity. The straightforward application of client requirements may not be wholly sympathetic with the building, so a feasibility study to examine the options may be needed, thereby shifting the focus to detailed design and implementation rather than the type of use (2.1).

Conversely, people may have a particular building in search of a new use. Organisations with a property portfolio may seek new uses, either to improve on the viability of an existing building or where use has ceased altogether. Estates in rural areas may use redundant agricultural buildings to diversify their activities (2.3). Whereas urban estates, supported by increasing property values, can afford to consider dramatic conversions to new use (Victoria Quarter, Leeds, 7.3). An institutional dimension is added by public authorities. Forced to adjust their activities in response to changing demands and new technologies, they must also find new ways of using their building stock (2.2).

Ultimately, the potential user might identify opportunities for re-use by actively seeking out properties that are available, or potentially available. A typical example

Example   2.1

USE: Castle/Ducal Palace, Nottingham
Scheduled Ancient Monument bedrock foundation of eleventh century fortress, with 1675 Ducal Palace Grade I. Burnt out Corn Law Riots. Converted 1870s T.C. Hine to first public art gallery.

TO: Modern museum/art gallery
Reconfigured as part of a phased masterplan with new disabled access connecting all six levels (the lower two through the bedrock). New shop, restaurant, temporary contemporary galleries, restored Victorian gallery, education and teaching rooms, and externally an artwork pavement using two sculptors and six poets.

A: Latham Architects

Lift and staircase designed as an obvious addition, i.e. not part of the original fabric. (*Stuart Blackwood*)

The contemporary gallery. Screens hung on rail can be located as required or stored out of sight. (*Stuart Blackwood*)

The shop with all fittings designed as free standing furniture. (*Stuart Blackwood*)

of this is illustrated in the case study for Matlock Bath Station as a Whistlestop Wildlife Centre (15.28, Volume Two). The search for buildings such as these is aided by directories and other publications, available for new owners and new uses, either as estate agents particulars listing the larger properties of vendors who are willing to pay for inclusion; or free publications, such as those published nationally by SAVE[1], and SPAB.[2] Some local authorities maintain a register of properties that are empty, neglected or in need of repair: i.e. listed buildings at risk.[3] Many local authority

Example   2.2

USE: Town hall, Croydon
Nineteenth century Grade II, brick, stone and slate, Italianate Gothic, five-storey complex of buildings with campanile, with extensions to the original.

TO: Civic and cultural facilities
Centrepiece is an elongated atrium or arcade created by glazing over the no man's land between new library and old town hall.

A: Tibbalds Monro[4]

Town hall refurbished.

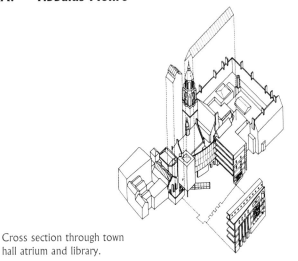

Cross section through town hall atrium and library.

Library extension.

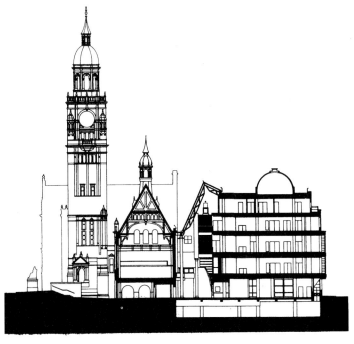

Axonometric showing how the new building fits into the old.

Example 2.3

USE: Farm and outbuildings, Rowthorne, Hardwick, Derbyshire
Seventeenth century Grade II coursed rubble stone walls, stone slate roofs, derelict house and barn ranges around farmyard.

TO: Residential
Four dwellings in outbuildings with large barn doors glazed to provide galleries and bedrooms. House rehabilitated as one dwelling.

A: Latham Architects

Before.

After. (*Stuart Blackwood*)

Example 2.4

Before – the last remnants.

USE: Barn, Cotswolds
Dilapidated. Stone walls on three sides with open oak posted colonnade, King post roof. Unusual two-storey design.

TO: Residential (single house)
Front wall, clad in timber, set back to preserve colonnade whilst new concrete lintels were textured by lining the shuttering with leaves.

A: R.H. Hyne[5]

After – ground floor accommodation is recessed to allow the barn bays to remain open.

economic development departments include properties not at risk, but simply on the market, in a database published quarterly of potential commercial buildings, whether vacant or for sale.[6]

■ BUILDING-LED

It remains possible to find properties requiring a new lease of life just by looking for them. A popular project for many couples is the scouring of remote areas of picturesque countryside in search of a building to convert into a country cottage. Already many old barns have been converted (2.4, 2.7), and many of those that have not are restricted by planning constraints. Consequently people now seek more unusual buildings to convert such as a water tower or folly (2.5, 2.6). It is now necessary to look down forgotten lanes or other routes such as old railways or canals, or in the corner of less developed villages where the intensity of use does not reach urban levels, and an old tractor shed may yet make a cottage.

| **Example** | **2.5** |

USE: Water tower, Appleton, Sandringham
Grade II, Robert Rawlinson, double octagonal plan, neo-Byzantine polychromatic brick/Carstone with cast iron tank.

TO: Holiday house
The original self-contained accommodation has been altered with living/kitchen and shower room on ground floor with bedroom over and extended upwards to include the second floor 'picnic' room as a bed/sitting room with the original stair access now acting as a means of escape.

A: Michael and Sheila Gooch[7]

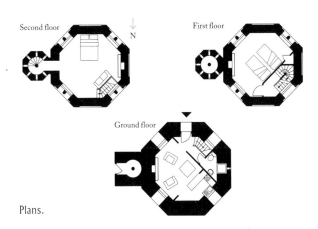

Plans.

Tower converted. (*George Wright*)

Example   2.6

USE: Bath house, Walton
1748 Grade II, Sanderson Miller. Plunge bath surrounded by cyclopean masonry and rocky vault surmounted by an elegant octagonal plastered room. Dilapidated, overgrown and structurally unstable.

TO: Holiday house
Following temporary support and a concrete 'butter' coat, a reinforced concrete slab was laid over the vault to stabilise the base of the room which was painstakingly restored with haired lime plaster, re-cast 'stalactites' and matching shell work. Conversion retains the room as a grand 'bed-sit', with the kitchen slotted into a small lobby and the bathroom into a void over the entrance, reached by a winding timber stair.

A: Hawkes and Cave [8, 9]

Bath house converted. (*Paul Gummer*)

Salon restored (with grotto bath under).

In less-desired areas, such as former industrial districts, it may be easier to find property for conversion and these can still offer attractive or potentially attractive locations, especially in the context of the immediate environment. Thanks to past policies of land reclamation and current institutionalised changes within our society, many areas previously despoiled by slag heaps and waste tips are now covered in lush fields, hedgerows and woodland, creating an ironic contrast to the stark, treeless monoculture of many agricultural areas. Old industrial districts have a variety of buildings laying dormant. Pit-heads, engine houses, workshops or storage buildings may await a new lease of life with which to invigorate the area (2.8).

Cities and towns can also offer potential buildings for re-use, though these may be less prominent than in a rural setting. Low value activities in the twilight zone of the inner city change as property values creep up, forcing people to move on (2.9). The commercial heart of the town hides a higher incidence of empty buildings than can be perceived by the casual observer. Some are hidden behind and above bustling shop frontages; some are in the upper levels of older office buildings without lifts;

Example **2.7**

USE: Barn, Kent

Eighteenth century, five bay, brick and tile timber-framed aisled barn. Cross passage with doors double height to north and single height to south.

TO: Dwelling

Occupying only half the barn, with modern forms expressed in precise and geometric shapes inserted to create a sequence of spaces of increasing scale. Externally the southern mid-storey opening has been heightened to include a window and an oriel looks into the unrestored half.

A: Thomas Croft[10]

Exterior.

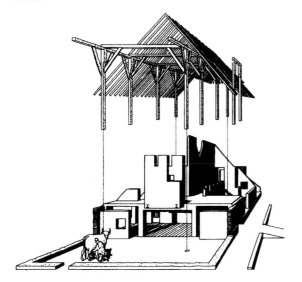

Dissected perspective.

Interior.

Plan.

First floor.

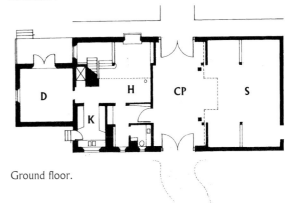

Ground floor.

Key

B	bedroom	K	kitchen
H	hall	L	living
D	dining	S	store
		CP	cross passage

Example **2.8**

USE: Bottle kilns, West Hallam
Nineteenth century, Grade II, brick bottle
kiln and works. Derelict.

TO: Craft centre
The kiln repaired and used for display, the
adjacent works were rebuilt re-using bricks
and tiles for a gallery for paintings, a café,
and a cards, gift and interiors shop.
Landscaped, the yard is now used as a tea
garden with a barn converted to the
proprietor's dwelling.

D: Nic Stone[11]

Before. (*Derby Evening Telegraph*)

After.

some are landlocked down small alleyways inaccessible to service vehicles. These
properties may only be used in part, and the part in use is likely to be the one return-
ing the most profit most easily, with the use of the remainder requiring investment
which offers insufficient return by itself. Such property often belongs to investment
companies, making decisions based on management accounts rather than structure,
space or use, not realising how much of their asset they are wasting. A more enlightened approach to this investment disincentive in city centres, where buildings
frequently co-join, may be solved by uniting ownerships through comprehensive
acquisition in order to divide them again, vertically or horizontally, to enable different sections to accommodate different uses. Such mixed uses are gaining favour with
planning authorities (2.10, 2.11, 2.12, 2.13).

Example   **2.9**

USE: **Power house, Stamford Brook, London**
1901 Grade II William Curtis Green (after John Belcher). Neo-Baroque, brick with Portland stone dressings built for London United Tramways but abandoned by 1917 and used only for storage since. 18 m wide engine room.

TO: **Residential and recording studio and offices**
Nineteen maisonettes were 'sleeved' in between the steel-framed roof trusses, with glazed elevations behind the parapet. As the site was restricted, one part of the building is used for car parking, while the other is used for a studio with three mezzanine levels of offices.

A: **David Clarke Associates – David Clarke**[12]

Entrance hall to offices with modern internal glazing contrasting with the original ironwork.

Key
1. Residential
2. Parking
3. Office studios

After – with living units just visible in the roof.

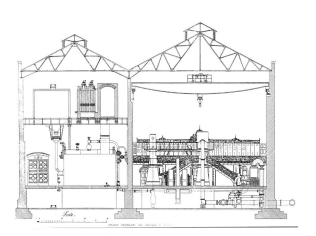

Section before.

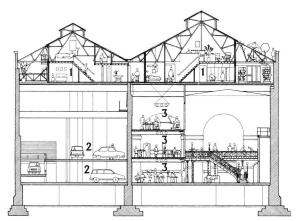

Section after.

Example 2.10

USE: Warehouse, Berwick upon Tweed
Eighteenth century, Grade II, five-storey, stone/harling with pantile roof accessible at level one for alleyway and level three from quay wall. Derelict.

TO: Mixed use
Level one, with poor daylight, became workshops and storage; level two offices accessible from alleyway; level three flats; levels four and five maisonettes accessible from quay walls with new lucams in the roof providing a prospect for upstairs lounge.

A: Latham Architects[13]

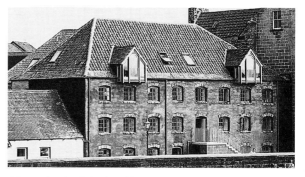
After – showing introduced lucams.

Section.

Key

1. Upper maisonettes	5. Workshops
2. Lower maisonettes	6. Quay walls
3. Flats	7. Small courtyard
4. Offices	8. Passage through wall
	9. Wharf

Example 2.11

USE: Offices, Bride Street, London
c1900, brick, five-storey block with basement.

TO: Restaurant and flats
Cellular offices on the upper floors converted easily to flats. The ground floor was removed and the resulting volume converted to a double height pizza parlour accommodated on a series of platforms spiralling down via ramps and steps from street level.

A: David Clarke Associates

Basement and ground floor during conversion.

Basement and ground floor after conversion.
(*Paul Ratigan, Photo Graphics Ltd.*)

Example   2.12

USE: Shops, town house and cork warehouse, Mansell Street, London

1720, Grade II Georgian, three-storey (plus basement) brick parapeted, stone dressed, five bay fronted, derelict, fire damaged with three-storey (plus basement), four bay brick warehouse at the rear with pairs of loading doors centred on each floor.

TO: Offices/studios

Rehabilitation of the house differs on each floor. Ground has three arched spaces off entrance reception to accommodate fire escape requirements; first has fully restored original fabric; second is open plan with exposed timbers; and third (attic) retains 1880 workroom remodelling with sand blasted timbers and wrought iron ties. Underpinned and partially rebuilt, rear and side elevations are now adjoined by a double curving glazed atrium roof linking to the structurally sound warehouse at the rear simply refurbished by including a new steel stair and lavatories in an internal service core.

A: Trehearne and Norman[14]

Linking atrium.

Georgian street frontage after.

Warehouse at rear converted.

Example 2.13

USE: Congregational Church, Belsize Park, London
1883–4, Grade II Alfred Waterhouse. Brick medium-sized church, church hall and missionary school. Disused.

TO: Recording studio
Integration of high-tech facilities while remaining sympathetic. The main hall is well lit with new recording booths tucked under the balcony. A central 'stack' of three control rooms in double isolated dense concrete boxes, over a plant room in an excavated basement, provides the nerve centre between the main hall and studios on each level.

A: Heber-Percy and Parker (devised by interior design consult, Madcap)[15]

Combined live concert hall and recording studio.

Double isolated studio one.

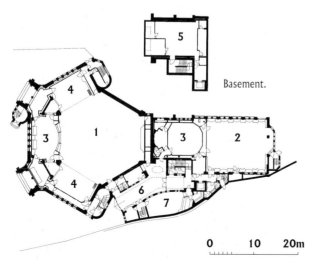

Basement.

Ground floor plan.

Key
1. Main hall
2. Sudios
3. Control rooms
4. Booths
5. Plant
6. Reception
7. Dining
8. Anteroom
9. Office

0   10   20m

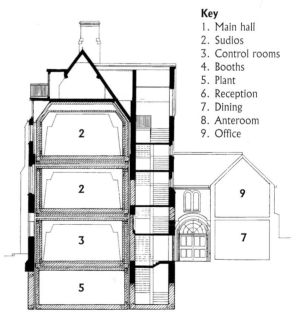

Section showing double isolated structures.

Example **2.14**

USE: Granary: Granary Wharf, Leeds
1777, Grade II*, four-storey, nine bays, stone, Leeds and Liverpool Canal Company.

TO: Offices
Outside a studied restraint in the handling of windows is complemented by an interior which displays the restored queen-post roof structure and coffered ceilings. The entrance is highlighted by a slated canopy and glazed tower protecting the original loading bay openings.

A: Building Design Partnership[16]

After conversion – little change toward the canal.

After conversion – but on the other side, a dramatic glazed intervention announces the new use.

Solutions may be infrastructural. Canalside warehouses and railway maintenance buildings, originally constructed to be accessible only by canal or railway may find themselves 'landlocked' by these transport routes. Lack of access by road may well have prevented the property from finding a suitable new use: this is resolvable by improvements to the surrounding infrastructure, and is not always expensive. A footbridge to a car park and the ability to trolley goods from a service area may be the simple keys to unlock a building's potential.

Stagnating industrial buildings may carry a legacy of pollution restrictive to their use. This could be affecting the structure, with chemicals corroding or soaking into masonry – chemicals that need neutralising – or the pollution could contaminate the surrounding ground, meaning that wholesale removal is needed, or a sealing in process, before re-use can take place. Using the 'Polluter Pays' principle, existing owners may be persuaded to fund the cleaning up costs, especially with the prospect of attracting a new user to rid them of their liability. If the legacy is old and the

---

Example   **2.15**

USE: **Hospital (Royal Free), Islington, North London**
1848, Charles Fowler. Principal buildings listed. Four acre site, two/three-storey, brick with stone dressings.

TO: **Residential**
Largest housing association project tackled – 200 plus homes. Exemplar combination of new build and conversion.

A: **Levitt Bernstein Associates for eastern half and Pollard, Thomas and Edwards Architects for western half**[17]

New build viewed through the old – pedestrians have priority.

Hard landscape with useful artwork provides a suitably urban setting.

polluter has gone then the restorer picks up the tab, as at Cromford Mill which had been misused as a colour works so the cleaning and neutralising costs fell upon the Arkwright Society.

■ POLICY-LED RE-USE

In recent years a number of institutional buildings have come onto the market. The advent of telephone banking, the modernisation of health services, and the slimming down of our armed forces have rendered these buildings surplus to requirements, creating opportunities everywhere, whether in the heart of towns and cities, or on large sites in the suburbs and open countryside. Some military installations placed on the market – ports, airfields and army camps – are the size of a small town, and made up of a wide variety of buildings.

Changes to planning and development policies of local government also provide opportunities by allowing commercial activity to spread into a new area, possibly by

Example	2.16

USE: **Warehouse (fruit and vegetable), Covent Garden**
Nineteenth century, two/three-storey, brick with stone details, corner building.

TO: **Retail studio (graphic centre)**
New cast iron, riveted staircase, set diagonally, accesses first floor with additional flight painted onto the wall to provide an illusion of a larger space. Stainless steel counters, lit underneath, appear to hover above the retained York paving.

A: **Paul Brookes Architects**[18]

Concept sketch.

Interior stairs and trompe l'oeil create an optical illusion. (*Chris Wood*)

relaxing restrictions on mixed use, or otherwise relaxing constraints enabling older buildings to be incorporated into new proposals.

The opposing approaches of redevelopment and re-use may become so polarised that high profile arguments result, as was the case with No 1 Poultry in the City of London, where two sides, one supporting a new Miesian tower, and the other supporting skilful rehabilitation, fought their case at appeal and in the High Court. Each situation for re-use creates its own dynamic for the property's future. If the challenge of bonding together the needs of the user and the building in its context is to be met, then the case should be a clear and positive statement.

REFERENCES

1. Save Britain's Heritage; the campaigning organisation that uses the media to lobby public and government opinion.
2. Available from the SPAB, 37 Spital Square, London E1 6DY, this includes a short description of their features.
3. Usually available from the County or District Conservation Officer.
4. Spring, M., Court Favo, *Building*, Vol cclx, No 11, 1995, pp 42–8 and Tibbalds Monro.
5. Hyne, R H., 'Conservation of a Dilapidated Barn into a Dwelling', *Building Conservation*, Vol 2, No 1, 1980, pp 18–20 and Edgington, Spink and Hyne Architects.
6. Usually available from the Council's Development Department. These are not comprehensive as they rely upon owners or agents volunteering information.
7. Cantacuzino, S., *Saving Old Buildings*, The Architectural Press, London (1981), p 181 and The Landmark Trust. The Landmark Trust is an independent preservation charity that rescues and restores architecturally interesting and historic buildings at risk, giving them a future and renewed life by letting them for self-catering holidays. Details of all 166 buildings are in the Landmark Handbook, available from Shottesbrooke, Maidenhead, Berkshire, SL6 3SW (01628 825925).
8. Ibid.
9. Civic Trust Awards, 1995.
10. McIntyre, A., 'Born Again Barn', *Architects Journal*, 3 April 1991 pp 40-5 and Hale, M, 'The Barn House', *Country Life*, 23 July 1988, pp 74–7.
11. Owner, Nic Stone, DE7 6HP and *Derby Evening Telegraph*.
12. Johnson, A., *Converting Old Buildings*, David and Charles, London (1988), pp 196-200 and David Clarke Associates.
13. Author, (Project Architect: David Bagshaw).
14. *Building*, Vol 255, No 15, 13 April 1990, pp 46–8 and Tony Weller of *Building* Magazine.
15. Thompson, J., 'Music Boxes', *Building Renewal* (a supplement of *Building*), 26 August 1994, pp 10–15, also Heber-Percy and Parker, and Gardner and Theobald Management Services.
16. The architect and Ian Bruce.
17. Cowan, R., 'From Hospital to Housing', *Architects Journal*, Vol 196, No 3, 1992, pp 20–3 and the Civic Trust and English Heritage.
18. *Architects Journal*, 10 October 1996, p 44.

From: The Thermal Baths, Buxton
         'Buxton in the Swim'[a]
To: The Cavendish Arcade

Now Grade II listed, in an Outstanding Conservation Area, the Thermal Baths were built for the Duke of Devonshire in the late eighteenth century by architects Henry Currey and Joseph Paxton. Adjoining the famous Crescent, they were highly fashionable and immensely popular with all classes. These single-storey spa baths are unique, comprising a series of triple cubicles along two corridors, a public bath at the rear, and a three-storey pumphouse. Fronted in stone the baths originally had a glazed 'ridge and furrow' roof. After the First World War they fell into disuse and decay. Derelict for nearly 30 years, and having changed hands several times, the property ended up with the local authority who were unable to find funds for conversion to a tourist information centre. Faced with a potential purchase, and the subsequent demolition of all but the front façade, by Kwik Save supermarket chain, the authority asked the Derbyshire Historic Buildings Trust (DHBT) if it could rescue the building. The shopping arcade was completed in 1987, winning a Europa

Nostra Award and priming the pump for re-use in the neighbouring Crescent and the Devonshire Royal Hospital. 'The construction cost of £750,000 represented value for money which no new building could have matched.'[b] The re-use relied upon the following creative factors:

■ **Feasibility study**

Other potential uses were studied, but as the building was aligned between the shopping and the tourist area, the option chosen was to create an arcade of interest which might attract people looking for specialist shopping or simply sightseeing. The architect's appraisal showed that with some grant assistance the project could break even and still retain the majority of the original corridors, some of the original bathing cubicles, a display of the specialist bath for invalids, and even allow for the repair or replacement of the tiling.

■ **The creation of a central glazed space to provide a focus indoors**

A central space was taken from the originally planned form of the building to create a small atrium providing a refuge from Buxton's wet weather. To compensate for this loss a part of the roof area was used as lettable space. The use of light through stained glass was an integral part of the design, adding colour to counteract

The baths converted to an arcade with the cylindrical roof reflecting the curve of the Crescent and the dome of the hospital behind.

Stair hall before.

Buxton's grey skies. The barrel vault window straddled more than the small, forum-like area created at ground-floor level; incorporating the pumphouse as well as a first floor, flowing out at the previous roof level and providing a restaurant space overlooking the forum.

■ DHBT persistence in the face of difficulty

Persistence on the part of DHBT was vital. The break-even ventures previously operated by the Trust had been in the residential sector. For a retail venture the Trust found it almost impossible to raise capital unless there was a substantial profit margin. Presentation and negotiations, with two investment companies fell through before agreement was reached with St Modwen to acquire and manage the project upon completion. The practicalities of the project were not easy either, as the River Wye runs diagonally underneath the building and there were two enormous water storage tanks which no one knew about underneath the building. Divers were sent down to investigate what was supporting the Baths and they resurfaced with it in their hands: corroded iron and mud. Foundations for the barrel vault had to be supported on this. The tanks were drained by the Fire Service as a training exercise; the structure strengthened; and the contingency fund

drained too. The party wall between the Thermal Baths and the adjacent shops in separate ownership proved to be a major difficulty when it was discovered to be of timber stud construction and riddled with both dry and wet rot. Part of the roof support, it moved when pushed, and its reconstruction in blockwork had to be undertaken outside trading hours to keep to schedule.

■ Innovative techniques of repair to keep costs down

The turquoise tiles were crazed and many were damaged or missing; a specialist firm, Maws of Newcastle under Lyme, was called in to produce precise replicas. The cream tiled architraves presented a different problem. They were also severely crazed, but the cracks went deeper than the glaze, and in the end had to be replaced by new tiles. New ceramic tiles replicating the variety of intricate mouldings could not be afforded within the budget so were specially made of fibreglass. Visitors can only tell the difference by knocking the tiles and listening for the hollow sound of the replacements.

■ Retention of the original features

The original Joseph Paxton roof was said to be a glazed 'ridge and furrow roof' so the decision was taken to add one glazed pitch of the roof slopes over each original corridor, even though these were of a later design than Paxton's. This created a light and airy quality in corridors that were previously dark and forbidding. Interior planting was used to emphasise the high-level break between the restored walls and open ceiling. The original changing cubicles have been turned into shop units; alternate doorways converted into shop windows displaying wares as if in a glass jewel box. Those facing onto the central forum were left to be fitted out by incoming tenants. Simple interpretative boards were designed and fitted to assist the understanding of the history of the building, and there is a hapless figure in a ducking chair hovering over one of the original baths as if preparing for a plunge. Carpet finish was selected as the corridors were originally carpeted. In the new atrium area the carpet pattern gives an archaeological pointer to the location of the lost walls.

■ Use of the first floor as a restaurant

Upstairs are the restaurant and coffee shop, the balustrade of which has been glazed with the old etched glass from the windows of the thermal baths. Shoppers and visitors can relax here, bathed in the glowing light from the stained glass roof, designed by the celebrated artist Brian Clarke.

■ The attraction of a major work of art

The stained glass barrel vaulted roof is an attraction from near and far. Its cylindrical form acts as a counter point to both the curving Buxton Crescent and the

Corridor after – with glazing over and alternate cubicle doorways converted into showcases.

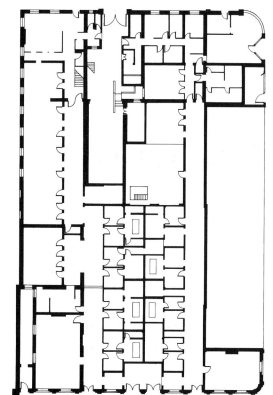

Plan before, showing cubicles and baths.

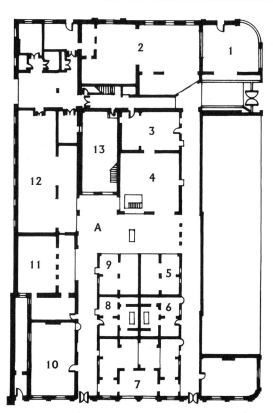

Plan after, showing shop units (unit 13 links to first floor restaurant).

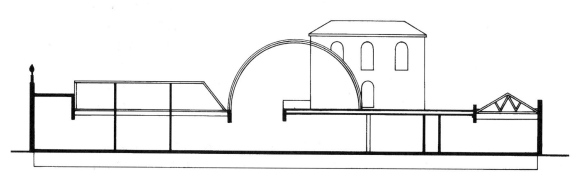

Diagrammatic section showing new cylindrical roof.

dome of the Derbyshire Royal Hospital. Colours from sap green through ultramarine blue to orange and opalescent white bathe the interior of the shopping arcade by day, and at night create a radiant landmark for Buxton. Constructing the frame for the 3,000 sq ft roof was a delicate matter. Seven 40 ft wide, three ton steel arches were lowered by a giant crane and bolted by a team of spidermen. An outer skin of polycarbon has been stretched over the stained glass to protect it from the ravages of the weather.[c]

Also see colour plate 2.

■ References

a. 'Buxton in the Swim', *Building Magazine*, 12 February 1988.
b. *Leisure Management*, December 1990, p 31.
c. Project Architect: Paul Glowacki, Latham Architects.

CHAPTER 3

The Challenge of Creative Re-use

The context of re-use is multidimensional. Re-use plays a role within the conservation debate and this is reflected in government policy. Changing attitudes to historic buildings, witnessed by an increase in the numbers of listed buildings have also drawn attention to the extent of building underuse or neglect.

For those working in conservation, the challenge has shifted. Whereas early campaigners fought to safeguard buildings from loss, their successors are ensuring that buildings will continue to survive by containing an appropriate, if not an original use. For campaigners the emphasis has changed towards the identification of new uses; ones that can provide an economic impetus for successful conservation. In a rapidly changing situation, the emerging challenge is to find a creative response to re-use, to reject the previous short-sighted attitude that a new use must be special or precious to be worthy of the building being conserved. The customary solution – offering a museum or heritage centre function as a new use – is now not necessarily a viable option.

Such attitudes continue to threaten many buildings and the need to promote newly identified uses is pressing. A position on the Executive Committee of the Council for the Care of Churches over a number of years meant that I witnessed many fine and substantial churches proposed not just for redundancy but for demolition. On occasion this was because just a few thousand pounds of expenditure was needed – sums beyond the means of a small group of parishioners yet insignificant as part of a large rehabilitation or conversion project. Nearly all of the church buildings subsequently demolished had the capacity for re-use, if only sufficient people had been alerted to the possibilities (see St Michael's 1.3).

The solution for obsolete buildings does not lie in uninspired tours of their dark and empty shells, but in the widespread encouragement of a new attitude that 'buildings are useful – buildings can be re-used'. A building does not have to be precious to be kept. The quest for sustainable approaches to meeting our development needs

Example   3.1

USE: Railway goods depot, Liverpool
1874, Grade II, three-storey, curved façade in decorative brick with gothic style stone dressings and a central sloping street for moving loaded wagons, 600 sq m with generous ground floor ceiling heights.

TO: Art conservation centre
Museum, offices, library, conservation studios and staff facilities are housed in the original office building. Exterior unaltered, except for double glazing, roof renewed, and interior reconstructed to accommodate demanding service requirements with robust detailing creating a cogent strong building fit for its purpose: a factory for art. The painting conservation studios are located on the top floor, maximising the use of natural light through new sloping glazing.

A: Ken Martin Architects[1]

Before – first floor.

After.

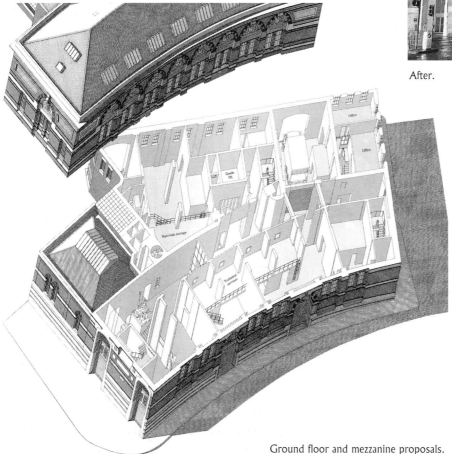

Ground floor and mezzanine proposals.

now embraces even quite modest buildings as suitable subjects for creative re-use. This will contribute to the diverse re-use of buildings becoming more widely accepted, reflecting a growing ethos that new uses should be seen as an opportunity rather than a threat.

Re-use is not typically conspicuous; a building that has been successfully re-used rarely draws attention to itself. Exceptions occur when the brief requires some particular notice to be taken of the new use (3.2). An exhibition centre, by its very nature,

Example   3.2

USE: Fruitmarket, Market Street, Edinburgh
c1900, Grade II, steel frame, timber floors, non-structural stonework, above railway tracks for transfer of fruit from rail to road, 30 × 16 m.

TO: Gallery
First converted early 1970s, remodelled late 1970s the property was renovated and reopened in 1992. The upper floor suffered a low ceiling height with no natural light, accessible by concealed fire escape and an elevation 'reminiscent of a bunker'. Three significant architectural interventions transformed the building; the flat roof replaced by a winged roof increasing hanging height and introducing north and south clerestory light; a drawbridge staircase placed centrally; and the ground floor façade opened up to a new café and bookshop, with glazed sliding door and hoist in a new opening over the entrance.

A: Richard Murphy Architects

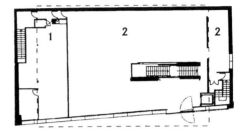

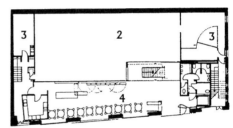

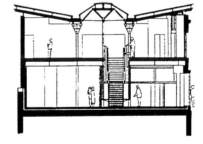

Key
1. Offices
2. Galleries
3. Plant
4. Café/bookshop

First floor plan, ground floor plan and section.

Before.

After – showing new 'butterfly' roof and openings in the façade.

Example | **3.3**

USE: **Church, Trinity, Aberdeen**
Nineteenth century, Gothic, granite, derelict.

TO: **Maritime museum**
Extended from the adjacent Provost house and linked to it by a new uncompromising glazed entrance extension, the church interior was gutted and four *in situ* concrete floors inserted on profiled steel permanent shuttering on a steel frame treated as a series of overlapping planes with voids between, allowing views through to different levels.

A: **Property Services Department, Aberdeen County Council**

Third floor plan. The design had to accommodate the voids necessary to house some of the huge exhibits and the different levels between the three buildings. (*Mike Davidson – Positive Image*)

Key
1. Temporary exhibition
2. Harbour design
3. Oil industry
4. Model of oil rig (through 3 floors)
5. Helicopter safety
6. Plant room
7. Void
8. Store
9. Office

The new link between house and church clearly displays its function. (*Mike Davidson – Positive Image*)

may want to publicise its presence, similarly an occupier may wish to promote some unique, possibly corporate, identity by dramatic exterior intervention (3.3). Unfortunately, successful re-use can give the misleading impression that the adaptation process is easy, resulting in an apparently simple and obvious conclusion. This is far from true, as the effort taken to achieve the end result is hidden, going unseen – and perhaps unvalued – in the eye of the beholder (3.1).

■ CHANGING ATTITUDES VIA LEGISLATION

The increasing number of properties listed as buildings of special historic or architectural significance is a demonstration of the growing need both to protect old, as well as many more recent structures, and to increase our resourcefulness in finding new uses to ensure their survival.

In 1991 an assessment of the state of the nation's historic building stock was completed in the form of English Heritage's Buildings at Risk survey. Although updated in 1998, the original was conducted along the same lines as the Derbyshire Historic Buildings Trust survey of 'Buildings Empty, Neglected or in Need of Repair' undertaken seventeen years before. It stated that 'the majority are the everyday buildings of the past which make up the character of England's towns and countryside . . . most in reasonable condition but a significant minority are at risk from neglect and others in a vulnerable condition and in need of repair.'[2]

Anticipating re-use rather than redevelopment, the same survey also described unlisted buildings within Conservation Areas as having a collective 'group value', so that their overall massing, form, scale and texture are worthy of retention as a setting for the listed buildings. Taken with other buildings outside Conservation Areas, these are of intrinsic interest, with local though probably not national significance, and are sometimes recognised by local authorities in a 'non-statutory local list of properties' that they refer to when considering planning applications.

The major factor leading to neglect is lack of use, and this often arises because the building's spatial layout or structure may be hard to adapt to appropriate new use. For instance: tall buildings (such as water towers) (3.4), large buildings (power stations), monumental buildings (castles), low ceilinged buildings (maltings), small buildings (dovecotes) and buildings inherently incapable of economic use (tombs and monuments).

The type of use may no longer be of value as a result of changes in population, processes of production, or economic policy. The location may be a deterrent to use due to remoteness, inaccessibility, site security, bad neighbours or pollution.

Very likely there will be ownership difficulties caused by inheritance, bankruptcy, disputes, avarice or parsimony.

Example **3.4**

USE: **Tower (folly), North Wales**

1821, extended 1859, Grade II, six-storeys, stone, castellated, Gothic style. Timber windows changed to cast iron frames on the later three added storeys.

TO: **Residential**

Walls over window lintels stitched with concrete and repointed. Original documentation showing intended use as a study retreat was used to avoid a change of use application – and a requirement for an additional external stair. Floors and stair were upgraded to 1 hour fire resistance. Heating pipes are avoided by using low voltage under floor mats.

A: **Adam and Frances Voelcker**[3]

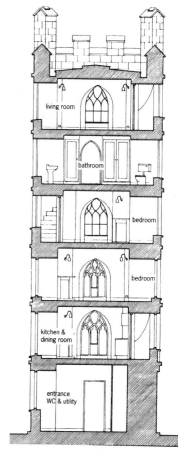

Bathroom with a view.

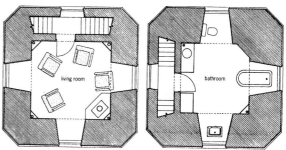

Plans and sections.

Simply as a result of its numerical superiority the largest category at risk is domestic buildings, but the greater concern is for agricultural buildings, warehouses, industrial mills, and wind and water mills. To this must be added increasing concern for military buildings, hospitals and the full range of utility buildings which no longer have a use. (All of these are considered more fully in Chapter 15, Volume Two.)

■ FUNDING PRIORITIES

The extent to which buildings are at risk immediately raises the question of resources and how they might best be deployed. The limits on funds available for heritage restoration have a decisive effect on the action taken. Whether the funding comes from government endowments, fund raising activities, or reinvestment within a wider estate, the net result is a constantly debated set of priorities, and the effect of this is to create a hierarchy of buildings from castles and cathedrals, down through significant industrial archaeology and ending at the humble cottage. This is not a static hierarchy: building subcategories now move both up and down the scale as the controlling funding responds more to a mixture of need and opportunity, rather than academic category. Within this increasingly fluid funding situation re-use, in bringing a financial investment through its plans for repair, can contribute more to the opportunity part of the hierarchy calculation. Re-use not only introduces money into the equation but also creates the dynamic of intervention, requiring a payback for its investment (3.5). The greater the intervention, the more likely it is that the re-use will have to fund all the repair; whilst the greater the limits on creativity, the more likely it is that the re-user will look to the government (or other community) purse for assistance.

■ RANGE OF POLICY INITIATIVES

In DoE Circular 8/87 prominence was given to the consideration of re-use.[4] Alternative uses were considered as an essential element of the armoury for action to protect buildings, to the point of exhorting local planning authorities to adopt flexible policies towards changes of use. The circular even reinforced the need for listed buildings to be genuinely offered for sale at a reasonable price before demolition could be entertained. Its general tone reflected continuity and greater clarity in the Government's policy towards preserving historic buildings and was closer in nature to the new form of Planning Policy Guidance notes (PPGs) published from 1988 on. In 1994, *Planning and the Historic Environment* was issued as PPG 15, the title reflecting a broadening of scope compared with Circular 8/87. Publication also allowed the provisions of the 1990 Town and Country Planning Act to be included.

A significant change in emphasis was introduced in PPG 15, relating to the re-use of historic buildings and offering a more positive regime than its predecessor. More criteria are included; against which to assess possible alterations or demolition of a listed building.[5] These embrace the need for flexibility when the original use for which the building was designed cannot be retained or reinstated. Whereas Circular 8/87 had indicated that new uses should be sought which would not damage the historic fabric, PPG 15 is less strict, commenting that a new use may be the key to the preservation of a listed building, especially where the building is functionally obsolescent.[6] The guidance goes on to suggest that where a new economic use can be achieved it may be possible for sensitive alterations to be made that would secure long-term preservation.[7] The fourth criterion for proposed alterations to vacant or obsolescent buildings offers positive advice:

> The extent to which the proposed works would bring substantial benefits for the community, in particular by contributing to the economic regeneration of the area or the enhancement of its environment (including other listed buildings)[8] (3.5).

Example   3.5

USE: **Corn exchange, Kings Lynn**
1854, Grade II, with handsome three bay stone façade of giant Ionic order fronting a long brick 'shed' with delicate iron trusses supporting a glazed roof.

TO: **Concert hall and events space**
The intervention necessary to retain the historic fabric is clearly displayed externally by the new brick piers supporting the flank wall either side of the new steel columns supporting the new roof. The roofs overhanging eaves protect a timber clad 'clerestory' expressing the acoustic plenum over the auditorium. A brick, parapet gabled, slated roofed, rear extension of similar scale accommodates the back of house facilities in an unmistakably up-to-date style, with a balcony to the administration suite overlooking the Staithe. Internally, the delicate iron trusses have been retained to support a steel gauze inner skin on the line of the original glazed roof. High quality bleacher seating allows flexibility of seating, performance and activity areas, whilst the consistently robust yet elegant detailing of handrails and theatrical technical paraphernalia provides the only decoration needed in the Auditorium. The ground and mezzanine foyers behind the front façade are adorned with artwork as hangings, blinds and sculptured metalwork balustrades. The clean beech floored, designer style interior provides a friendly café bar and accessible booking office. Understandably, this is a popular venue attracting a wide range of performers and activities.

A: **Levitt Bernstein Associates[9]**

Cleaned and restored front. (*Matthew Weinreb*)

New extension to the rear. (*Matthew Weinreb*)

Interior retains much of the original character. (*Matthew Weinreb*)

Axonometric

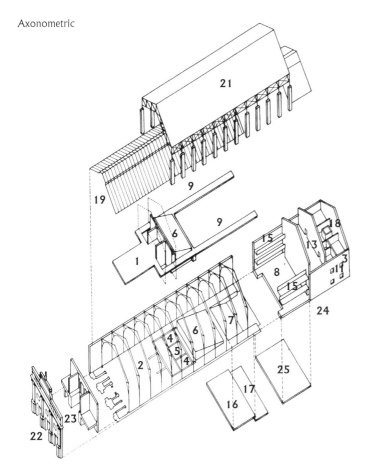

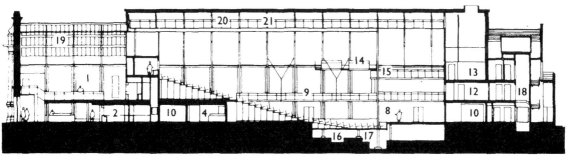

Longitudinal section: concert mode

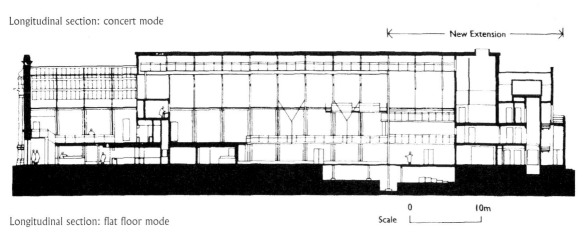

Longitudinal section: flat floor mode

New Extension

Scale 0   10m

Creative re-use of a building is not normally served by demolition and reconstruction behind a retained façade; PPG 15 also states that, 'the preservation of façades alone, and the gutting of and reconstruction of interiors, is not normally an acceptable approach to the re-use of listed buildings; it can destroy much of the building's special interest and create problems for the long-term stability of the structure.'

However, there may be occasion where the building's historic interest is low but environmental streetscape quality high. In such circumstances redevelopment behind façades may be an acceptable method of re-creating sustainable activity as part of an area wide regeneration. (See Jewellery Business Centre, 6.4.) Contemplation of the total demolition of a listed building meets with three further assessment criteria in PPG 15. As might be expected, these are considerably more refined than those in Circular 8/87, and require more evidence to be provided by the owner to justify the grant of listed building consent. They include demonstrating that every effort has been made to continue the present use or find an alternative use.

Case Study	3.6

From: Repton School Sanatorium
To: The New Music School

This case study demonstrates that neither the use nor the ownership have to change dramatically to apply the concept of creative re-use. This Edwardian sanatorium, two-storeys in red brick and roof tiles, had three short, interconnected wings. The structure was sound but the services obsolete, so modern healthcare provision had rendered it redundant. Re-use relied upon seven key factors, detailed under the following headings.

■ **Combining two apparently unrelated initiatives**
The school governors were inclined to demolish the sanatorium but they engaged architects to identify whether a viable new use was possible so that the property could be sold to advantage. Coincidentally, the school was raising money for a new music school to be built on a green field site, but costs for a new construction were too high. The brief for this accommodation was similar in size to the existing sanatorium. So this brief was applied to various conversion alternatives on the sanatorium. Initally the task seemed impossible: the spaces did not fit and the circulation requirements would not work.

■ **Gutting the central section of first floor to enable construction of the rehearsal room**
The breakthrough came with the raising of the roof over the centre wing of the sanatorium. This was then extended on the first-floor level to the doctor's house at the rear, being large enough to accommodate the rehearsal space. This allowed circulation to pass underneath along the original corridor with a new entrance at the rear of the building which ultimately provided a more direct route to the school campus. By careful analysis and manipulation of the existing structure, the music school brief was fitted room by room with the footprint of the old sanatorium to within a tolerance of plus or minus ten per cent. If the project was to be a success however, something more had to be achieved. The 'old san', as it was known, was disliked by the pupils and its conversion to a music school was unlikely to inspire.

Rear of the sanatorium before.

After – as the entrance to The New Music School.

■ **Re-orientating the building with a new entrance facing the school campus**

The sanatorium sat in front of a sunken lane with high hedges. Access from the main school was across the playing fields, negotiating a mix of paths and unkempt boundaries. Curiously, the sanatorium was accessed by entrances at each end of the long corridor, giving an impression of insularity and even of foreboding, appropriate only for an isolation ward for contagious diseases in a pre-antibiotic era. The solution was to re-landscape the rear garden to open the site up towards the playing fields and lead to a new central entrance at the rear of the building. This was designed to be open and inviting, using a glazed timber screen to allow the inside to be easily visible from without. The entrance roof sweeps down to ground-floor level, reducing the apparent scale. The landscape was then opened up to reveal the building's new aspects.

■ **Utilising the heavy masonry construction to provide sound insulation**

With an internal arrangement that placed stores between rehearsal rooms and classrooms, sound proofing was restricted to sand pugging between the floor joists.

■ **Avoid the use of air conditioning**

Trials within the building showed ambient noise levels from outside were preferable to the hum of air conditioning; reducing costs.

■ **Interior design to present the building as a new music school**

Internally the need to achieve acoustic control and sound absorbency, even in the corridors, was used as an excuse to introduce carpeting. A varied, and sometimes controversial, colour scheme was adopted

Auditorium.

throughout. Together with new lighting, this added interest and a vivid intensity to transform the image of the interior. This was preceded by an early trial colour scheme in various rooms of the building, upon which comments were received: a technique of client consultation, which is always a possibility when re-using existing buildings, but hardly possible when designing new buildings, other than at the last stages before occupation.

■ Empathic alterations and additions

In undertaking these substantial alterations the design philosophy became critical. A direct copy and extension of the original Edwardian character would only reinforce the severe monumentality of the building. On the other hand a strong contrast would devalue the original by laying too much emphasis upon the new elements. The solution adopted was to use roof slopes of the same pitch and same natural red clay tiles as the existing,

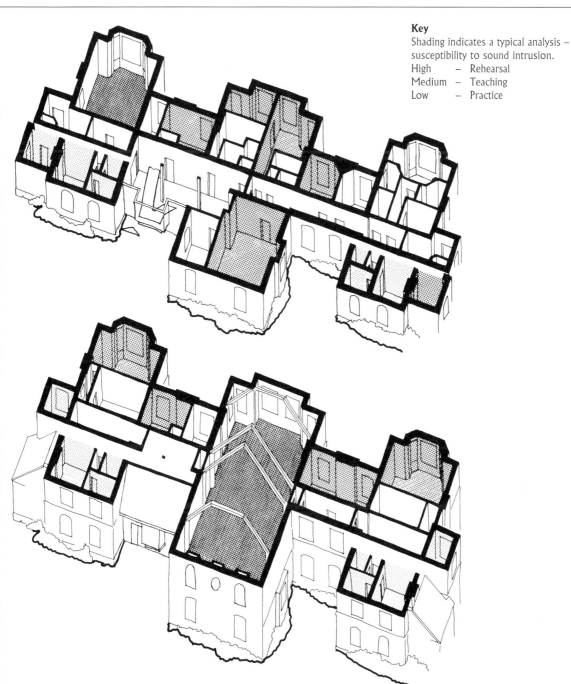

Key
Shading indicates a typical analysis –
susceptibility to sound intrusion.
High   –   Rehearsal
Medium –   Teaching
Low   –   Practice

Axonometric viewed from rear.

both to roof the new rehearsal room and to sweep down over the new entrance. Monumentality was avoided by using a glazed clerestory around the rehearsal room between the original and amended eaves height and a glazed screen across the entrance. The division of the glazing with mullions, transoms and glazing bars followed a varied rhythm derived from the 'Fibonacci' scales which form the basis of much musical rhythm. This produced properties sympathetic to original glazing patterns, though quite dissimilar, so expressing the new use of the building rather than simply copying from the past.[a]

Also see colour plate 3.

■ Reference

a. Project Architect: John Goom, Latham Architects.

■ SOURCES FOR INSPIRATION

Owners and practitioners can find inspiration from many sources. In the first instance they are well served by the range of amply illustrated publications which show re-use projects that have taken place over the past twenty years. Early examples tend to emphasise the architectural attributes of conversion projects that involve a wide range of uses selected internationally.[10] These had, and still have, an important role in inspiring others to consider new possibilities. Later writers have explored the methods of conversion,[11] or specialised in particular types of buildings.[12] The wider impact of re-use activity has also been addressed, indicating how it can act as a catalyst for other social or economic benefits or extend to very large complexes of buildings.

Opportunities for re-use have a chronological and historical context. Solutions applicable in the 1970s may be out of place in the new millennium since available building types and potential uses respond to changes in culture and the economy. Nevertheless, early examples still remain useful for inspiration and encouragement because the principles, if not the detail, still apply. Moreover, a retrospective glance at situations which have become unfamiliar with the passing of time, can assist lateral thought, stimulate new possibilities and increase the breadth of information available to the practitioner faced with the practicalities of re-use. Whilst we can learn from earlier examples, as circumstances change the copying of solutions from the past is not an option. This makes it essential to appoint competent professionals who will survey, analyse, interpret and propose contextual solutions for re-use appropriate to the current cultural and economic climate.

■ THE CHALLENGE

The case for re-use can be viewed as part philosophical and part practical, engaging or promoting re-use as set out in the following chapters. Having interpreted the context that has developed from preservation through to conservation, it is time to address fully the issues of re-use. The challenge of creative re-use is wider than heritage conservation: the reasons for retention are multiple. Although the distinction between those reasons can be blurred it is important that those proposing and those appraising re-use, should recognise the breadth of the spectrum from the rosy tints of history, through the multifaceted rainbow of community action to the clean green of environmental concern. The challenge is to broaden the applicability of conservation whilst increasing its effectiveness.

REFERENCES

1. Mulhearn, D., 'A factory for art rises from the ashes', *Architects Journal*, 13 June 1996, pp 45–7.
2. 'Buildings at Risk a New Strategy' and Buildings at Risk Register, English Heritage, 1998.
3. Singmaster, D., 'Gothic High-Rise Beats a Holiday Retreat', *Architects Journal*, 13 June 1996, p 49.
4. Circular 8/87, *Historic Buildings and Conservation Areas – Policy and Procedures*, Department of the Environment.
5. Pickard 1996.
6. Paragraph 2.18, PPG 15, DoE 1994.
7. Paragraph 3.13, PPG 15, DoE 1994.
8. Paragraph 3.15, PPG 15, DoE 1994.
9. Singmaster, D., 'Cornucopia in Kings Lynn', *Architects Journal*, 14 Nov 1996, pp 43–5 and Levitt Bernstein Associates.
10. Cantacuzino, S., *New Uses for Old Buildings*, Architectural Press, London 1975.
11. Markus, T., A., *Building Conversion and Rehabilitation: Designing for Change in Building Use*, Butterworth, London, 1979.
12. Johnson, A., *Converting Old Buildings: Homes from Barns, Churches, Warehouses, Stations*, David and Charles, Newton Abbot, 1988.

PART TWO

THE ROUTE TO A SUCCESSFUL PROJECT

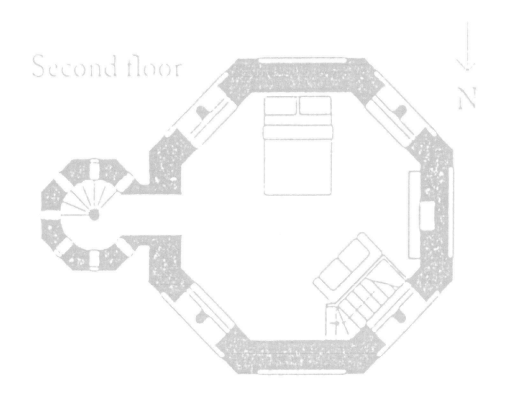

Second floor

CHAPTER 4

Initiating Action

An examination both of the appeal exerted by older buildings, and of the sustaining role played by creative re-use, defines the core audience whom the re-use process seeks to serve. Further analysis is required to establish the balance of knowledge, skill, and decision-making power that will initiate a process requiring a genuine team effort. Without the promoters, directors, actors and technicians there can be no production. Teamwork is essential if all the pitfalls of surveying, briefing, conceiving, designing, costing, engineering, approving, funding, detailing, specifying, pricing, implementing, commissioning and occupying are to be undertaken successfully.

PLANNING THE ROUTE TO A SUCCESSFUL PROJECT

A successful outcome for re-use means following a carefully and systematically planned route. Attention to detail at each of the key stages in the process is vital. Once a property has been selected as the subject for re-use, there are eight identifiable stages involving a mix of players, where critical risks arise and important decisions have to be taken.

Acquisition
Buildings of all types and sizes should be considered for re-use, but the first pivotal issue is the control of the building. Unless the promoter of re-use and the owner are one and the same, ownership will have to be secured. The purchase of an option for a period may be worthwhile to make time for a thorough feasibility study, ensuring that all the potential re-use's parameters can be met. The consent of an owner makes

purchase a benign issue, but aggressive tactics such as compulsory purchase orders or even company take-overs are all legitimate. However, outright control will be of little use if the initial appreciation of the building and its setting are unrealistic. At the outset it pays to be cautious of taking an over aggressive approach to gaining control if this is only driven by enthusiastic over optimism.

Understanding the building
The architect draws on a wide range of skills in evaluating the architectural merits of the building, its condition, exterior movement and stability. Desk research will be required, even some opening up on-site to examine structure or services. A landscape architect or urban planner may also need to analyse the property's wider setting, and the historic building architect to research a

Conservation Plan. There is more to this than just surveying and recording. A synthesising process leads from the many facts gathered to an understanding about the building. Sometimes problems arise from unexpected discoveries e.g. historic wall decoration, or something of new archaeological significance in the building's remains. The historical evidence may even point to potential structural problems that may redirect the efforts of re-use.

The user's brief

Briefing is a two way process. First time users can benefit from the significant help on offer from their advisers. A speculative venture will require market research to identify a 'dummy' user creating a typical profile against which decisions can be made. If the type of user remains unclear then a flexible 'parachute' brief will be needed. There are user groups other than the client to consider as buildings have an impact on visitors and the general public, entering or just passing by. It is critical to establish the requirements of all the users. A well considered brief will avoid later problems if it is user, not building, oriented.

Cost and finance

Bearing in mind that potential income must exceed expenditure, an accurate cost plan by a Quantity Surveyor is essential. This may be difficult to achieve in the early stages as comparing costs per square metre with other conversions may be misleading. A market analysis to assess commercial viability, and the availability of grants to cover part of the project costs both lend support. But external factors, such as inflation, should not be relied upon to resolve an otherwise unrealistic financial analysis. The antidote to unrealistic expectations at this embryonic stage is in part available through professional advice; but the key to success or failure may still hinge on the entrepreneurial skill of the client. The client may also have a preference for the form of funding, if not the source. In sum, the difficulties may include a vendor with unrealistically high hopes who fails to understand the true costs of re-use; or failure to find a backer sympathetic to the type of project. In the latter case, the presentation of a sound proposal via a feasibility study is critical to raising funds.

Design

In working with the building the professional team must develop the design together, and may involve craft trades in the project planning and evaluation to establish the all-round technical feasibility. The client must be willing to take ownership of the design at this stage, to be satisfied himself that the design matches the brief, signing this off

to avoid costly variations during the later stages of detail design or work on-site. Any tendency to compromise or doubt expressed by the client in taking 'ownership' of the design needs to be fully aired if the vision is to retain its clarity. Otherwise the truth of the original concept may be lost and an unsympathetic design imposed for misguidedly pragmatic reasons. To this end the critical direction of the project is dependent on the production of accurate information, presenting a clearly transparent and acceptable design solution. Recognition of the real issues means that problems arising from there being either a famine or a feast of information are less likely to lead to later variations, side-tracking from the main direction of the project.

Approvals

Legislation was not necessarily written with re-use in mind. The proposal will now be exposed to wider scrutiny by a variety of bodies. Each area of regulation brings a different perspective and degree of authority. One response is to seize the onus of responsibility, presenting strategies which invoke the spirit rather than the letter of the legislation. However, much as the team may try to influence the outcome, these decisions are in the hands of others. The consequences of the failure to win approval are delays, costly appeals or significant alterations to proposals. Such a possibility should be allowed for in the project timetable especially if the proposals are contentious. Optimistically – for re-use in general if not some particular projects – innovative solutions may well result which can provide guidance for future strategies.

Production

The overall design is now fixed and the detailed design can be developed, gaining client approval in stages. The production team must be left to get on with the paperwork: a legal document describing every detail of the proposals. The critical elements of the production stage are: time to prepare adequate information, the choice of procurement route, good co-ordination between consultants, the selection of the contractor and preparing and maintaining a realistic programme. Additional fee costs and programme delays are likely if client requirements are changed that cause design variations.

Implementation

Once works are opened up some of the soundest assumptions can be changed by evidence on-site. The prospect of a respectful, co-operative and productive dialogue between design team and contractor is what makes it possible to do justice to the preceding phases of the project. All the inspiration, research, planning, diplomacy, discussion, design, detailing, and production must be pulled into focus to inform the work necessary on-site. The end result still depends upon any unforeseen implementation being in accordance with all that has gone before. The delegation of responsibility should harness where possible the skills of particular operatives or craftsmen ensuring that design concepts are communicated to the hand that will implement them.

The appointment of a Clerk of Works might be considered as the works are likely to involve a wide range of trades. As they are likely to remain unseen, it is important that those which have the greatest impact upon the long life of the building (foundations and structure) and its performance (services) are properly supervised. At the end of the project it is the finishing trades that are evident and the importance of good preparation work for painting and decorating cannot be overemphasised: internally the majority of what can be seen is likely to be paint. Adherence to the proposals, clear decision-making and clear communication are critical if work on-site is to progress smoothly and costs be contained. There are times when it is more cost-effective to alter the finished product rather than amend the contract.

Occupation

Following this route, the journey is completed when the building is handed over and occupied. But this is not the end of the re-use story. The building needs to be maintained and kept in readiness for changes that will inevitably occur. A maintenance manual will be useful. Good management will be required if the facilities are to continue to serve the user well.

■ CATALYSTS

The process may begin with individuals who can show the way or provide an example for others to follow. Individuals such as Marcus Binney, working through SAVE Britain's Heritage; publishing books and catalogues, organising press campaigns to put country houses, churches, mills, hospitals and barracks to good use. Binney has demonstrated the waste, mismanagement and ignorance of some authorities and owners. Entrepreneurs like Kit Martin have shown how country houses and mansions can be successfully adapted for residential use; rarely subdividing existing spaces, so that the resulting apartments have an idiosyncratic mix of room sizes but each with its own front door (4.1).[1]

The rescue and adaptation of large, derelict, mill complexes for commercial use also requires vision and great zeal. Two notable relationships: that of Sir Ernest Hall with the re-use of Dean Clough Mills (4.2), and of the late Nathaniel Silver with Titus Salt's Mill at Saltaire (16.3, Volume Two) are noteworthy. Not only did these structures survive, but they now employ more people within their walls than at any time since their industrial heyday. Many less prominent individuals have initiated smaller projects to secure the re-use of modest but worthy subjects for conservation, demonstrating how widespread is the belief that change is possible for those who have the conviction and stamina to take their vision through to completion.

Change of ownership is often enough to trigger the process of re-evaluation. A prospective purchaser often brings a fresh input of ideas, or a new approach to a previously intractable problem. Not untypically there are resources, financial or otherwise, in support. From the creative re-use perspective such new owners become agents for change. They are catalysts to the process, regardless of whether

Example   **4.1**

USE: **Country house, The Hasells, Bedfordshire**
1720, remodelled 1791 by Martin Cole for
Francis Pym, Grade II*, two/three-storey, 7
× 11 bays, brick, stone dressings, parapet
and simple doric portico, sash windows,
extensive outbuildings. War-requisitioned,
then used as a hospital, left semi-derelict,
application to demolish was refused.

TO: **Residential**
Converted to three principal houses in the
south and east front to avoid dividing the
main rooms, cottages in the former stables
and flats in the three-storey kitchen block.
Access is from existing doorways and all
residences have their own garden as well as
shared use of 15 acres of communal park
and woodland. Together with the conversion
of Dingley Hall, this became the prototype
country house conversion.

A: **Malcolm Leverington for Kit Martin**

Courtyard. (Mark Fiennes)

Key	V	Void	S	Study
B	Bedroom	U	Utility	D	Dining
Ba	Bathroom	L	Living	t	toilet

South and west elevations restored. (*Mark Fiennes*)

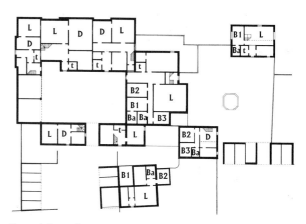

Ground floor plan.

First floor plan.

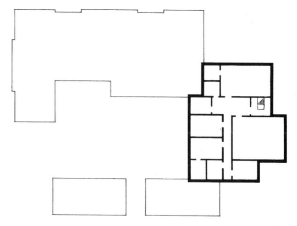

Second floor plan.

Example . **4.2**

USE: Mills: Crossley Carpets, Dean Clough, Halifax
1840–70, 1,000,000 sq ft in a series of stone mills between three- and six-storeys. Business ceased in the late 1970s and the building lay empty in 1982.

TO: Offices, workshops, galleries, restaurant and theatre
Re-occupation and re-use was the vision of Sir Ernest Hall, led by creating studio space for artists along with a series of talks and events that has continued to grow. Occupants vary from small companies to major corporations, entrepreneurs to voluntary groups. The reception and circulation space forms the gallery whilst viaduct arches have been converted to a theatre space.[2]

The Mill complex fills the valley.

they are individuals or organisations (companies, trusts or local authorities). In taking this role they may act on the advice of a team of professionals who can encompass a wider range of ideas and offer an objective assessment of the possibilities. To form a team, however small, can be the key to achieving results. In its own way, the team may need a catalyst, a project champion to project the vision, to maintain momentum and stay on course. This might be the owner, perhaps a developer looking for a commercial solution, or could include a campaigner seeking to safeguard a building's future. As the project progresses it is not uncommon for this role to transfer to another individual; one who has the time or particular skills needed to fulfil the task.

■ INHIBITORS

The first hurdle to overcome may be individuals or organisations who by their attitudes or actions frustrate or inhibit re-use. Twenty-five years of advising historic building trusts in their efforts to save old buildings has led me to believe conclusively that there is no such thing as a problem building, only problem owners. A building is or will become a problem if certain attitudes are encountered in the owner. The owner may be unsympathetic, misguided, impecunious or recalcitrant. The problem might lie in the lack of ownership. This may be intestate, disputed or unclear. The owner may be absent; remote from the daily management of the property.

Whenever a building is seriously neglected it is because an inactive owner no longer has a use for it. As neglect causes increasing deterioration the owner should decide how best to use the property. Failing that, they should let it or sell it. Occasionally owners are difficult about trading their property and a few even practise wilful neglect out of some misguided and selfish sense of proprietorship. Sometimes it is not the building itself that is the victim of a problem owner, but the surrounding land. Prevention or discouragement of access to or from the building occurs by withholding a right of way or operating an incompatible use (which even if unauthorised can be difficult to stop). Some owners are simply unsympathetic and require persuasion through explanation of the benefits they could realise from change or improved use of the building.

In contrast, the misguided owner can often be enthusiastic, with grand but inappropriate ideas. Understanding by example; visiting comparable properties; meeting other owners can all be effective remedies. SPAB even runs courses for owners who wish to learn. It does not follow that clear intentions are all that are needed. Avaricious owners or entrepreneurs have clear intent, but not one that will benefit the building. This may arise from underestimating the costs of proper repair or overestimating the value of the property. Recalcitrant owners may only respond to both positive and negative treatment; the incentive of grants combined with the threat of a repair notice.

Quite often, owners do not realise how much their property has devalued owing to the lack of repair. A responsible owner ought to have a real understanding of a property's worth. They will have maintained it in reasonable order, and in carrying out alterations or extensions in accordance with the appropriate consents, taken care not to compromise the character and qualities of the original. In this way, the value will have been retained or enhanced (13.1). However, the value put on a property by one owner can differ from that put by another. Faced with the demise of an existing use, the current owner may have to realise that time and money must be invested to secure a new use, if not by them, then by someone else. A review of the property holding, whether a single building group or a wider estate, can open up the possibilities for alternative use. In such an informed situation, realism ought to prevail in the assessment of current value and discussions about sale prices. The process of re-use can then be embarked upon with the objective of maximising the value of the property.

Over-zealous enthusiasts, even experts, defending a personal belief or corporate objective may lose the ability to hear or understand another point of view. Behind such dogma usually lie alternative solutions to a problem. Representatives of official bodies should at least be prepared to consider a different, well-presented argument from a professional with a proven record of achievement. After all, government guidance encourages wider discretion on matters of detail in order to achieve broader conservation goals.

■ TRUSTS

Strength in numbers brings confidence in a common cause. From the commitment and actions of a single person can come the capacity to forge a team or group who share similar objectives. Anger at the threat of demolition, or despair at the waste of dereliction can create sufficient pent up energy for a group to take control of an unsatisfactory situation. Many such groups have formed a trust to achieve their objectives.

Building preservation trusts are not a new idea. Both SPAB and the National Trust started with the objective of saving a building. Their value is in being the purchasers of last resort, taking on problems that other organisations have failed to resolve. They are non-profit making and run mostly by volunteers. They fulfil an amenity and conservation role with the important element of financial accountability. As charities operating to achieve specific ends, they also act as a catalyst for wider improvements and certainly open doors that would be closed to others. The key mechanism to a trust's success is the revolving fund. Money is raised to fund one project, the returns from a sale at its conclusion can then be released for a subsequent project. A national revolving fund operates with the support of the Architectural Heritage Fund and acts as the primary mortgagor to more than one hundred trusts in Great Britain.

Using actions rather than words most trusts work with a local knowledge, earning considerable respect through their ability to solve problems thought insuperable by others. A few concentrate upon a particular building type e.g. the Industrial Buildings Preservation Trust. Others like the Vivat Trust, Phoenix Trust and Buildings at Risk Trust tackle large, national projects such as country houses, old hospitals and barracks. Some act with single, specific purposes; like enabling use as a community facility (Park United Reformed Church, Halifax), heritage centre (Silk Mill, Wirksworth, 8.6) or a museum (Ironbridge Gorge, Shropshire). Many private schools and some universities are also charitable trusts or foundations, holding property for educational uses and for investment purposes. The Derbyshire Historic Buildings Trust was set up in 1974 and over twenty years undertook twenty projects, from individual properties to whole groups, to a total value of £2 million from starting capital of just £14,000.

Of particular interest for creative re-use are the trusts that regard the preservation and use of heritage property as their primary role. Unique in the scale of its operation and the independence of its action is the National Trust. Managing its estate as an exemplary landlord, the conservation value of its properties and landscape attracts millions of visitors annually. The Trust is therefore involved in the leisure and tourism industry, the act of caring for the individual properties becoming the re-use for which visitors regularly return. Smaller trusts fulfil a similar role. The Landmark Trust is pre-eminent amongst these, acquiring the most unlikely structures over many years. Factories, forts, follies and farms, monuments and moated houses have all been converted; fitted out as holiday homes and furnished appropriately (2.5, 2.6).

Public authorities and agencies do still play a role in saving buildings and providing amenities, but owing to reduced resources this is increasingly likely to be advisory. Their role is more as an enabler, frequently extending to partnerships with one another, private owners, developers or housing associations to help clear the way for the desired outcome.

■ ENGLISH HERITAGE

Exemplar properties at English Heritage, the ancient end of the spectrum, are witness to the value of their knowledge, skill and commitment over the years. Even so, as this quango takes on an ever widening remit, presumption of its omniscience could be misleading. It needs to clarify just where it reigns as the ultimate arbiter of heritage taste, and where it only has a catalytic or commentary role. With properties in care it can present exemplars of its philosophy, but where outside investment and other operators are involved its role should remain advisory. English Heritage also offer grant aid, this may be used as a lever to ensure its advice is accepted. This is less of an issue now as funding for historic buildings is primarily through the Heritage Lottery Fund, though still advised by English Heritage.

| **Example** | **4.3** |

USE: Country house (Theological College), Kelham Hall, Newark
1863, Grade II*, George Gilbert Scott, Victorian Gothic brick seminary, stone mullions and parapets, tiles. 1920s Byzantine chapel. Charles Clayton Thompson.

TO: Council offices
Using the carriage court as a reception; the dining room as staff restaurant; the Cedar Room as a committee room; and, the climax of the design, the music room as the council chamber, the house now accommodates more activity than at any time in its history. Other rooms are in use as ornate and lofty offices. Staircase safety required additional handrails with close spaced balusters and lightweight glazed partitions acting as enclosures. This is the latest in a series of changes, e.g. the carriage court became a conservatory, a chapel, and a refectory, before becoming a reception.

A: Newark and Sherwood District Council[3]

The carriage court over the years as conservatory, . . .

The original house with its seminary extension.

chapel, . . .

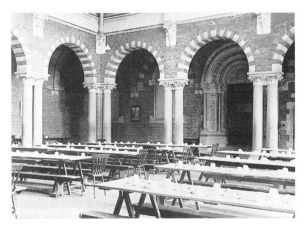

refectory . . .

and reception.

(*The Society of the Sacred Mission*)

■ LOCAL AUTHORITIES

Local authorities, no longer the funders of all public projects, work hard to attract grants or broker deals with the private sector. Occasionally through reorganisation or rationalisation, there may be an opportunity to change their own accommodation and re-use a local building of significance (4.3, 7.1 and 15.54 in Volume Two).

Local authorities also give advice through their conservation officer. It is essential that all front line guardians of our heritage retain an open mind, understanding that there are different valid philosophies, and that their role is to identify which are acceptable and which are not. Where buildings are empty, neglected or in need of repair, the potential applicant for listed building consent should be in a position to choose at the least between two acceptable philosophies. The private practitioner, working for a wide variety of clients and with different officers through the country, knows just how wide that range of philosophies can be. The conservation officer that best serves their community, and their building stock, will have removed any blinkers, thinking laterally, and discussing openly, when dealing with informed and honest applicants.

■ AMENITY SOCIETIES

It is the role of the statutory amenity societies to comment to local authorities upon the proposals and actions of others. Without the educational influence and political pressure of amenity societies much of our heritage would be lost or significantly reduced in historic value. However, a society which values criticism more than action creates an inherent inertia that stifles creativity. Now, more than ever, we need to nurture creativity in the use and preservation of our buildings, if preservation is not to become the dead hand that takes away their vitality. A new direction is required; grown from within to ensure these societies motivate as well as criticise, inquire as well as commentate, co-ordinate as well as specialise, and lead as well as procrastinate. As doyens of the conservation movement they must set an example by embracing a vision for the future of our heritage, and not just the maintenance of its past.

■ ENGLISH PARTNERSHIPS/RURAL DEVELOPMENT AGENCIES

English Partnerships and more recently the RDA's have shifted direction from the provision of industrial sheds to a more holistic approach, aimed at regional and inner city regeneration by workplace creation. Rehabilitation of existing stock in these areas is high on its agenda; converted to housing, workshops or leisure amenities. In pursuit of this goal English Partnerships set up a joint initiative with the Urban

Villages Forum in 1997 to promote the mixed use of land and buildings. The partnership of these two organisations is an acknowledgement of the role creative re-use can play in both economic and community regeneration. Development Corporations, City Challenge, Single Regeneration Budgets and other limited life regimes and organisations are set up in areas of particular need to help deliver outputs of regeneration such as new jobs, reduced crime, better standards of living, and an enhanced environment, e.g. Canal Basin, Sheffield.

■ DEVELOPERS

Developers are skilled in spotting the potential of a location, and in order to maximise profit whilst containing risk they choose the buildings with the widest capability, in the best condition for the price. One frequent factor effecting a building's change from redundant to active usage can be a developer's limited timescale. Unfortunately low cost derelict buildings do tend to attract opportunist developers with no track record and little skill, aiming to turn over a quick profit. This is bad news for historic problem buildings. Individual developers with some sensitivity towards problem buildings, and who have built up a good track record of projects have a vital part to play. Their capacity to take on challenging projects still seems to be outstripped by the supply of buildings awaiting attention; a skills shortage evidenced by the recent loss of so many hospital and asylum buildings to redevelopment.

■ PROFESSIONAL ADVISERS

Any but the simplest re-use project requires a team with design, management, technical and implementation skills. To set the context, an archival researcher or historian will reveal the past history of the building in all of its aspects, drawing on desk research into a wide range of sources in both the public and private domain. An archaeologist may be needed to record the standing archaeology and evaluate the historic merits of these elements; or on occasion to undertake tentative underground investigations which may reveal information about the building's history and structural movement.

■ Architects

The creative part of re-use is often provided by the architects in the team, even to the extent of architects regularly being the individuals who act as catalysts, finding the properties, identifying appropriate uses and networking to put together a team of people to implement the projects. Two different skill types are required of architects. Building carers need to be analytical, methodical, enduring and pragmatic. Creative re-use architects need to be empathic and understanding, yet entrepreneurial in outlook and inspired in vision. Every team advising on an historic building should include within it a suitably qualified and experienced conservation architect. Perhaps this could be required in the same way that the CONDAM Regulations require Health and Safety Planning Supervisors. The Sackler Gallery certainly benefited from an alliance between Julian Harrap, as historic building carer, and Norman Foster as visionary.

■ Surveyors

There are several categories of surveyors who may have a role to play.

Land agents have a duty to advise major landholders. Redundant buildings that they once considered a liability are now seen as an asset with capacity for conversion.

Building surveyors, who maintain building stock may conclude when scheduling works of repair that a more interactive solution is needed to secure the future for an underused building.

Land surveyors also measure buildings and with today's computer technology their specialist expertise is needed at the earliest stage to plot accurate plans and elevations of the building (and its surroundings) identifying floors that are not level and walls that are out of plumb.

Quantity surveyors who have experience in rehabilitation and re-use can advise on the build up of cost plans. This is a more complex and difficult task than for new build, as apparent cost comparisons may turn out to be misleading, making it more of an art than a science.

Valuers and estate agents can be crucial in determining the likely income if a property is to be sold once converted, or establishing the value to an investment institution if the property is to be retained. Their valuations of a completed project must fall somewhere between that of an eager purchaser and a forced sale. Owners always consider such valuations too low, and banks too high. Over-valuation sometimes occurs where unrealised repair costs have not been deducted.

■ Engineers

Structural engineers assess existing structure and design any new structure required for conversion. Understanding the way older structures stay up comes with special experience (not by simply measuring and calculating) – it helps avoid over design and leads to cost-effective solutions which respect the buildings integrity. Appoint only engineers with relevant experience.

Mechanical and electrical engineers designing installations for lighting, heating and ventilation must understand spatial characteristics related to a building's thermal mass and think innovatively about routing cable, pipe and duct runs if they are to retain a building's character.

Specialist use may require an acoustician or sound engineer.

Traffic, highway or civil engineers may be required to advise upon access or parking requirements.

■ Designers

Few interior designers celebrate the existing character of a building's interior, but their creation in response to a client's requirements can transform an interior of little value. The loose fit of such design allows the interior to change with fashion without affecting the building's structure, enabling its continued use in the future.

Lighting designers may advise which exacting standards must be met or if a particular ambience is required.

Exhibition designers create a form of theatre set, capable of changing quickly and easily to new configurations and layouts independent of the building's structure.

■ Other professionals

Landscape architects can enhance or recreate a building's setting.

The planning supervisor may be an architect or surveyor monitoring the Health and Safety plan as part of a quality control methodology which professionals should always apply.

Clerks of Works, monitoring quality on a day-to-day basis are unfortunately utilised less frequently than in the past. They support the 'get it right first time' attitude which is the hallmark of a successful team approach.

Solicitors may be required, not only to purchase the property either free from constraints or with all easements and covenants revealed and agreed, but also to advise upon other legal matters during the project's progress.

Accountants who understand tax implications alongside financial propriety will be essential to all but small projects.

■ Contractors

The contractor, subcontractors, craftsmen and tradesmen complete the team who will implement the project. Their relationship with other members of the team will depend upon the form of procurement adopted. This could result in an adversarial relationship, or a team approach. The latter requires trust and may not be demonstrably the cheapest approach. But the benefits of teamwork based on trust may reduce the time taken, avoid disputes and deliver better value for money (see Chapter 11).

■ Project managers

Where time is not of the essence the architect can lead both the vision and the production to achieve a thoroughly consistent end result. However, to avoid the conflicting demands created by a fast track deadline an independent project manager may be appointed to manage all members of the team; cajoling them to meet deadlines, maintaining a tight grip on cost targets and taking expedient decisions when the unexpected occurs, being equally tough with both contractor and client. This is an aspect not always appreciated by clients at the outset. It is the reason why, once appointed, the project manager must be independent. This should not be confused with the role of Client Liaison Officer whose job is merely to clarify client requirements and communicate these to the team. The liaison officer may be unable to deter the client from delaying instructions, or prevent amendments at crucially disadvantageous stages in the contract.

REFERENCES

1. Binney, M., and Collett-White, J., 'Rescue of the Hasells', *Country Life*, 4 July 1985, pp 16–20 and Kit Martin.
2. Dean Clough Limited.
3. Margaret Moakes, Newark and Sherwood District Council.

Case Study	4.4

From: Derelict railway cottages, Derby
To: Thriving urban village

These are the earliest known railway company cottages in the world. The significance of the cottages, built in 1840, was unrecognised until a campaign by the Civic Society drew attention to their existence filling a triangular area of ground by Derby's 'Tri Junct' Station. Empty, vandalised and ready for clearance, rehabilitation of the cottages was too expensive for the council. The Derbyshire Historic Buildings Trust purchased them with a view to creating an urban village. Employment and public transport were in plentiful supply, but the cottages were situated directly onto the pavement, fronting the busy station approach with no room for parking. How could these terraced properties be transformed into a desirable inner city area where people would want to live? The key factors were:

- Listing of the properties as of special architectural and historic interest.
- Designation of a Conservation Area.
- Declaration of a General Improvement Area.

- Realigning the main road, purchasing land opposite from British Rail, to enable front gardens to be created.
- Road closures of half the width of the other two roads forming the triangle. This made the greatest contribution to independent front doors and secure car parking.
- The demolition of a small workshop to provide six lock-up garages.
- The demolition of three properties to improve daylighting conditions for thirteen more.
- The demolition of an end of terrace, gutted shell to provide a parking area and rear access for parking to ten properties.
- The re-use of bricks, slates, window frames, doors, floorboards, skirtings, architraves, joists, rafters and even chimney pots from the demolished properties both to match repairs and contain costs.
- Variety within the development of 55 houses using fifteen different house types.
- The restoration of the original railway inn to act as a social focus. This Free House serves Real Ale and now runs its own micro brewery.
- The development of an adjacent site by an independent non-profit making company for new starter homes of sympathetic form.

Railway Terrace before.

Midland Place after.

Calvert Street dining kitchen – before. . .

- The retention of the shop unit, with flat over, as a hairdressers.
- The provision of a maintenance manual.
- The creation of a residents' association.

■ Before

The Cottages were vacated as unfit in the late 1970s and fell into dereliction. The Derby Civic Society considered their plight, and campaigned for their use as council houses, assuming that the local authority would rescue them; it did not. The alternative of rehabilitating the cottages for sale on the open market was faced with problems. The cottages were scheduled for demolition; were in the line of a proposed inner relief road; and in an area not zoned as residential by the planning authority. It was clearly not to be easy. Agents also advised that there was no market for terraced housing in Derby: everyone wanted a detached or semi-detached house. In 1979 values of terraced houses in Derby stood unimproved at £5,000 and improved at £8,000. The first valuation of the properties, once rehabilitated, stood at £8,500. Taking account of the preliminary projected costs of £10,500 this equation produced a negative value of £2,000. The rehabilitation of the houses themselves was not the problem. This would cost money, but presented a straightforward repair and conversion exercise, though requiring particular care over details.

after.

The problem was in the market potential. Unless the value of the properties upon completion could be raised there was no likelihood that income would be sufficient to fund repair costs. The key to this conundrum lay in identifying what the market need was and delivering a product that satisfied that need in a unique manner. This was identified as: conveniently located, having a decent sized garden, attractive two and three bedroom houses, of compact but not minimum size with generously proportioned rooms, economic to heat, with a car parking space immediately adjacent, in an attractive environment, and with defensible space outside the front door. Yet the area, having been a notorious district, was far from attractive. The existing properties fronted directly onto the street, rear gardens were divided from the houses by access ways that led through to 'mizzens' (toilet blocks), and an old rope way was fashioned between the backs of all the gardens.

Calvert Street before.

■ The alternative

There was only one area in Derby at that time where terraced houses were accepted. This was in the old village, and desirable suburb, of Darley Abbey where three-storey Mill Workers Cottages were gathered in picturesque groups. The aim was to market the Railway Cottages as an equivalent area, demonstrating the economy that living in a terraced house offers and yet providing the modern amenities every new householder sought.

Ways were sought to improve the physical context of the properties. The triangular site fronted directly onto the highway on all three sides. The only way of expanding the site was to move or close the roads. This was done at a cost to the whole rehabilitation exercise of £1,000 per terraced property. The environmental improvements, together with the unusual facility of a dedicated parking facility for each house, enabled the valuation to be increased to £11,500 making the equation even. As a valuation exercise undertaken to assess feasibility this was successful. In actuality the costs of undertaking the environmental improvements were underestimated, but so was the market upon completion.

Reconfiguration of the street with parking bays and planting beds.

■ The campaign

The original campaign to save the Railway Cottages from demolition took a high profile in the City of Derby. Presentations made on behalf of the Derbyshire Historic Buildings Trust to the Planning and Estates Committee failed by a narrow majority to convince them that they should reverse the previous policy of demolition. The issue was presented to the local media, the local newspaper, radio and television, through a public awareness campaign. Television and radio interviews

Railings create 'defensible space'.

culminated in a phone-in programme on the morning of the Full Council Meeting at which the Leader of the Council acknowledged he had received more mail on this issue than on any other. At the end of a two hour debate the proposals were supported. The Council had

Parked cars on one side, pedestrian/vehicular street on the other.

unwittingly given an excellent start to the project's promotional campaign.

■ Rehabilitation

Of the 55 houses retained for conversion the vast majority fell into two simple types: two bedroom and three bedroom. A means of inserting a bathroom into each of these at first floor level was effected without reducing the number of bedrooms. As might be imagined the three bedroom houses were of more generous proportions than the two bedroom, but in both cases total space standards were above that being built in starter homes or small family housing at that time. Reorganisation of the access to gardens by re-routing pathways along the bottom of the garden rather than against the house introduced real privacy. Garden space standards for many of the houses were also above those to be found in the high density new development that was occurring on the outskirts of town. Also the Railway Cottages were within walking distance of the town centre and immediately adjacent to the station for people who might wish to travel. No other area of housing could offer this dual advantage in terms of location.

■ Original character

Just three small houses were left without parking spaces, located on a cul-de-sac in the middle of the development. The cul-de-sac was clearly big enough to park three cars, but after some debate it was decided to close this cul-de-sac to traffic and to accept that three of the houses would not have parking spaces. The cul-de-sac was left as a replica, representing the street's original character when the properties were first built, uncluttered by cars. This was further celebrated by the engraving of the Derbyshire Historic Building Trust's symbol onto the blank, brick, first-floor, wall of the property terminating the street. It was the Trust that had the courage and the conviction to back the architect's initial idea for the rescue so that faith rightly becomes part of the history of the property. All front gardens were planted, the cohesion of the design bonding the terraces together as the planting changes along the street. Re-using stone kerbs, steps and paving, as well as gravel dressed tarmac, and the careful selection of street lamps, enabled a quality period character to return without creating anything either too brash or too precious of heritage. To emphasise the property's uniqueness the original colour schemes used by the Midland Railway Company were applied to the exterior of the houses so that all front doors were the same colour.

■ Marketing

To maintain the public interest, following the well reported stormy debate in Council, items of interest for the media were planned at periods of six to eight weeks:

Sheffield Place during replacement of gas, water, electricity mains.

- The number of skips of rubbish (113) to be removed from the 55 properties.
- Historical research into the original occupants and what their jobs were.
- The discovery of an elderly ex-resident who was related to one of the original occupiers.
- Points of interest like the signalling style alarm systems under the eaves going to each bedroom to wake householders when it was their shift.
- Selective demolition including saving for re-use, doors, floorboards, whole soldier brick arches, roof slates, bricks, sills, chimney pots and windows.
- Building work, e.g. a wall that was leaning nine inches out of plumb was retained and tied back into the existing structure rather than demolished and rebuilt.
- The unusual decision to split the contract, to allow three medium- or small-sized contractors to undertake the work rather than a large regional contractor. This reduced cost whilst competitively enhancing quality.

On completion 'restored' to its original character.

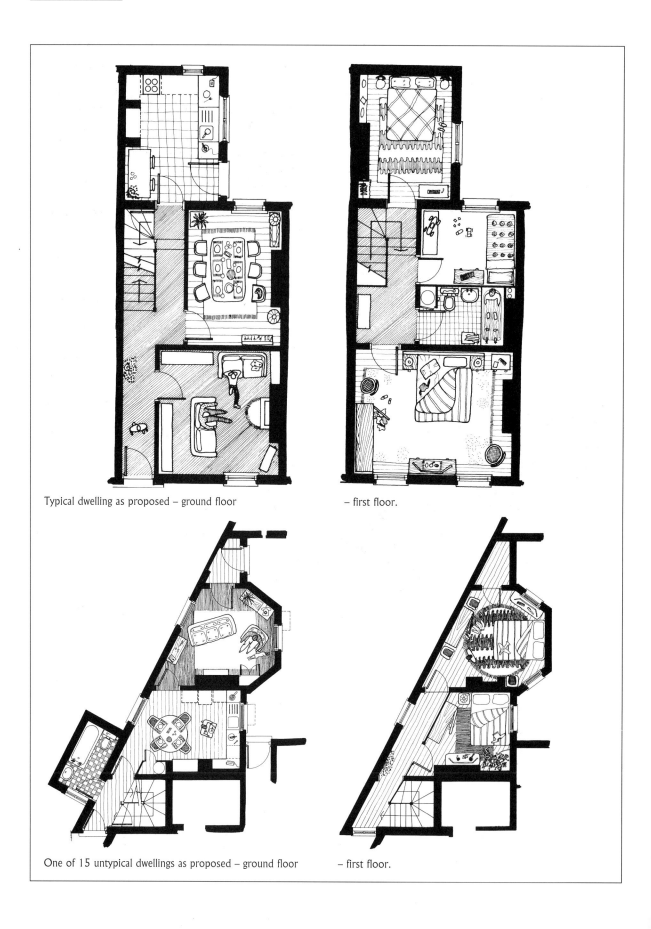

Typical dwelling as proposed – ground floor

– first floor.

One of 15 untypical dwellings as proposed – ground floor

– first floor.

- The skill of craftsmen in re-using original materials, e.g. a slater, a joiner and a glazier.
- A window repair demonstration to illustrate how such windows can be economically repaired rather than replaced.
- Explanations regarding the road closures, with drawings showing how half the road would be closed and turned into parking spaces and front gardens.
- Warnings regarding the impending road diversion to create front gardens on Railway Terrace and the potential problems of disruption due to roadworks.
- Photographs and interviews of the personnel working on the road works. All the work was done at night so as to reduce the disruption caused to traffic.
- A garden and ironmongery feature on the design of the railings and front garden planting.
- An article about the decor showing: feature walls newly dry lined, being wallpapered, different paint colour schemes internally to ensure that no two houses were alike.

This constant promotion ended in major publicity for the opening of the first cottage completed and the release of the first six cottages for sale. The agents had been registering interest during rehabilitation and had identified ten keen purchasers for the 57 cottages, but had yet to establish a realistic market price. Price was more dependent upon the building societies' valuation than upon the means of the purchasers. The building societies were not keen to support the £12,750 sale price now needed, so three chief executives were shown what had been achieved, including the environmental improvements. Two remained unconvinced but the third supported the valuation. This building society was introduced to the purchasers and the sales were confirmed. That these properties were to sell ten years later for five times this figure vindicated this approach.

The first phase of six houses was released and publicity of the plight of the four disappointed customers generated a queue, sleeping on the pavement overnight outside the agent's office, when the next six houses were released a month later. The consequent national publicity which arose ensured the sale of subsequent releases as well. The price of later phases was raised to £13,500 to create a small project surplus and confirming everyone's belief that the properties were in high demand.

The new owners formed a residents' committee, and the area is still popular two decades later. Of interest is the wide range of residents including solicitors in chambers in the town, plumbers in the building trade, postmen working at the nearby post office, actors and actresses at the nearby theatre, salesmen also travelling by train, young couples starting their new home, divorced couples reforming theirs and retired couples remaining in the town centre.[a]

Also see colour plate 4.

■ Reference

a. Project Architect: David Bagshaw, Latham Architects.

1.
St Michael's,
Derby –
the staircase
in a fire
protected area.

**See Case
Study 1.3**

2.
Cavendish
Arcade (formerly
Thermal Baths)
– the restaurant
on the roof
enclosed by the
new barrel vault
of stained glass.
*(Michael
Ord-Clarke)*

**See Case
Study 2.17**

3. New Music School, Repton (the rear of the old sanatorium) viewed from the school campus across the playing fields. (*Stuart Blackwood*)

See Case Study 3.6

4.
Railway
Cottages,
Derby –
a barren
terraced street
transformed
by 'pocket'
size gardens.
*(Stuart
Blackwood)*

**See Case
Study 4.4**

a.

b.

c.

d.

5.
The Jewellery
Business
Centre,
Birmingham:

a.
Old windows
(re-used as a
re-built wall)
viewed through
the new.
*(Stuart
Blackwood)*

b.
New windows
(for Jewellers'
Workshops in
the new rear
extensions)
viewed through
the old.
*(Stuart
Blackwood)*

c.
Detail of
'The Gates'.
*(Stuart
Blackwood)*

d.
A rear extension
in reclaimed
bricks. Light
fittings and
handrail relate
to 'The Gates'.
*(Stuart
Blackwood)*

**See Case
Study 6.4**

6.
Victoria Quarter,
Leeds:

a.
County Arcade
'restored'
showing new
lighting and
shopfronts.
*(Stuart
Blackwood)*

6.
Victoria Quarter,
Leeds:

b.
County Arcade
'restored'
showing the
new mosaic
floor and colour
scheme.
*(Stuart
Blackwood)*

6.
Victoria Quarter,
Leeds:

c.
Queen Victoria
Street 'covered'
with new
stained glass
roof and re-
landscaped.
*(Stuart
Blackwood)*

**See Case
Study 7.3**

7.
Midland House,
Derby:

a.
Original
staircase
'restored' and
protected with
new fire screens
and doors.
*(Stuart
Blackwood)*

7.
Midland House,
Derby:

b.
Access
balconies to the
lift in the new
link block.
*(Stuart
Blackwood)*

7.
Midland House,
Derby:

c.
The main
entrance in the
new link block.
*(Stuart
Blackwood)*

**See Case
Study 9.4**

8.
King's Fund
Headquarters,
Cavendish
Square, W1:

a.
The
Conservatory in
the courtyard
uses a unique
form of 'bow
and arrow' truss
allowing clear
glazing without
mullions.
*(Stuart
Blackwood)*

b.
Basement bar
under the
courtyard
accessed by
steps in the
new lightwell
within the
conservatory.
*(Stuart
Blackwood)*

**See Case
Study 12.4**

CHAPTER 5

Understanding the Building

The starting point of any successful philosophy of creative re-use is to understand that *re-use must work with the building and not against it*.[1] An understanding of the building must therefore be reached. Only then will the architect be able to convert space in a manner appropriate to the new use, and avoid the conversion working against the building and detracting from any inherent industrial or economic value. Re-use loses meaning and purpose if there is too much imposed change: if too much of the original is lost then what is there to retain? If changes enhance the essential qualities of a building then the result will be a synergy that benefits the building and the user.

Evidence of the successful generation of this synergy may not easily be seen. It would be naive, and perhaps conceited, to assume that the impact of re-use on an existing building will always be immediately obvious, either externally or internally. The need to consider carefully the design issues and the impact of altering or extending an existing building can encourage novel if highly sympathetic solutions, even developed to a level of sophistication that exceeds most stand alone modern buildings. Re-use offers an alternative to the total replacement of a building. Of course there are times when a building *in situ* blocks an apparently more dramatic and technologically innovative replacement: Norman Foster's unsuccessful proposed replacement of Langham Buildings in London's Portland Place with a new headquarters for the BBC is a case in point. It is equally fair to say that plenty of buildings lacking in design qualities have replaced originals of more appropriate scale and character. These replacements might display only a fraction of the design ingenuity that is required to successfully alter and extend existing structures of character. There may be a lack of vision, sympathy and effort shown here that would explain why rehabilitated or adapted older buildings are more popular amongst the general public than are many new ones. The lack of any glaring visual evidence of re-use should not imply a lack of public appreciation of that re-use: after all, one creed of modern architecture is 'less is more'.[2]

■ APPROACHING THE BUILDING

■ Emotional value

The first step is to absorb the atmosphere of the building; let subjectivity take control for a moment before the objective takes over. In that moment a personal, emotional value should emerge for the building. Get to know the building's personality. It is common enough to hear people say they love a building or have a love for buildings, yet many professionals are too busy being objective to allow this to influence their judgement. This is wrong: other than architects, few people think about architecture, but many people do feel it. Christopher Day calls this moment listening, likening it to that of a physician listening to his patient, 'listening without any judgement, even listening to the unpalatable.'[3]

Atmosphere of a church compared with a factory

Church	Factory
tall, lofty space	wide, expansive space
changes in level between spaces	each floor level throughout
single storey	single or multi-storey
often dark (if glass is stained)	usually daylit along two sides
hierarchy of spaces	no hierarchy
axial	non-axial
large columns defining spaces	light slim columns within space
solid masonry walls	infill panels
tall, high windows	wide, low windows
natural materials	stone, brick, concrete or steel
ornament, craft, value	system built, plain, worthy
strong shapes and forms	rectilinear
distinct character	common character
ancient	modern
inflexible	flexible
quiet	noisy
calming	enabling
awe inspiring	usable
beautiful	anodyne

Each of these are attributes to be enjoyed, harnessed or overcome dependent upon the proposed use. The less that have to be overcome the more appropriate the new use may be.

For the architectural building – one with high architectural ideals – absorbing the atmosphere is more difficult. The building may contain highly charged emotive art in paintings and sculpture, or even be a work of art in its own right. It will even carry the weight of studied appraisal, criticism, and reappraisal. These buildings are often built to rules: proportion, geometry, differing interpretations of a classical language or historical style. The beholder then needs to judge whether these rules are being transcended; are they experiencing high art or the music of architecture? Does the whole created exceed the sum of its parts? Reaching this judgement should involve the realisation and adoption of a personal fundamental truth about the building, and should include some analysis of general criticism to understand why others – cognoscenti or general public – think the building to be important. Somehow, once captured, this personal truth must be cherished as a constant guide through all the ensuing processes of design, re-design and construction, regulations and costing, programming and completion. These first impressions will be important at a later stage.

■ The building's story

When preparing a design brief for work to historic buildings it might seem too obvious to suggest that the story both of that building and that place should be taken into account. Yet there are plenty of examples to show that research into, let alone any understanding of a building's history is often overlooked. An able conservation architect will of course turn to evidence of the past – published reports and a written history – before proceeding to develop the remainder of the design brief. This will include an examination of previous re-use of the building. However, it is important that such historical analysis and investigation is undertaken without forgetting that it is not only the building itself which is important but its surroundings.

Vernacular buildings are somehow easier to understand. They are invariably more natural and unabashed as reflections of their place and time, responding to climate, locally available materials, social form and tradition. Familiar in feel and use to their owners when first built, there is an appeal to the senses from the tactile quality of the materials, visual texture, and spaces which evokes warmth or security. The difference between the architectural building as against the vernacular one is that the former is more likely to have a written history in a known social context, while the latter has a built history within an assumed social context. Many properties fall between these two extremes but there are lessons to be learnt within the distinction. Firstly, avoid the influence of too much desk research for architectural buildings, instead look harder at the building. Secondly, for vernacular buildings, research more around the building for greater context. The vernacular building is a direct product of its context, more so than a high architectural one. Reading the story of such a building demands we also read the story of its context.

■ Consider past re-use

Re-use is hardly a new phenomenon. Since the abandonment of the earliest buildings people have re-used them with just enough alteration to satisfy their needs. At first alterations were to expand basic accommodation for a larger family or clan, or to house more diverse activities such as a byre for animals, or a workshop for production. In times of strife property was fought over and the new occupant might strengthen fortifications. In times of peace acquisition by purchase reflected a more stable social structure where new owners might consolidate their social standing; consolidation often limited to the erection of a new façade. This might suggest a wanton disregard for past structures, but when new building was an expensive commodity the façade was the most economic and practical means to an end. Even if expansion was not required and the building shell was sound, new façades were added cosmetically in response to a new stylistic fashion. It is not uncommon to find half timbered buildings fronted in dressed stone, and when brick was the fashionable import from the continent, rubble stone buildings were sometimes fronted with imported brick.

Up until the nineteenth century, towns and cities were restricted in area. Buildings co-joined, lending support to each other to form continuous façades. For most people at the time relocation was not an option, so the only route to more space was to build up and out. New storeys were added by trial and error without improvements to foundations, leaving the building to settle in relation to its neighbours and redistributing stresses within its own structure as well as that next door. If it didn't fall down then, it would remain until the next change. Changes do not always reflect expansion through improvements in economic and social circumstances; they also reflect contractions, down turns and loss of standing. A wealthy merchant's house might be reoccupied by several families, or middle class housing be taken over for workshops (as with the Jewellery Quarter in Birmingham). In the process re-use sometimes results in some clear signs of deterioration of purpose giving the appearance of makeshift adaptation. Of greatest importance, it also shows how re-use has always been an active part of the economic scene and how it has affected the buildings we seek to re-use again.

■ Step back from the building

Study of the historic development of the locality, through the interpretation of growth patterns from a sequence of old maps and a reading of its social history, provides a foundation of knowledge. Follow this by interpretation on foot, with sketchbook or camera, to identify what remains of the original locale; see what continuum remains. If the property in question had a specific economic use then acquire knowledge about that industry, or activity: its growth and decline, its patterns of trading, and the part the building may have to play in such a role. If the building was commissioned and designed by a known architect, then study that architect's work and the social background of both the architect and the client.

Where appropriate reconstruct, mentally and visually, the relationship of the building to other buildings in the past. Was it larger than adjacent buildings when first built? Did it stand alone? Was it a different character, or did it blend in? Was it innovative? Such questions need to be asked for each stage of the building's life if it is to be understood. The fact that these were stages in a building's past suggests that it is important not to assume that one context or story can necessarily be set against a constant contemporary situation. Indeed the reason for understanding history and context is to comprehend the dynamics of the site: the way it has, and may continue, to change. If context is valuable then this is not an optional stage.

■ A STRUCTURAL RESPONSE TO CHANGING USE

If creative re-use is sensitive to the history of a building and its context then it should also be sensitive to future re-use. The creative insurance policy for this can be found in a response to the building's structure that allows for further dynamic re-use yet safeguards as many elements of the original building as possible. The physical survey of the building will bear this in mind.

■ Allow for future change

The project to be undertaken will have an assumed life span. This could vary from ten years for a simple refurbishment or emergency repair, to more than a hundred years when repairing the fabric of an ancient monument. The normal life of a new building is between thirty and sixty years. A quick comparison with past changes over a similar period illustrates the significance of the changes in context which can occur. The speed of change in residential areas may be slower than in some commercial areas, but change is nevertheless always evident. This is the dynamic that has to be taken into consideration when preparing a brief to repair or re-use an historic building. At a particular moment in time one has to attempt to understand the nature of the changes that have occurred and are still occurring, and allow in some way for further change in the future. It is not so much a question of being clairvoyant, predicting the future, but more, understanding the possibilities and influences that may be brought to bear and try and make some allowance for them.

■ Long life or loose fit?

Buildings change because their users and their needs do change, often unpredictably and without regularity. The preparation to allow for this lies in a carefully considered response to the building's structure, elements and fittings. We begin by separating the requirements of 'long life' from those of 'loose fit'. The long life elements form the core; ones common to a wide range of users and which are unlikely to change. These are distinct from those elements particular to the user; ones dependent on current technology, or relating to patterns of occupation. The perception of differing life expectancies for different elements is a key to the creative part of re-use. It assists not only our understanding of why changes have occurred to the building over previous years, but its scope for change in the future. It outlines the capacity for the building to accept change, and what is the relative permanence of fixtures needed to accommodate the user.

■ Extending the life of an element, e.g. timber

The life expectancy of different elements will vary within a building. This depends upon the quality and nature of the material used; its specification; and the design of the details by which it interacts with other materials. This can be illustrated by taking just one building element, timber, as an example. An untreated softwood bearing plate simply placed upon the soil, as it is under a garden shed, will quickly rot away. The same in oak or elm would last a lot longer. Specify heartwood of oak or elm and the longevity is increased further. Alternatively, the longevity of the softwood could be increased by impregnation with preservative to resist insect attack and fungal growth. These timbers will still be subject to a regime of soaking and drying out, heating and cooling. To last, timber needs to remain as stable as possible; continual movement causes splits or cracks and the breakage of joints with other members or materials.

Having selected the nature of the material, its quality and its specification, we can improve the situation further by detailed design. If, for example, we raise our base plate timber above the ground by placing it upon a solid foundation of stone, and we place a damp-proof membrane of mortar and tar between the stone and timber, then we will prevent the water from the ground soaking the timber. If above this timber we have a roof of thatch to stop rainwater coming from above, and place a rainshield of lime wash on the outside and a warm living environment for people or animals on the inside, then the life of our timber will be increased further still. This prolonged life depends upon that of the damp proof membrane and the continued maintenance of the limewash and thatch, and these in turn depend upon the continued use of the property. Improve this with modern, long-life damp proof courses, waterproof roofs and effective rainshield systems. Add insulation externally; constant heating systems internally; a vapour barrier to prevent the ingress of any products of occupation; then gently ventilate as a fail safe so that when any of the other materials, or details fail to some degree the effect upon the timber will be minimised until the problem is noticed and rectified. Indeed once the timber is so well protected it becomes difficult to see when conditions have changed and deterioration may result. This is why electronic monitors are sometimes placed within a structure, set to inform, or even alarm, the occupants, if and when conditions do change. With all these actions the life of our timber could have extended to a thousand years or more.

An analysis similar to this can be applied to the timber in existing buildings. Conditions can be changed to preserve the structure, or panelling by ventilation, air conditioning and monitoring. Theoretically at least, every element of every building could be designed to last that length of time. However, this would be wasteful. Even

Example   5.1

USE: Castle, Riber, Matlock

A Victorian 'Castle', Grade II, designed in a simplistic oversized toy-fort style, John Smedley, with robust and repetitive details of fenestration from elevation to elevation, Riber was in fact a folly in more ways than one. It dominated the hilltop skyline, and was a business failure as a hydro, the predicted water supply not being available. The shell was therefore fitted out with relatively low cost materials to form a large house for Smedley but his lack of building construction knowledge led to leaking and dry rot. Collapse of the roof was followed by fire removing all but the gargantuan, hewn, gritstone shell. After decades of being open to the weather from both sides, cracks were observed in the free-standing structure.

TO: Hotel

The proposal was to build hotel accommodation within the shell tying back the free standing structure with bedrooms and corridors around the perimeter, on all three storeys, creating a cellular structure internally, whilst the central reception and restaurant space remained within a full height central atrium, lit from above.

Over 100 feet high, at the break of the slope, expensive to scaffold. The repetition of the original design enabled substitution of one elevation for another in terms of dimensional drawing so the problem was how to use a limited fee to obtain accurate information upon the extent of the cracks in the structure. This was undertaken by helicopter (cheaper than scaffolding) flying along each elevation within only a few feet of the building taking photographs at right angles to each window opening. Once back in the studio, the photographs were enlarged to create an elevation 1/10th full size to enable the extent and breadth of the cracking to be measured to ± 1 mm.

Key
B   Bedrooms
Ba   Bathrooms
L   Lounge
St   Store
V   Void over reception and dining areas

Riber Castle – a true folly.

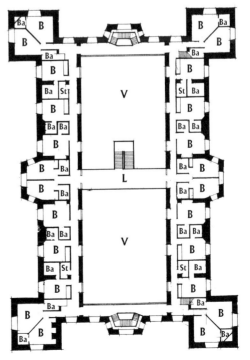

Proposed hotel conversion – first floor.

in a long lived, monumental building such as a cathedral, the heating and lighting systems are likely to change, floor coverings will become worn in places, and the nature of the activity taking place within will change also. Nevertheless most elements of a cathedral are expected to be long life, unlike a school or an office block, whose requirements might change dramatically over the centuries and even the decades.

■ Measuring long life

The nature of the change made differs with each element and its life expectancy:

- The structure needs to stand for the longest period of time. For masonry buildings this might be assumed to be 200 years.
- The weathering materials, such as roofing slates which can be replaced and upgraded, follow at, say, 60 years after which period there may well be significant alterations to the form of the structure.
- Services, because of their reliance in part on mechanically and electronically working parts, and the increasing expectation of improving standards that changing technology brings, have a shorter life of, say, 30 years.
- Fixtures and fittings which directly relate to changes in working practices and living habits, as well as fashion and whim, may only have to last fifteen years.
- Corporate image, being dependent upon the life expectancy of companies, the success of trading outlets, graphics and marketing campaigns, might have only five years.

■ Loose fit

The interaction of user requirements with a building's capacity for change can be understood by applying a simple rubric: *the elements of a building that need to be conserved*, whatever they may be, *should be treated as long-life elements.*[4] What remains applies to particular user requirements only and falls into the loose-fit category. Conservable features are likely to include the structure; perhaps also the windows and doors, plaster surfaces, architraves and skirtings. In some cases even light fittings might comprise a long-life element for historical reasons. Once these are clarified for a building the user's requirements can be identified. Loose-fit features are likely to include the following: their life expectancy and degree of integration to be decided in individual cases.

- The need for additional accommodation: an extension or separate new building. The additional accommodation might be permanent, short life, or even temporary if its longevity is unpredictable or funds are short.
- Circulation changes: fire escapes, lifts. Lifts may only be essential for disabled access so might be resolved by a stairway chair lift or combined with a goods lift. Heavily trafficked circulation routes could be concentrated on new stairs rather than old.

- Improved insulation or ventilation: air-conditioning or ventilation may be achieved through a comprehensive system, hidden from view in fine architectural buildings, exposed in industrial buildings, or taken from stand-alone units.
- Improved lighting: this might be achieved through rewiring and relamping existing luminaries; fitting recessed, concealed light sources within the structure or behind surface finishes; or including uplighters and desk lamps as part of the furniture.

Whether a loose or a tight fit is best should be decided element by element. Ultimately the opportunities available will be constrained by the nature of the building. But the challenge of creative re-use is to take those constraints and turn them into opportunities; to transform the apparently greater constraints of historic buildings into values celebrated by the new use. For the more vernacular building the challenge is to be proactive, enabling the re-use to add vitality and new life; in some circumstances even a new or revitalised identity.

REFERENCES

1. cf Appendix in this Volume, page 215, Principles for Re-use.
2. Architect: Mies van der Rohe.
3. Day, C., *Place of the Soul: Architecture and Environmental Design as a Healing Art*, Aquarian Press.
4. cf Appendix in this Volume, page 215, Principles for Re-use.

SURVEY TIPS

Ownership
Check the extent of ownership – especially the boundaries and who is responsible for maintaining them. Ascertain whether there are any restrictive covenants. Request information from the solicitor in writing!

Check maintenance
The first commandment for the maintenance of any building is, 'thou shalt clean out thy gutters!' The collapse of many a building can be traced back to the origins of a blocked gutter especially if trees have been seen growing out of them.

Prepare and plan
Before you stride unwarily into a suspect roofspace as an intrepid building surveyor it would be wise to prepare and plan your approach beforehand.

Don't just 'look and record'!
Many a condition survey is simply a dictated visual record of the building room by room and elevation by elevation, which, because it lacks understanding of what is seen may well miss the significance of some apparently minor defects and misinterpret the effect of others.

Desk research
The usefulness of desk analysis of historical data is referred to in the main text. If available original plans, plans of alterations, old survey drawings, written up histories of the building, or earlier condition surveys are essential for comparison, anything which might give a better understanding of when, and how, the property came to be as it is now. Use 'as-built' drawings of recent conversions but beware old, proposal, drawings, as walls and particularly services may have been constructed in different locations.

Line and level measured survey
Where there are obvious discrepancies, or an absence of information, then a site survey will be required. This should be done by qualified architects, or building surveyors. Beware the credentials of the firm offering a

cheap quote. Prepare the survey specification carefully. Identify the different levels of information to be obtained. Only measure what is useful, but include all essential information. A detailed survey of both line and level, and condition, will include drawings showing plans, elevations and sections of the buildings indicating the construction, the levels of existing insulation, the location of services and the condition of the building by means of notes on those drawings, or otherwise a report including a Schedule of Dilapidation under five recommended repair headings: Emergency; Urgent; Necessary; Important; Advantageous. Identify what the school is spending on maintenance and running costs, so that revenue expenditure can be prioritised accordingly over the next five years. (It is often prudent to have the survey done by an architect or surveyor whom it is intended will advise subsequently, or have them draw up the specification, which will tie in the responsibility to one firm.)

Plan at each floor level

A measured and drawn survey is a major aid to understanding – the more detailed the better – particularly if it is able to offer an understanding of the building's structural integrity and even more so if the survey is accurate enough to show where the building is out of true, line or level. However, if this is not available and time is short a simple pencil plan, paced out and set to approximate scale onto a tracing paper pad over metric graph paper, with each floor plan overlaid can cause the surveyor to consider how the building is constructed, what happens to the structure and what roles certain walls and features play.

Think methodically

The information collected, whether comprehensive or minimal, should be analysed to see what problems might be anticipated. This is not to formulate preconceptions which might override other observations, but to heighten awareness and understanding prior to on site recording which might cause the surveyor to inspect areas that otherwise might be overlooked (e.g. the back corner of a particular storage cupboard if it is at the base of a valley gutter). With experience, such an analytical understanding becomes a sort of sixth sense when undertaking inspections. But this sixth sense will not be developed unless this more laborious and painstaking approach is adopted in the early years, and will in any event still be essential for the larger project where sixth sense can easily become numbed by fatigue, or more than one person may be undertaking the survey.

Organise

Take the time to organise the actual survey. Identify the order in which it is to be tackled, arrange for any neces-

sary access with keys and ladders being made available, torches, safety helmet, overalls if necessary.

Gain permission for physical examinations

Ask permission to lift manhole covers and inspection chambers, undertake some minimal destructive investigation – lift carpets, probe joinery and plaster, remove paint flakes etc. to enable a valid assessment to be made.

Arrange for access

A survey which is caveated by a statement such as 'no inspection was made of inaccessible parts, including the roof, roof void and basement' is not worth the effort typing up! If access cannot be gained to such areas then the client may be wasting money, as evidence vital for decision taking will not be available, so that any resultant conclusions might, at best be flawed and at worst misleading. If, say, access to roof space is physically not available because there is no ceiling hatch, suggest to your client that (with the agreement of the owner, if different) they pay for the installation of one. If the client owns the property (or decides to buy) it will prove necessary for good maintenance and if he does not own the property and decides not to buy because of what is discovered then it can be seen as a relatively cheap escape from a more expensive liability.

Opening up

An agreement with the occupier may allow certain 'opening up work' to enable measurement and assessment of hidden detail – the 'opening up' then to be made good until the current occupier terminates.

Look into voids

Tenant fittings may present a significant problem if, as in a shop unit, none of the structure or finishes that will be visible to the building team are visible to the surveyor. If certainty is required early, then an endoscope (a sort of miniature periscope) with video camera might be used to see into voids behind the interior fit out – a costly process.

Be safe

When undertaking a survey wear the right gear, soft shoes for roofs, boots for rough ground, helmets for constricted spaces. Always let someone know where you are going and how long you expect to be, especially if undertaking it alone. Accidents can happen but rescue can take place if others know your whereabouts and can raise the alarm if you do not return. If alone, take a mobile phone.

Work top down

Start at the roof, or at least in the roof space as this is where many troubles begin and symptoms further down the building may be better interpreted.

External elevations

Initial survey can be undertaken using a sketch book, notepad and a pair of binoculars. This enables initial identification of areas where symptoms have become apparent but, unless the problems are within easy reach from ground level, or by ladder, this does not provide measurement.

Photographic survey

A photogrammetric survey, or rectified photography allied to computer drawing, can provide a fair and accurate method of recording of elevations both internal and external if unobstructed views can be obtained. From these it is possible to record the decay of particular elements within the structure whether they be individual bricks, stones, mullions or beams but they are not normally sufficient to accurately record the extent and width of cracks. If known beforehand the brief can include the recording of cracks from which measurement can subsequently be taken (5.1).

Gaining access to high façades

Where access is available at ground level adjacent to the façade then a 'cherry picker' (used for cleaning street lamps, etc.) can be used to undertake detailed survey work. With electrically powered hydraulics there are machines small enough to be taken into courtyards and even buildings to provide access to internal elevations. Lightweight models attain three storeys, larger vehicles attain five, beyond which a mobile crane and bucket is required. A tower scaffold can provide access to small areas requiring prolonged study. Over heights greater than two storeys this should be tied back into the structure to ensure stability but care must be taken not to damage the structure. It has been known to use helicopters to gain access for visual inspection of inaccessible façades (5.1).

Annotate drawings

Use a drawing (the pencil sketch referred to earlier or a reduced photocopy of the survey) plans, sections and elevations, if available, upon which to draw lines, notate rooms, doors and windows, write relevant apparent dimensional variations/discrepancies and locate cracks, discontinuity lines, movement directions, falls, fixings and services, with different coloured dotted, pecked, broken or full lines, hatched areas, or shading.

Dictate

Record description on a cassette recorder in a predetermined sequence of walls, floors, ceilings, windows, doors, fireplaces, joinery items and so on starting with the north wall and swinging clockwise in each room. Writing longhand notes soon palls and the notes become briefer and may miss out key elements due to mental fatigue. Dictation is quicker and usually because of the lack of effort, more comprehensive. The eyes can remain on the subject matter and in addition to noting the key points, frequently other less obvious, but important details can be observed, which add to the understanding.

Look for evidence – research

Avoid jumping to conclusions – like the surveyors report that recommended underpinning the western half of a single storey building that had 'settled'. Desk research showed that the eastern half had been built where an old railway embankment had been removed shortly before. In fact the western half had remained stationary and the eastern half had risen slowly after the embankment had been removed (and after the building had been built). Movement, apart from a minor annual cycle, had long since ceased.

Look for evidence – on site

Similarly, properties condemned by the health inspector as unfit because the rear extensions had subsided until walls were 200 mm out of plumb over two storeys, were found upon inspection of the cracks to have settled during construction. The evidence? Original plaster fitted exactly into the cracks in the internal brickworks.

Look for evidence – ask questions

Recent history, however anecdotal can also be pertinent; knowledge of a burst water main or corroded heating pipes since repaired can explain otherwise mystifying staining that might be interpreted as rising damp. Knowledge of the location of hidden services can also be invaluable. In one instance, a strange form of wet rot fungus on a skirting board in an empty property on the market was initially interpreted as rising damp. In fact it was a heating pipe buried in a new screed, perforated by a 'gripper tack' which had only caused a leak when the fitted carpet was removed together with the 'gripper rod' and had not been noticed because the building was empty.

Record pollution

When surveying old industrial sites use desk survey, observation and ultimately physical analysis to establish the extent of any pollution and ensure this is registered so that future groundwork operatives can take necessary precautions when renewing or repairing services.

CHAPTER 6

Understanding the User's Requirements

When planning a re-use proposal, it is essential to consider the needs of the potential user. Creative re-use projects are started for many different reasons. It may simply be that the owner wants the building converted, but there could equally be a pressure group fighting to save a building, or a government agency wanting to use an existing property as part of a regeneration programme. Sometimes a potential user looking for space acts as a catalyst and inspires the idea for a re-use.

Planning authorities often treat the building as more important than the prospective user. We must, however, recognise the user's needs at the beginning to reduce the likelihood of further changes too soon after the conversion programme is completed. Ideally, a major project should be designed with enough scope and flexibility to survive without further change for at least 30–60 years. Consult the user early on and increase the chances of a building being protected in the long term. If you do not know who will use the building you must be open-minded about the uses to which the building may be put.

■ FINDING A NEW USE FOR THE BUILDING

Think laterally about the uses to which the building is to be put.[1]

We must accept that while it is usually reckless to demolish a building that still has a structural life, there are times when, due to expansion plans for the surrounding land, it becomes imprudent to retain an incompatible building.

Assuming the building is to have a new life, however, after surveying and analysing the building, brush away your preconceptions and start to think of it irreverently. If a new use for the property is not pre-determined, keep your mind open to future possibilities for the building.

Weigh up the constraints with the opportunities offered by the property itself. List the strengths and the weaknesses for later re-appraisal. When rejecting a potential use, record any objections in detail. Some of these obstacles may become surmountable at a later stage, perhaps due to acquiring adjacent land, another building, a change in planning policy or a new grant regime. An erstwhile rejected use could eventually turn out to be the most suitable.

■ IDENTIFY THE NEW USER

In the broadest sense, there will be many 'users' of the building in its new form. These could include the owner or developer, the tenant or occupier, the visitor or customer – even the public who pass by. We have to appreciate their particular requirements.

When a re-use project is started without a known user, it is almost as if the building were the client. The brief then is to find the most appropriate use. Efforts should be made to find potential users requiring space, or new investors. Alternatively, research could be undertaken to identify a need for particular facilities or specialist accommodation (e.g. loft apartments converted from old multi-storey factories or stores, cf 6.1). Building projects which have proved successful in other areas can be used as models.

It may be possible to advance an already successful form of development. One method would be to attract a successful venture as an anchor tenant in your space by reducing their rent and overheads. They may then draw in further tenants, particularly if there is a central theme to the development (e.g. The Custard Factory, Birmingham whose theme is the performing arts and supporting skills and businesses, 6.2). This can develop into a vibrant community with its own momentum. Avoid preconceptions, the more unpredictable re-uses are often the most successful.

Conrad Hilton is reputed to have said, 'There are just three factors essential to the success of a hotel – location, location and location.' So, however suitable a building may be for conversion into a hotel, even if that were its previous use, it may not necessarily be an appropriate one now; if it is in the wrong location.

Do some research into similar projects. Were they successful? Were the clients' needs fulfilled? If you cannot find this information from articles, books or lectures it may be possible to visit the clients themselves. The experience of others in any particular field of activity could be helpful.[2] For in-depth research, it is advisable to employ an expert who understands the market and can anticipate its dynamics.

Once the user has been found, their requirements can be identified in a specific brief. Start by defining the problem as a statement of need. Commercially, this could be: 'the need to provide space for x number of staff with varying roles', or in domestic terms: 'a home in which to play music without disturbing others'.

Example   6.1

USE: **Department store, Manchester**
Nineteenth century, unlisted comprising 144,000 sq ft in up to six storeys in nine different buildings. Empty since 1975.

TO: **Flats and shops**
81 flats and 21 retail outlets.

D: **Urban Splash**[3]

Atrium – before. (*Jonathan Keenan*)

Church Street/Oldham Street elevation before. (*Jonathan Keenan*)

Atrium – after. (*Photoflex*)

Church Street/Oldham Street elevation after. (*Photoflex*)

Example   6.2

USE: Custard factory, Birmingham
Late nineteenth to twentieth century, part
Grade II, five-storey steel and concrete framed
factory around a central courtyard employing
1,200 people. Disused since 1980.

TO: Business centre for creative industries
Studio workspace for art, dance, theatre, TV
design and crafts; galleries shops and cafes to
attract visitors; and student accommodation.
SPACE organises craft fairs, theatrical
performances and its own newspaper.

D: SPACE[4]

Courtyard (note wall sculpture).

Entrance.

The client, whether owner, developer or tenant can describe their needs directly to
the architect. A client requiring business use could appoint from their staff a client liaison
officer through whom requirements and needs can be communicated. Discussions will
be more focused if parameters can be established at the outset. Checklists (see RIBA Job
Book) can prove useful, but there is no substitute for an enquiring outlook.

If the proposal is for residential use and the tenants are known, as could happen in the case of local authority or housing association tenants involved in estate renewal, it will be necessary to involve the tenants in groups and ask them to appoint spokespersons. The objective is to generate maximum participation and encourage the tenants to maintain an open mind. However, it is prudent to explain to them the limits of the building and its possible changes, so they will accept compromises more readily.

If the prospective tenants are not known at the outset, typical tenant profiles can be created, whether commercial or residential, by comparison with similar schemes elsewhere.

While it is impossible to consult the general public en masse, their views are represented by such bodies as the amenity groups of heritage and conservation, local chambers of commerce, local societies and residents associations. Ultimately, the local council is elected to represent the public view as a civic duty but consultations with them need to be carefully managed. The interests of each of the different users, for example the owner, tenant and passing public, must be given sufficient consideration to avoid satisfying one group at the expense of the other.

Where a project is likely to be controversial, or of particular public interest, it may be necessary to conduct public meetings. This would provide an opportunity for them to voice their opinions and concerns; but be aware that the participants will be the most interested parties, and not necessarily representative of the public as a whole. Beware of raising expectations unrealistically regarding the degree of change they can effect.

■ PREPARING A BRIEF

The next stage in the project is to look at the business case for each option that arises. Then a strategic brief can be devised that sets out the key objectives of the project and identifies the criteria used to measure its success. The design team and client throughout the design stages will continually refer to this.

When preparing the brief, it is important not to concentrate on the detailed, practical requirements at the expense of the wider aims and aspirations. Encourage clients to think laterally, identifying the long-term consequences of current strategy, as well as the immediate implications.

Too often, with proposals for conversion, the brief is driven by the existing building, rather than by the client's real needs. When clients discuss a new building they often spend a long time deciding upon the physical format they need. They may refer to similar types of building, or compare illustrations of other buildings but they rarely expect a copy of another design. Conversely, with existing buildings, clients often measure up rooms, obtain plans and try to work out their own solutions. 'We thought this space might be particularly useful for the . . .' is a phrase often used by clients, without having looked into factors such as servicing, access, egress, uses of adjacent space, sound or thermal insulation, or aspect (although prospect is usually considered). As the clients discover the impracticality of their wishes, they tend to withdraw from decisions that really do require their input.

To avoid such communication difficulties, prepare the accommodation brief for the conversion as if it were a new building. Only the response to the brief should be different. Any references to the existing property should be kept separately from the accommodation brief. In this way, the two factors can have separate, identifiable influences upon the ultimate design. The weight given to each factor can then be varied to test the sensitivity and appropriateness of that design, for both the user and the existing fabric.

If the user has been identified, an 'ideal brief' can be drafted. This needs to be a comprehensive but realistic assessment of needs against possibility. If the client has a strong or clear view of the building's possibilities in advance of the commission, this must be taken into account. It will then need to be tested by preparing an accommodation schedule describing the design and building plans, a known management structure and predicted requirements. A full briefing that includes long-term strategy should facilitate the development of a master plan – a vision for the future that will accommodate all predictable needs in a co-ordinated and progressive manner.

The brief needs to be sufficiently sensitive to change to ensure that the design is still usable by the time the project is completed. Images, organisations and clients change with time. The marketing industry spends millions trying to predict changes in the market; it is equally hard for the client and architect to develop a brief that allows for future changes. I was once told, 'It is an architect's job to have hindsight before the event.' We try but don't always succeed!

In order to forecast likely changes, several factors must be taken into account including: an assessment of past patterns of change; targets; growth rates; space per person; efficiency; organisation (such as control by a parent company); external influences from competitors; a changing market place; and improving technology.

It should be possible to project five and ten years ahead – short periods relative to the life of the building. It is worth testing any predictions by consulting other professionals in the field; brainstorming with staff, gaming techniques with live players, or extrapolation and simulation by computer. The brief should be as far-sighted, comprehensive and broad in perspective as possible notwithstanding constraints of time, circumstances and resources.

■ Future activities in the building

Once a proposed use is decided upon, further creative thought needs to be applied to activities inherent in that use. This is the equivalent stage to the designer's 'bubble' diagram in identifying links and connections between activities in order to convert a brief into a design concept. In the case of re-use plans the creative element is in trying to apply the brief in as many different ways to the existing plan as possible, identifying the strengths and weaknesses of each option. A 'design think tank' session with several designers pursuing different goals can stack up a range of solutions for objective analysis. These can then be tested against the acknowledged user's needs.

The corporate image

As most corporate users consider image an important factor, they may decide to accept or reject a particular building at the feasibility stage according to its potential to reflect upon the company. When dealing with a strongly promotional client, a building, especially if listed, needs to be tested for its ability to shape up to requirements. Corporate clients can sometimes be persuaded to adapt their image to the building and environment.

McDonald's hamburger chain is noted for its strong corporate identity. When a branch is located as a stand alone unit within an edge of town retail development they will use oversized signage, on a distinctively designed building with predetermined roof shape, brick, frame colour and overall form. The 'Big M' is designed to stand out distinctly. This brash image would look out of place in any Conservation Area. Customers must be able to recognise the restaurant, yet it must blend in with the surrounding buildings and shops. This can be achieved by affixing an internally illuminated 'M' inside the building, which is visible from outside through a traditional window, or by a discreet sign adjacent to an opening. In these situations the architectural heritage is taken into account as well as the local authority planning controls, especially those applied under the Advertisement Regulations and Article 4 Directions. Thus the company's promotional image can be expressed through a logo which is assimilated even in the most sensitive locations (6.3).

Example   6.3

McDonald's Restaurant, Chester. The logo is displayed only from behind the shop window. (*Cloud Nine Photography*)

McDonald's Restaurant, Tower Hill – a small 'M' on the stonework is sufficient. (*Cloud Nine Photography*)[5]

Each company will have its own corporate image. Bankers will wish to emphasise their stature, insurance companies their opulence, designers their trendiness, engineers their innovative style and so on. The challenge is to successfully resolve the image of the occupier with that of the building's original character. Sometimes these are in accord, as with the splendour of the new roof over Queen Victoria Street, alongside Frank Matcham's County Arcade, Leeds (7.2); or in counterpoint, as the high technology entrance link to the sturdy railway company offices for Midland Inter-City, Derby (9.2). Sometimes the impact is restricted to the interior, as the internal street at the Derwent Business Centre, Derby (17.3); or the glazed vault at the Cavendish Arcade converted from the Thermal Baths, Buxton (2.17) or a symbol on the exterior, as the gates, forming a 'brooch' to the Jewellery Centre, Birmingham (6.4).

Case Study 6.4

From: Sweatshop Housing Block in Birmingham's Jewellery Quarter
To: Jewellery Business Centre, 'The Jewel in the Crown'

'The Prince of Wales has chosen well. There could not be a more appropriate venue for his first, personal, inner city venture than Birmingham's Jewellery Quarter . . . barely half a mile from the concrete jungle of central Birmingham. There are not only jewellers and silver-smiths, but electro-platers, metal spinners, stampers and piercers, casters, die sinkers and finishers. A ring may travel to two or three workshops to be finished. Many one, two and three man businesses exist entirely on subcontracting from larger workshops. Some craftsmen simply lease a bench.'[a]

Birmingham's Jewellery Quarter grew following the flood of cheap gold into the town after 1849. Centred in a residential area, small businesses multi-occupy the three-storey terrace houses, expanding and contracting so that flying freeholds have become the norm and every backyard has become filled with workshops, sometimes with only a metre between. Filled with ovens and machinery, and without adequate means of escape, these have degenerated into potential death traps. Some of the larger workshops, built as companies grew, are spread amongst the residential streets. To ensure the survival of the jewellery industry in this area, the replacement of premises for the numerous one-man trades, and small companies was really needed.

The worst affected block was the area bounded by Hockley Street, Branston Street and Spencer Street. Built around 1840, this consisted of two rows of character-istic terrace houses, a large Edwardian corner house, and a 1900 workshop block punctuated by large arched windows. These are the very staple of the Jewellery Quarter; well proportioned, but plain, and built of Midlands red brick.[b] The key elements for re-use were:

■ **A comprehensive proposal for the whole block**
Without losing the feel of the old Jewellery Quarter the aim was to create around 34,000 sq ft of first-class working accommodation, with plenty of daylight and full access for the disabled. Purchase and development funds of £3.8 million came from the Prince of Wales through the Duchy of Cornwall, to establish occupation

Spencer Street before.

Spencer Street after. The entrance archway replaces the most derelict building. (*Stuart Blackwood*)

by a range of small businesses.[c] The Jewellery Business Centre now comprises 60 self-contained units, ranging from 200 sq ft to 2,000 sq ft for jewellers, silversmiths and other related trades and businesses. The developers were Grosvenor Laing Urban Enterprise Ltd.

■ **Demolition of the rear and back extensions of all properties**

The opportunity was taken to unite the various frontages by clearing away the derelict, unstable, tightly packed workshops within the block and extend to the rear of both Spencer Street and Branston Street. These extensions increase the original depth of each frontage block and also project out in a staggered relationship to one another to form four spacious courtyards.

■ **Frontages are retained and a new archway identifies the entrance to the centre**

The only evidence on the street frontage that this development has occurred is the introduction of a new two-storey arch on the Spencer Street elevation which provides access from the reception area to the workspaces and to a landscaped courtyard.

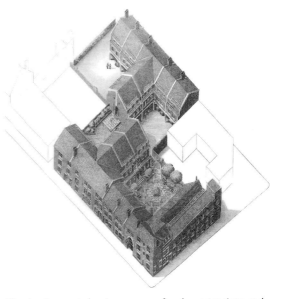

The development showing new rear façades, extensions and courtyards: two pedestrian, two at lower level for parking.

'Backyards' before.

■ Adornment with a symbolic jewellery related sculpture

Within the arch a pair of metaphorical gates signify security, but stand ajar in a gesture of welcome. These are made of hand-forged metal and cast glass, with images and techniques used in the construction of jewellery. Begun here, the theme is followed to the heart of the development with the design of handrails and light fittings. Symbols and artefacts have been included in the paving of the entrance area and courtyards, The hopper heads were also commissioned as caricatures of individuals connected with the project.

'Backyards' after.

The Symbolism of 'The Metaphorical Gates'.
(*Stuart Blackwood*)

New rear wall to 'factory' of reclaimed material.

The metaphor of the gates is one of security: something the jewellery industry cannot do without. It is also an appropriate part of architectural language. The large, arched opening in the façade creates a hierarchy in the fenestration denoting the entrance to the Business Centre. The sculpture within the archway dresses this entrance with a unique identity, more than just a vacant hole. The use of gates rather than doors allows the reception space to remain between inside and outside, acting as a link to the private courtyards within. Doors would create an exclusively internal reception space. One gate is in the open position as an invitation to the visitor. A fretwork or filigree allows views through the gates so that the Business Centre reception still relates to the public domain. The stainless steel and brass used are contemporary building materials relating to the traditional silver and gold of the jewellery industry. Similarly, cast glass nuggets are incorporated to represent gemstones.

The pattern of the sculpture represents geological and organic forms which have been the basis for Jewellery Design for millennia. The lower half represents the earth's strata containing the cast glass nuggets with roots seeking their way down to find them. The upper half represents the plant of progress with the faceted polished glass jewels. The sculpture is clearly a one-off, handcrafted work – as is good jewellery – and not a mass produced architectural screen. The metal-work is joined together as if a brooch had been magnified 100 times, so at close inspection all the welds at the junctions can be seen clearly. In fact, the design for the gates was reproduced at 100th the size and presented to the Princess of Wales as a brooch.

The concept and design of the sculpture was a collaborative process between architect and artist and the production the result of the sculptor's individual metal working skills. The artist/sculptor, Michael Johnson, puts it in his own words: 'The Gates are based on contemporary jewellery: young people with new ideas are the future of the jeweller's art, not mass produced imports. Minerals drawn through the roots produce fruit, similarly minerals worked by artists and jewellers produce art and jewellery.'

Hopper head of Latham the architect (plus the foreman, crane driver, project manager, etc., – but not HRH).

■ Explosion resistant workshop accommodation with enhanced daylight

New construction and reconstruction both utilise load-bearing cross walls, allowing higher storeys to step back and permit top lighting for workbenches as well as giving workers windows with views. The strength of these walls enables explosion resistant accommodation.

■ The re-use of materials blending the new with the old

Second-hand bricks were used both for reconstruction and new extensions. Cast-iron windows re-used in the rear 'factory' façade and blue paviours from basements cover the Spencer Street courtyards – laid out as quiet access and sitting areas for visitors and tenants.

■ Limited car parking

At a lower level the other courts provide parking space over part of the site together with covered parking under the Branston Street block.

■ The management of the centre has easy lease terms for small businesses

The relatively relaxed leasing arrangements help to ensure a thriving centre with up and coming design talent taking advantage of the location. 'The project has played a major part in the reinvigoration of the Jewellery Quarter and restored one of the city's traditional industries to this district of Birmingham. The artwork incorporated in the development is also helping to put it on the tourist trail, an important source of revenue for the tenants. Already, tours for foreign visitors to the new Birmingham Convention Centre are being diverted so that the Jewellery Business Centre and its gates can be seen and appreciated.'[d,e]

Also see colour plates 5a–d.

■ References

a. Binney, M., 'The Prince's New Showcase', *Country Life*, 5 October 1989.
b. Ibid.
c. 'Jewel in the Crown', *RIBA Journal*, June 1992, pp 36–7.
d. Ibid.
e. Project Architect: Neil Barr, Latham Architects.

In each case the user needs to discover how to exploit the inherent qualities of the building to foster its own image. Clients often find this quite difficult. Assuming they eventually accept that the building will suit their image, decisions can be made about alterations. If, for example, the interior of the building is not original, plans can be made to convert it to suit the client, whilst the exterior retains its original character.

An example might be in the purchase of a former bank, which suggests 'stature', and bedecking the interior with soft furnishings to create a feeling of warmth, or maple flooring to modernise it (6.5).

Example   6.5

USE: Bank, City of London
Classical colonnaded double height banking
hall in National Westminster headquarters.

TO: Art gallery
Light timber over the cleared floor area
combined with high light levels enables
artwork to be displayed on simple plain white
free standing screens.

A: DEGW[6]

The Lothbury Gallery.

Example   6.6

USE: Country house, Eastley End, Egham
Georgian, Grade II, with stable block, grange, and walled gardens in brick.

TO: Office
House and outbuildings retain their original character but were extended to form new garden elevations facing a court across which new offices are contained within a modern steel and glass single-storey, the roofs of which are covered with hedged gardens.

A: Edward Cullinan Architects[7]

A large complex extension is assimilated into the garden landscape setting.

The main house.

Example   **6.7**

USE: **Garage/coach house, Notting Hill**
Nineteenth century, brick and slate, double height, mews coach house converted to garage with large sliding double doors.

TO: **Workshop and design studio**
Retaining the coach house character, paint was removed from brickwork and doors made to hang on the existing external sliding mechanism. The doors open to reveal a new glazed screen set back to create a double-height lobby giving access to workshops at ground-, and studio at first-floor level.

A: **Powell-Tuck Associates[8]**

Externally the coach house has only been cleaned and repaired, but the doors open to reveal the new intervention. (*Dennis Gilbert*)

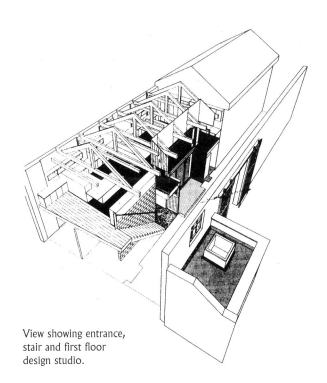

View showing entrance, stair and first floor design studio.

The paint was blasted from the old brickwork which contrasts with modern insertions. (*Dennis Gilbert*)

Contrasting themes can also be effective. A traditional country house may suggest permanence with a perceived past, yet building an extension that is engineered with innovation can symbolise progress (6.6).

In some cases, the contrast could be hidden initially, to create a serendipitous surprise to the visitor, as when only the interior is different in character (6.7).

COMPILING A BRIEF FOR A SCHOOL
(Given the opportunity to purchase and convert adjacent buildings)

An organised client

Identify the decision making structure – the relationship between staff, the head and governors. Appoint a chairperson and/or a client's liaison officer with the architect.

The liaison officer needs the authority to make decisions between meetings so queries can be dealt with firmly and speedily to ensure uninterrupted progress. The liaison officer has a key role to play. Beware of placing responsibility into 'expert' hands because it is true liaison with the client that is required. The ultimate client is the pupil. The teacher, head, bursar, governor and co-optee are all progressively further removed.

Identify the problem

Look at all the problems facing the school. Attempt to quantify them and prioritise.

- Shortage of accommodation.
- Temporary buildings (patched up service for decades).
- Old technology buildings.
- Shortage of assembly space.
- Poor sports facilities.
- Inadequate arts block.
- Leaking roofs.
- Faulty wiring.
- Lack of insulation.
- Poor accessibility.

These questions must also be asked

- How easy or difficult, costly or inexpensive, are the problems to resolve?
- How are the criteria established to identify which to tackle first?
- Do the management, head, governor, bursar and staff, all agree?
- Would the pupils also agree?
- Would it be more effective to refurbish the existing premises as new technology rooms or as simple, new classrooms?
- Where are the existing services – water, drainage, gas – and how would they connect to the adjacent buildings?
- Are there large-scale mains which might prevent extension?
- What importance do staff place upon car-parking space, now or in the future?
- What is the likely cost?

Also, think ahead. What happens when these current projects are completed? The school may become more popular or its status change (e.g. lowered entry age or raised leaving age). Will the decisions made now allow for these changes?

Survey

See 'Survey Tips', Chapter 5.

Inception

Select an architect on the basis of conceptual ability; design skill; the ability to complete projects on budget and on time; experience of schools; a track record in re-using buildings; an empathy with the school and its objectives; methods of working; and if possible one whose completed designs find favour with most of the governors and staff.

Appoint on the basis of the RIBA Conditions of Engagement, 'Architects Appointment'. Be clear about fees and how much work will be done for it. Sign an agreement. Define workload. A similar exercise should be undertaken to appoint other consultants.

Draft a brief for the consultants, inviting them to assist in the above analysis and the prioritising of the development of the whole school (unless this has already been done), i.e. anticipate needs rather than react to them as they arise.

Analyse

A head may identify a school by the pupils and staff while the architect may see it as the building. It is important to maintain the balance between these two views. Review the curriculum and the potential for future change, together with an audit of the human resources required before finalising building and equipment requirements.

The school will have a vision of the future education they wish to provide for their pupils, involving class size, special subject areas, particular ways of delivering the curriculum, pastoral care, and health and safety. All will form part of the business plan which should be the basis of the brief.

Calculate existing space and accommodation:

- Site areas.
- Recreation areas.
- Playing-field areas.
- Teaching areas.
- Number of toilets.
- Staff accommodation.
- Medical accommodation.
- Boarding accommodation.

Take account of the size, purpose and intensity of use of each space, and of the number of pupils on roll.

Identify both permanent and temporary accommodation even if not in use. List the spaces under one of four categories:

- General teaching (classrooms).
- Light practical (computers, art, science, music etc.).
- Heavy practical (craft/design/technology).
- Large spaces (hall, library, dining).
- Sport and PE.

Allocate a workplace number to each space according to its type of space and its area in order to calculate the capacity of the school

Analyse the current curriculum totalling the number of periods per week to be taught for each subject, and the number of groups to be taught in any one. Aggregate these totals via a matrix into the accommodation categories listed. Apply a loading factor (percentage of time in effective use) varying between, say, 70 per cent for a hall to 90 per cent for classrooms.

Detail the brief

From the analysis, a room schedule can be derived, forming the outline brief for the school, based upon the requirements of the curriculum. This is equivalent to the accommodation brief for the design of a new building. Compare the resultant room schedule with an analysis of the existing accommodation, to identify the additional accommodation and/or adaptation requirements, which will enable the curriculum to be delivered.

However, analysis should not be limited to the present, so prepare a likely curriculum timetable for, say, five years in the future, identifying likely pupil numbers and an assessment of the curriculum split at that time. A future room demand schedule can be derived from this and the implications taken on board by the architect to illustrate future development that may be required. In this way the analysis can respond to the dynamic of the school, anticipating the potential for change as well as the efficiency, or lack of it, of present use.

Now the client and consultant can write the brief identifying:

- The amount of accommodation required.
- The type of accommodation.
- What accommodation needs upgrading, or converting.
- How much further survey information is required.
- Targets for reducing maintenance and running costs.
- The perception of the school, and any resultant image sought.
- Potential for future expansion.

- The nature of the client organisation and the way consultants should report to it.
- The programme that everyone must adhere to.

Synthesis

Take time to consider the brief. This is when all the questions should be asked. Too often they are asked too late, causing expense, confusion and delay.

It may not be possible to quantify all of these, in which event the consultants will have to undertake a feasibility or master plan prior to proceeding with particular design solutions.

Test the brief. Assess the feasibility of the assumptions made by preparing different options for development. For presentation, the architect can interpret these in drawn form.

- Consult with statutory bodies on any matters of principle.
- Compare alternatives.
- Consider cost.
- Think about methods of implementation.
- View the possible programme.

Consult

This is the stage at which it is fruitful to involve the maximum input of technical staff and use their experience together to contribute to the thinking process.

A 'brainstorming' technique could be adopted. This can involve all staff and governors but may be more appropriate with just a premises committee and relevant heads of department. It is important that the 'body politic' of the school is involved so that everyone will accept responsibility for the final outcome. Involve as many relevant people as possible. It is better they speak now and their ideas be accommodated (or they understand why they cannot be implemented), than make suggestions later which, if used, would cause expensive changes to the design.

This process is not only part of the resolution of design problems, but also a way of getting the client body to become part of, and understand, the nature of the design process. Do not restrict the architect even at this stage to considering only one possible solution; involve the other consultant advisers to give advice on potential alternatives.

The brief should be agreed in writing between client and consultant before proceeding. It should be agreed between all those involved as it will later be used as the basis for analysing which alternative design solutions best meet the objectives.[9]

Sometimes the client cannot describe their desired image adequately. The architect may gain some clues as to a user's desired image by inspecting their current premises. This can prove a useful starting point for discussion not only about the building's conversion, but also to the type of maintenance and renewal that might be required. This discussion should be kept simple. Before putting pen to paper, the architect could discuss with the client a wide range of images of other buildings and projects, comparing the effects of old and new, famous and obscure, prestigious and ordinary, in order to help the client focus on their aims.

■ WHAT MAKES A GOOD BRIEF?

A good brief is more than a set of space requirements. It represents the user's needs, hopes and aspirations. It incorporates past experience and current influences yet anticipates the future and accepts change. It will be flexible, take account of the building's capacity for change, and be conscious of the image presented upon completion.

It will propose a timetable which must be planned, programmed and co-ordinated. If for any reason the deadlines need to be brought forward, it is not sufficient to merely apply more labour or spend more money on it. More teamwork and earlier commitment by all parties may be required particularly by the client who may have to accept that decisions are irreversible after each stage.

Time, commitment and hard decisions will be required of the client and their advisers. Inevitably the brief will develop as the project proceeds, the design will have to be 'signed off' before the production stage is reached, in order to ensure prudent cost management.

REFERENCES

1. cf Appendix in this Volume, page 215, Principles for Re-use.
2. Markus T.A., *Building Conservation and Rehabilitation: designing for change in building use*, Butterworth, 1979.
3. Rose, V., *Catalytic Conversion: REVIVE Historic Buildings to Regenerate Communities*, SAVE, AHF, IHBC and UKABPT.
4. Ibid.
5. McDonald's.
6. 'Monet, Monet, Monet', *Building*, 21 February 1997, p 14.
7. *Building*, 7 December 1990, p 45.
8. 'Coach-House of Many Colours', *Architects Journal*, 13 March 1997, pp 44–5.
9. Latham, D. and Smith, D., *Capital Building Bids: Procurement and Commissions*, GMSC, High Wycombe, 1994.

CHAPTER 7

Enhancing the Value of Property

A re-use project clearly has to be financially viable, and there can be financial rewards from working with old buildings.[1] Yet there are specific problems that can arise with conservation and adaptation.

■ EVALUATING IN A UNIQUE CONTEXT

Valuation is crucial at the briefing and feasibility stage to establish the parameters for action. Yet a valuation is usually based on knowledge of the sale price of properties of a similar type, condition and location, making adjustments for differences where appropriate. In the commercial field these adjustments involve analysing a matrix of data, rental values, capitalisation and deferment rates, the quality of tenants attracted and strength of covenant. Historic buildings, however, have such a unique context, character and arrangement of space that it is difficult to find a suitable comparison.

These unusual qualities often depress the value. Potential purchasers are not sure how to appraise the property, how to maximise its use, or to what extent restrictive controls will prevent them from undertaking certain activities. Occasionally chronic disrepair or even dereliction makes the building look an even less likely proposition. At this point buildings may have a 'negative value', their low price attracting interest from an undesirable type of entrepreneur. These venturers are sometimes misguided; they may perhaps be looking to profit from a quick sale, or even want to occupy such a large property themselves. In many cases they are unaware of the costs involved, or the grants available.

Only a few agents specialise in historic buildings and conservation work. They usually advise upon properties to be marketed nationally. Local historic properties and sites may therefore require special advice.

Commercial buildings can be valued by looking broadly at the physical possibilities within the shell, and what other marketable building solutions exist.

The conversion of Covent Garden from a fruit and vegetable market had a seminal influence upon the conservation movement. This was not only because of its excellent conservation, but because it demonstrated a market acceptability for such re-use. Although this was not a unique project (Faneuil Hall in Boston had shown the way), it was the first influential project of its kind in Britain. In this case, the valuation was only made after combining knowledge of what had been achieved elsewhere, with a clear understanding of local economic activity, and the building's physical potential.

There may be a discrepancy between the physical potential of the property and the perceived market requirements. If this occurs, identify whether the property can be expanded or constraints removed so the full value can be realised although this may prove difficult in the case of listed buildings. But, for example, it may be possible to acquire land adjacent to a large residence for extra garden space, garaging, a paddock or ancillary accommodation. Perhaps a restrictive covenant or right of way could be removed, although this may prove difficult in the case of listed buildings.

■ The value of listed buildings

'Listing is unlikely to devalue your home (unless you happen to possess a decaying mansion). Some argue it adds to value. Estate agents are not averse to mentioning the fact in their particulars – so presumably it is a benefit. There has been no research to establish what effect listing has on house values but the general consensus is that it has little impact: if anything, it adds to value.'[2]

The value of commercial buildings can be affected by listing. In 1993 the Royal Institution of Chartered Surveyors (RICS) and English Heritage (EH) jointly commissioned research from Investment Property Databank (IPD) titled, 'The Investment Performance of Listed Buildings'. The report is updated annually and its findings surprised many in the property industry.

In the 1996 update IPD stated:

> Listed office buildings out-performed the office market generally – both in Central London and across the whole of the UK for the second consecutive year, in 1995. However, this recently stronger performance has not been sufficient to compensate for the much poorer relative returns at the depth of the recession (in the early 1990s) and so the medium term three and five year figures still show under-performance by the listed stock. Over the full fifteen year period, for which measurement is possible, listed office buildings continue to show marginal out-performance . . .
>
> The relative advantage over the last two years reflects underlying causal patterns which have typified the full fifteen year measurement period. The listed office buildings produced stronger returns, through the early and mid-1980s, largely as a result of stronger than average rental value movements. Yields contributed modestly

but were never the driving force. By the same token the relative collapse of the listed buildings' returns in the early 1990s reflected only very modest adverse yield shifts and huge discrepancies in terms of falling rental values. It would, therefore, seem likely that future superior returns to listed offices cannot be expected to spring from further relative yield adjustments and must await underlying rental growth at rates in excess of those supported by the office markets generally.

Figure 7.1a shows the annualised total return (i.e. combined capital growth and net income) for the UK office investments in IPD's databank, broken down by age and listing status. It shows that between 1980–1995, pre-1945 listed buildings performed best (as they also did in 1995), but over the past three and five-year periods they have been out-performed by post-1975 buildings.

Figure 7.1b illustrates that rental levels for listed buildings now lag about ten per cent behind rents for modern office buildings, after rising to much higher levels in the late 1980s.

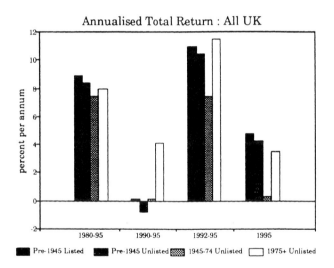

Figure 7.1a

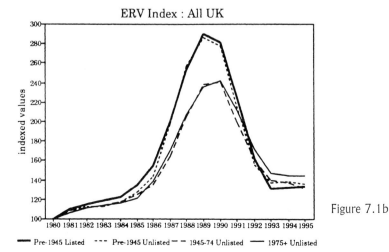

Figure 7.1b

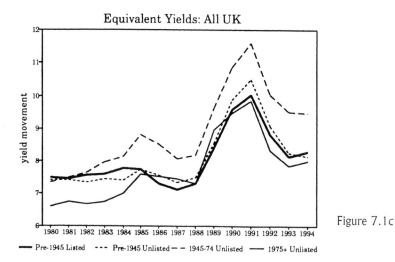

Figure 7.1c

Figure 7.1c indicates that yield rates are only one quarter per cent behind those for modern office buildings.

Although IPD's report suggests that listed buildings for office use make good investments, their figures do need qualifying. The sample taken was small. The returns are measured net of recurrent costs, including repair costs (where these are borne by the occupier rather than the owner). When institutions acquire listed office buildings for their investment portfolio they tend to choose the best available rather than typical ones. Many of the buildings studied were in city centres, which are more valuable locations.

As the costs are not factored into the IPD research, the RICS, EH and the Department of National Heritage (DNH) asked Dr Christine Whitehead at Cambridge University's Department of Land Economy to assess the effect of listing on commercial buildings. Her findings were different to those of IPD. The following are extracts from her report:

The immediate objective of the research undertaken by the Property Research Unit was to examine 'worst case' scenarios, where private costs could be expected to be the highest, in order to give an estimate of the maximum cost which might be incurred. In the vast majority of cases, especially where listed buildings are located in conservation areas, the extent of these costs can be expected to be very much less. Indeed, in many cases, there may be significant benefits to owners as well as to society as a whole. The importance of the research is its attempt to measure the extent of those costs that do exist in order to ensure that they are properly taken into account in the formulation of policy. What is just as important is then to attempt to measure the true social and wider economic benefits, so that policy can be fully informed.

In some circumstances the listing of income-producing non-residential buildings does reduce their market value by eliminating potential development value.

This is a one-time cost normally borne by the owner of the building at the time of listing and should not affect subsequent performance. The effect appeared most marked for small buildings located in areas with high development pressure and outside conservation areas.

Owners of listed buildings know they are extremely unlikely to receive permission to demolish their buildings and few apply to do so. Listed buildings may therefore simply deteriorate if a suitable use is not found. Draft PPG 15 [now PPG 15] stresses the importance of keeping a building in economic use.

The results of the Cambridge study partly explained why property owners are wary of investing in listed buildings, as they believe the added restrictions involved can suppress value.

English Heritage was not only interested in the economic aspects of listing. They, together with RICS and DNH, asked the University of Reading and DTZ Debenham Thorpe to look at the social and economic benefits of listing.

When looking at all the reports on listing buildings, a picture emerges of benefit to the community at large, funded mostly by the owners of historic properties. The nation's heritage will only truly benefit when we have merged the objectives of conservation with sound economics. Society wants to retain its best period buildings and areas, and property owners seek a fair return on their investment (or, if an owner-occupier, beneficial use).

■ A realistic approach to valuation

All parties need to take a flexible approach. Some adaptation or change of layout and facilities may be required if the owner is to get a fair commercial return on his investment. The owner/investor still has to respect the history of a building. Solutions and techniques must be sought which intrude as little as possible into the fabric of a building. Applications like full air conditioning and unnecessary floor strengthening should be avoided.

The planning officer and committee should also be flexible about use. They are primarily interested in land use, but will have to weigh this against the importance of the building. It is better to put a redundant building back to work than leave it empty and decaying. Planners may need to seek valuation advice if the owner insists economic viability of the building depends on change of use or alterations. Conservation officers, who are primarily interested in the building fabric, will then be able to take economic factors into account as well as architectural history.

The private sector will only invest cash if they can clearly see an economic return. Good conservation must recognise commercial factors, or possibly put the building at risk.

Figure 7.1d shows how owners and conservation officers can reach an agreement. As values rise higher up the vertical axis, the need to create value through repair and change diminishes to the left of the horizontal axis.

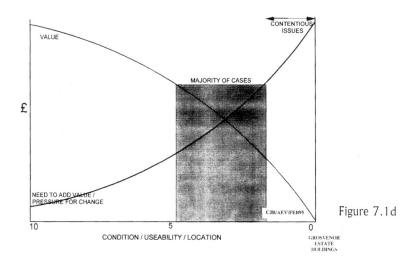

Figure 7.1d

If a building is usable, well located, in good repair and attractive to an occupier, its value will be relatively high as it stands and there will be less need to alter the building. Conversely, as the value falls down the vertical axis, the need to create value through repair and change increases to the right of the horizontal axis. If a building is unusable, badly located, in poor condition and unattractive to an occupier, its value will be relatively low and there will be more need to make alterations.

Most cases probably occur towards the centre of the graph, either at or close to the point of crossover of the curves. Difficult issues arise to the far right hand side of the graph, where the owner may seek extreme solutions such as façade retention or even demolition.

At the time an application is made for listed building consent and/or conservation area consent, the applicant could call for the opinion of a reputable local valuer to propose to the local authority where the building should be positioned on the graph. The local authority may accept this advice if the valuer is known and highly respected. Alternatively, local valuers acting on each side could agree where on the value curve a building should be placed (taking into account local values). Both owner and conservation officer should then find it easier to agree on the extent of change or adaptation that should be allowed to a particular building. For listed buildings, occupation is the key to good conservation. Occupiers bestow value and provide care. This should be reiterated to the Conservation Officer.

■ Appraising the Project

Market conditions may vary considerably in different locations. A rehabilitation project that proves commercially successful in a city may not be appropriate in a provincial or rural location. Owners of under-used or vacant property may not recognise this factor; with unrealistic expectations, they could hold out for a high sale price[3] especially where their advisers are seeking the best return for their client.

At the time of writing, this misguided optimism is common with government agencies and statutory undertakers.

One remedy lies in negotiation based on an informed view of the risks and costs likely to be involved, although by the time this information is amassed, the project may become financially unfeasible. A better answer would be for such owners to instigate an investigation into the creative re-use of their property. A realistic approach must always be taken when appraising the project. What are the economic aims of the owner/developer and how do these apply to the project?

Established developers are more likely to take over a property in good condition and refurbish it for a similar use or convert to another use. They prefer a well-maintained property of known condition and capacity rather than a low cost purchase with unknown risk. They will pay a higher price for being more certain of the maintenance costs, and faster conversion work. The value of the building is retained as the degree of intervention is reduced. The result could still vary from simple change of user, to a full gutting and re-cladding of a sound structure to reposition and re-present the building in the market place, thereby extending its life significantly.

The key to valuation of such properties is to assess the real costs and the potential. This is no simple matter. Early estimates are difficult to produce, which may be a problem when seeking financial support. Repair costs of neglected properties are particularly difficult to quantify. A proper schedule of dilapidation, repair costs, a health and safety survey and, if desired, an energy audit must be undertaken by the potential purchaser or his architect and structural engineer, and qualified by a specialist quantity surveyor.

The means of funding the project must be ascertained. What funds can the owner obtain? A trust or other charitable body constituted in a different way to a commercial operation or a private interest will approach the project in its own way.

A local authority that uses their legislated power unreasonably may reduce a property's value to the point where re-use becomes uneconomic. If this is unavoidable, the authority could make regulation more acceptable if a grant is made available.

■ **Available resources**

Before taking action, we should assess the resources available. We must understand market forces, to avoid buildings lying derelict. A market campaign is needed to find the user for the building. Market research must be undertaken to identify the likely customer, quantify the size of the market, clarify the product range and look at the innovative ways in which buildings can be re-used. The product must then be promoted in the relevant media.

One of the first steps is to check whether grant aid is available for all or part of the project. Seedcorn money may be available to re-use projects to fulfil social or historic objectives where there are insufficient market forces in the area. The AHF and historic building trusts acting as 'honest broker' may assist in this.

Where there is a recognised social or cultural need, public funds can support projects that cannot be provided by market forces. Not by creating a museum or arts centre merely to use a redundant building but in response to a demonstrable need which would otherwise have necessitated a new building. The public can at the same time be made aware that re-use can be just as effective and exciting as a new building. Government, local authorities and statutory undertakers can set an example by re-using buildings wherever possible (7.2).

Example   7.2

USE: Woollen mill, Ebley, Stroud
1799 and 1840, G. F. Bodley, 1819, four-storey double-width stone built mullion windowed Long Mill plus 1840, five-storey large cast iron windowed stone block with higher ceilings, separate staircase turret and boiler room. 56,000 sq ft, closed 1981.

TO: Council offices
Purchased in 1986, conversion utilised the roof space of the Long Mill by incorporating a continuous dormer. A 15,000 sq ft hexagonal extension accommodated council chamber, meeting rooms, staff restaurant, computer suite and print room. Bringing council activities under one room from six locations in the town enabled redevelopment of the centre, ensured the survival of the historic mill, and, as an exemplar, acted as a catalyst to encourage the conversion of other mills in the area.

A: Niall Phillips[4]

Arrival area with the continuous dormer just visible on Long Mill.

Inside the fourth floor attic storey.

There are a variety of funds available for the repair, conservation, and use of historic structures, buildings, art and artefacts. These include the Heritage Lottery Fund. The possibility of re-using existing buildings can make many previously unthinkable projects financially viable. Arts theatres can be economically housed in converted buildings. Sports and leisure space could be found in converted warehouses and so attract Sports Council funding. When considering large-scale projects with the aim of regeneration or social improvement, European funding could even be a possibility. This would need to be applied for under the umbrella of an active local authority.

Even after extensive research has been undertaken, there is still a need to maintain a flexible approach. Economic climates, method of working, company structures and even companies themselves can change, bringing about new constraints. However ideal the current brief seems, there must always be a fallback plan, a 'parachute brief', in case the owner or occupier needs to pull out. Even if the design is specific to a particular client, whether office headquarters, research laboratory or arts venue the building may have to be let or sold, and as such will need to be as broadly attractive a proposition to the open market as possible. Such back-up scenarios are not always possible with historic buildings and one should never underestimate the economic risks taken in such projects.

Valuation is a complex science, and specialist advice should be sought. In order to succeed, all parties must understand the market conditions and work jointly to secure funding and grant aid.

REFERENCES

1. Houghton.
2. Colin Redman, *Does Listing Affect Value*, Tony Walker, *Conserving Value*.
3. Johnson 1988.
4. Stroud District Council.

Case Study	**7.3**

From: Victoria Quarter Leeds: run down arcade
To: Prime retail quarter

Frank Matcham designed the County Arcade as a fashionable shopping centre in the Edwardian heyday of Leeds. By the 1980s it had lost its upmarket appeal and consisted mainly of shops selling second-hand goods. The owners, Prudential, who had acquired the Leeds Estate, sought to invigorate their investment and invited a limited design competition. However, the key to this reinvigoration was not 'tarting-up' by design add-ons, but by appraising the whole Leeds Estate, which included the Cross Arcade and adjacent Queen Victoria Street, to re-establish the original core shopping area. They needed to re-create a prime shopping zone in the city. This was achieved by:

1. The decision to include a wider area and enlarge the critical mass.
2. The covering over of Queen Victoria Street with a new glazed roof in a modern but empathic manner to double the covered retail area.
3. The development of appropriate fire strategies.
4. The repair and cleaning of the original terracotta faience finishes and painting of ironwork to a new colour scheme so the original architecture could be seen and appreciated.

County Arcade before – tertiary shopping. (*Simon Corder*)

Queen Victoria Street before – pedestrianised.

5. The careful restoration of all Edwardian mahogany shopfronts throughout the estate.
6. The rigorous control of signage and graphics.
7. The use of artists: a sculptor blacksmith for new light fittings, seats and kiosks; a sculpture mason for the fountain; a ceramic artist for the terrazzo flooring; and a stained glass artist for the roof.
8. High quality design and workmanship of paving, landscaping and fittings to Queen Victoria Street.
9. A lettings policy to create a balanced mix of tenants.
10. The promotion of the area as a whole with a new identity, 'The Victoria Quarter'.

The following description is taken from an article written by Martin Spring, first published in the Refurbishment Section of *Building*.

Three out of Leeds' four surviving shopping arcades were built around theatres or music halls, and share their florid stage-set decors. But unlike the staged effects of today's shopping malls, the arcades rely environmentally on natural daylight and fresh air.

By far the most sumptuous of the arcades is County Arcade. Completed in 1904, it was designed along with the adjacent Empire Theatre and two other shopping streets by Britain's most prolific theatre architect of all time, Frank Matcham.

A Byzantine level of embellishment in terracotta, green-glazed faience, cast iron multi-coloured mosaics and mahogany is lavishly draped over every visible surface. The style is no less prolix, with Baroque, Jacobean and Art Nouveau motifs lifted directly from the catalogue of Blumentoft, the local terracotta manufacturer. In a continuous frieze below the eaves, a unifying motif takes the highly appropriate form of the pomegranate, the Moorish symbol of fertility.

By the mid-1980s, County Arcade was creaking with age and under a chaotic overlay of plastic and neon shop fascias. More disquieting for its owners, the Prudential, it was also losing trade to the new artificial shopping malls in the West End.

The Pru therefore decided it was time for a comprehensive revamp. Rechristening its development Victoria Quarter, it invited ideas from the retail interior designers, McColl, and the conservation based architects, Latham Architects.

County Arcade as proposed – restored shop fronts – new lighting.

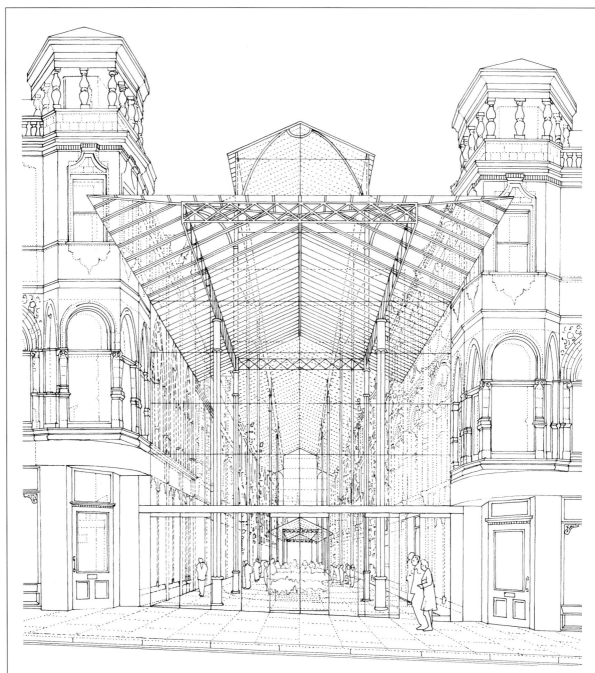

Queen Victoria Street proposed as a covered street.

Derek Latham could ensure a workmanlike job in restoring Matcham's County Arcade, but he is no rulebook conservationist. His clinching concept was to continue in Leeds' grand theatre tradition and create a brand new shopping arcade along the adjacent Queen Victoria Street by pedestrianising and roofing it over in glass.

The County Arcade and neighbouring streets form a direct link between the office area to the west and the extensive markets and bus station to the east. With a constant throughput of potential customers, it would be hard to imagine a better location for shops. The intent was to make the arcades and streets a destination rather than a route.

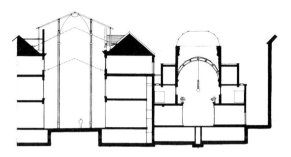

Section through Queen Victoria Street and County Arcade as proposed.

Concept sketch for central section with self supported roof above the façades.

Hence the new arcade, which encourages passers-by to linger by protecting them from the elements. Even more inviting are the restaurant and wine bar that spill out on to the pavement within the new arcade. Not least, added is a range of art objects that transform a shopping chore into a delight for the senses.

The Victoria Quarter has much in common with the recently completed Princes Square in Glasgow [16.8, Volume Two]. Both developments create new naturally-lit shopping arcades by glazing over an existing space between buildings, and both are embellished with art objects.

Princes Square is more radical in concept, as it creates three floors of shops and galleries out of the blank building elevations, while in the Victoria Quarter all 90 small shop premises are existing. On the other hand, Princes Square suffers from a stylistic clash between the engineers' steel structure and the artists' Art Nouveau- inspired balustrading and mosaics, while the Victoria Quarter succeeds with works of art that are both more in keeping with their surroundings and more inspired in their own right.

Stylistic clashes have been largely avoided at the Victoria Quarter because all artist craftsmen were chosen and commissioned early on by the project architect Stuart Hodgkinson – an enthusiastic advocate of art in architecture, who said, 'Anything new should be in sympathy with the original but made using contemporary crafts'.

At the Victoria Quarter, 'sympathetic but contemporary' means that the new artistic insertions have a presence of their own within the flamboyant ethos established by Matcham. The crafted new elements culminate in Brian Clarke's breath-taking technicolour stained-glass roof of the new arcade in Queen Victoria Street.

Of the artist-designed elements, by far the most spectacular is Clarke's stained glass lining to the new arcade's glass roof. Totalling 750 sq m in area, it was the largest secular commission of stained glass windows in the world, and described in Clarke's own words as 'an unending floor of liquid colour'.

The other art elements are less flamboyant, mosaic roundels set in the floor of the restored County Arcade were designed by Joanna Veevers. In ancient Roman tradition, Veevers weaves tiny squares of

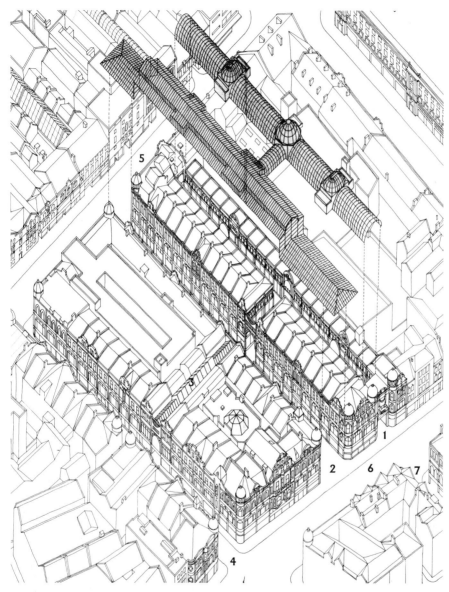

Key
1. County Arcade
2. Queen Victoria Street
3. Cross Arcade
4. King Edward Street
5. Briggate
6. Vicar Lane
7. Site of Matcham's Theatre replaced by 1950s arcade, now reconstructed as Harvey Nichols department store

The whole Leeds Estate, designed by Frank Matcham with Latham's new roof.

Italian marbles and granites in a spectrum of natural colours into complex geometric patterns plus a few stylised forms of fruit.

The result contains both a regular pattern that fits into a repetitive building fabric and a richness of design and colour that matches but does not mimic Matcham's decor.

A bit cruder, perhaps, are the wrought iron lamp pendants and litter bins by blacksmiths Alan Dawson and Jim Horrobin. Significantly, though the Pru's refurbished Victoria Quarter now has a double core

of glorious arcades, it has a much more amorphous edge to the development, which merges into the surrounding city fabric. Once the Victoria Quarter proves commercially successful, it can then expand by an organic and environmentally friendly ripple effect to rejuvenate surrounding areas of the city centre. [In fact, this has now been achieved with the opening of Harvey Nichols Department Store on the site of the old theatre.] What dark satanic mills of the 1980s – those new shopping malls with artificial lighting, air conditioning and car parking decks – can claim that?

Vicar Lane before.

■ Restoration underpins inspiration

Underlying the inspirational highlights of the refurbished Victoria Quarter is a painstaking task of basic building restoration. Working from Matcham's tantalisingly sketchy original drawings and a handful of early photographs, the architects set about scheduling all repairs to each shopfront based on a series of photocopied drawings.

The first task was to clean all exposed walls. Repairs were then carried out that entailed lifting all faience copings and refixing them with no fewer then 2,600 stainless steel pins. Small screw-holes and cracks were patched with colour matching epoxy resin.

Nearly all the shopfronts in mahogany and glass needed total renewal. Fortunately, an original example – the superb Chapman's Corsetieres – remained (and still does) in pristine condition and served as a model for hand-carving the ornate mahogany frames and reproducing the original gilded Art Nouveau lettering.

Restoration was not without some judicious fakery. To the architects' relief, even Matcham's revered original revealed its share of cost-cutting artifice. For instance, what were assumed to be ornate mahogany finials within each shopfront were in fact cast and painted plaster.

In this tradition of artifice, modern replacements for the original marble pilasters were fabricated out of glass-reinforced plastic by Alan Butcher and Associates. They were filled with concrete to prevent the telltale hollow sound if knocked, and the marbling was imperceptibly painted by one of Butcher's in-house craftsmen.

Vicar Lane after. (*Suart Blackwood*)

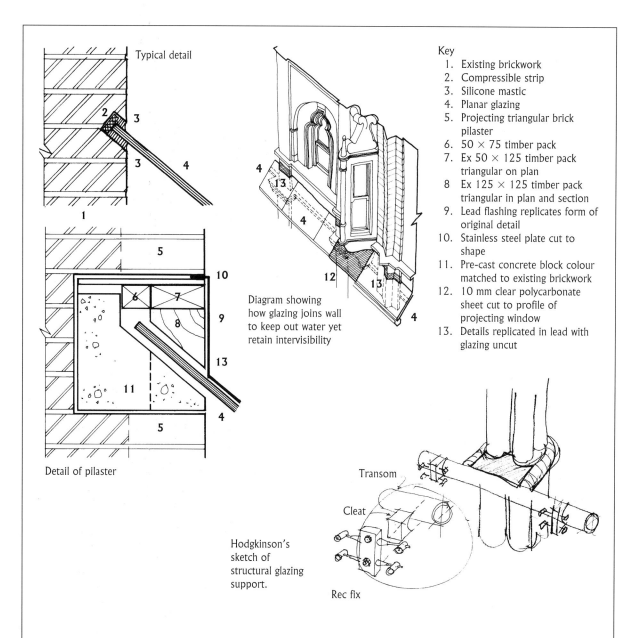

Typical detail

Detail of pilaster

Diagram showing
how glazing joins wall
to keep out water yet
retain intervisibility

Key
1. Existing brickwork
2. Compressible strip
3. Silicone mastic
4. Planar glazing
5. Projecting triangular brick pilaster
6. 50 × 75 timber pack
7. Ex 50 × 125 timber pack triangular on plan
8 Ex 125 × 125 timber pack triangular in plan and section
9. Lead flashing replicates form of original detail
10. Stainless steel plate cut to shape
11. Pre-cast concrete block colour matched to existing brickwork
12. 10 mm clear polycarbonate sheet cut to profile of projecting window
13. Details replicated in lead with glazing uncut

Hodgkinson's
sketch of
structural glazing
support.

Transom

Cleat

Rec fix

The bane of any building restorer is how to comply with strenuous modern building regulations and environmental standards. Here, the overriding problem was means of escape from fire. The local fire authority insisted that each shop inside the arcade had two separate means of escape. An elaborate system of two levels of fire compartments, automatic smoke vents and a maze of fire escapes was devised by the architects and fire consultants FiSec of Newark.

In County Arcade, the new means of escape from all upper floors of the shops incorporates the original gallery that led to staff toilets. The galleries have now been connected up into a continuous passage-way by forming two new bridges across the arcades. In its traditional arched cast iron form clad in faience and fitted with cast iron balustrades, it is hard to imagine the new bridge is not part of Matcham's original fabric. The plain truth though is that it too is constructed in GRP.

Derek Latham is not above hyping up Matcham's original decor to appeal to our more technicolour era. Thus, the pomegranate frieze in murky green faience has been picked out in bright green and orange paint. The cast-iron arches to the barrel vaulted roof have likewise been painted green and gold.

In Latham's pattern of things, repairs plus the occasional extrapolation (such as the new gallery bridge) are carried out to the letter of Matcham's original, whereas new insertions are freely and creatively designed in the spirit of Matcham's embellishments, as in the new stained-glass, mosaics and wrought ironwork.

Also see colour plates 6a–c.

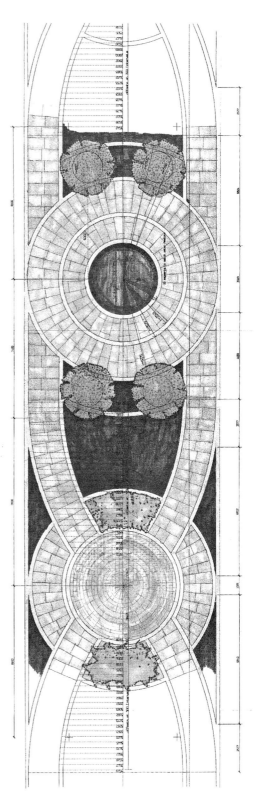

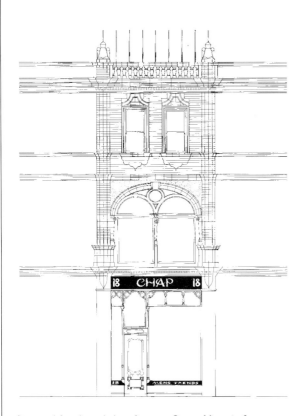

Restored façade and shop front to Queen Victoria Street.

Paving layout to Queen Victoria Street.

CHAPTER 8

Design: Working with the Building

Once we are satisfied that we understand the building, the project is financially viable, and the user has been found, we can develop the design. We need a plan of action that is sympathetic to the building and appropriate to its new use. At this stage we must involve both the client and the funding institution.

■ PLAN OF ACTION

The plan of action will involve deciding the form of re-use, clarifying the brief, interpreting the needs of the user and identifying the criteria for access – all within the context of our times and the building's location. Any such plan will have to stand up to scrutiny and criticism and have the capacity to respond to changes of circumstance.

It is, therefore, useful to listen to other opinions at this stage, which the design team can absorb before setting and following their own brief, checking their designs against the agreed criteria, and reworking and refining where appropriate. It is, however, advisable for all members of the project team to work to an agreed philosophy which will help them focus on their aims and suggest what practical steps to take.

■ MAKING ALTERATIONS AND ADDITIONS

Use sympathetic material where new additions are to be made, either as an extension of past techniques, or in contrast to them, dependent upon the nature of the brief, context, setting etc.[1]

At first, this seems like a contradiction in terms. On the one hand you may be trying to match in concept and detail the alterations or extensions to a 'crumbly' historic building; on the other you are taking a modern, design-led response apparently imposing new values, ideas and materials upon an existing fabric. In fact, both concepts can be applied depending on factors such as the brief, the context, and the setting.

Many purist building conservation groups and professionals only consider the building fabric when appraising potential major alterations and additions. Their aim is to make any 'new event' indiscernible except upon close scholarly inspection. They treat the building as an inanimate object, a precious artefact in a museum, allowing its interpretation but restricting its use. But buildings without people to use them are mere monuments. In defining an ancient monument under the Ancient Monuments and Archaeology Areas Act 1979 (s1(3)), it is said, the Secretary of State 'may not include in it any structure that is inhabited (except by a caretaker)'. In contrast, listed buildings are historic buildings that are used for a purpose and not just remaining for their own sake.

Example	8.1

Use: Repton School Sanatorium

TO: 'The New Music School' (see case study 3.6)

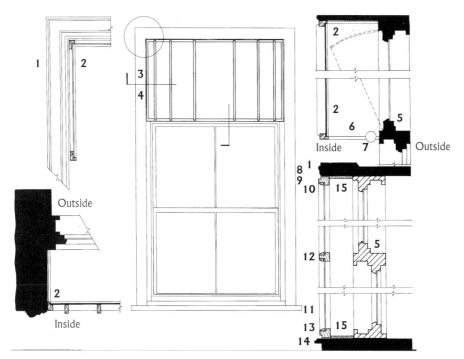

Key
1. Existing architrave
2. 10 mm Rockfon Dekor lay-in tiles butt jointed and glued to plywood backing, pinned and glued to linings and relocated timber frames
3. 25 × 38 rebated framing set flush with face of existing window linings
4. 19 × 38 applied battens notched into framing
5. Sliding sash window
6. 12 × 12 stop bead to acoustic lining
7. Location of roller blind
8. Frame set in flexible bedding compound and screwed to existing lining
9. Ex 38 × 50 head
10. 19 × 10 glazing bead
11. 5 mm clear glass set in non-setting compound
12. Ex 38 × 50 transom
13. Ex 38 × 50 sill set in flexible bedding compound and screwed to sillboard
14. Existing sillboard
15. 10 mm Rockfon Dekor lay in tiles cut to suit and pinned and glued to existing lining between sash frames and new frames
16. Existing sash window

To reduce sound intrusion whilst gaining ventilation, without resorting to air conditioning, special external 'hoods' were created over selected sash windows to provide sound baffles.

Key

1. Existing architrave and lining
2. Mastic seal plywood/architrave
3. Fanlight removed and opening filled with 6 mm plywood in existing rebates with 12 mm edge and vertical edges full depth beading. Rocksil R32 (roll form 40 mm) quilt insulation compressed and sealed with 6 mm plywood sheet
4. 25 × 10 twice splayed bead planted on and mitred in to architrave
5. Existing door leaf made good and adapted as necessary – panels internally filled solid with plaster and covered with 6 mm plywood glued and screwed to existing. 6 mm hardwood lipping applied to top edge and vertical edges
6. Continuous blocking piece pinned and glued to existing panel prior to plaster fill
7. 25 × 6 splayed architrave bedded in mastic
8. 19 mm rebated hardwood lining
9. 6 mm clear glass
10. Additional planted bead to give min. 25 mm rebate where doors are to be FR
11. 'Schlegel Rolled' or similar seal fixed to face of rebates at head and jamb
12. Threshold with adjustable contact strip (ACS) screwed to face of door
13. Carpet finish to existing flooring
14. 25 mm ground to suit plaster thickness
15. 12 mm blockboard panel full width and height of architrave, hardwood lipped on exposed edges architrave re-fixed to blockboard backing. All voids to door linings grouted solid
16. Fanlight removed and opening filled with 6 mm plywood to existing rebates with 19 × 12 beads. Apply insulating quilt and seal complete with 12 mm blockboard
17. Existing door leaf made good and adapted as necessary. Panels internally filled solid with plaster and covered with 12 mm blockboard. Door rehung on 11/2 pair 'Parliament' hinges
18. 6 mm bead on 12 mm hardwood frame
19. Bottom splay to transom but square to accommodate seal
20. Proprietary neoprene seal in aluminium holder screwed to threshold, linings and transom (Sealmaster Type JC or similar). Ex 100 × 38 timber threshold screwed to continuous bearer
21. 100 × 50 continuous softwood bearer under threshold. Fixed to brickwork through isolation material
22. 25 × 50 battens
23. Carpet finish on 21 mm T & G boarding
24. Mineral quilt insulation
25. Existing boarding
26. Existing joint may continue through opening.

Doors were also upgraded to different levels of sound reduction dependent upon activity.

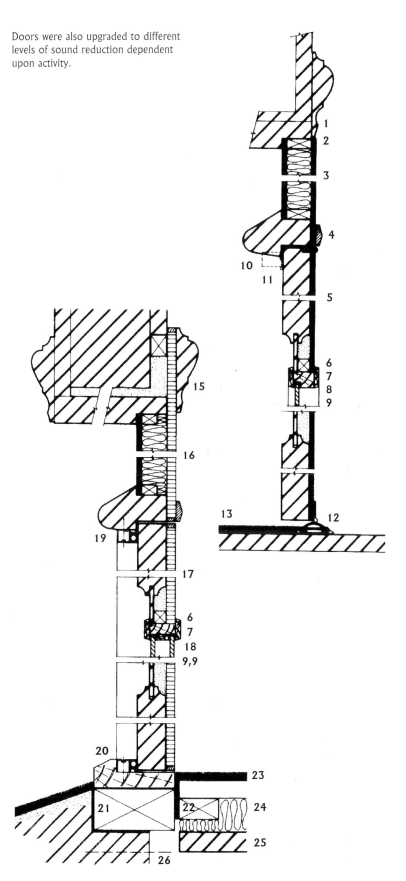

Example   8.2

USE: Warehouse: merchants, Castlefields Basin, Manchester
1827, Grade II, four-storey 20 × 41 m, brick, slate roof, thick cross walls dividing into six unequal bays. Half burnt, derelict since 1971.

TO: Offices 1997
To be flexible to let as four units improving daylight and permeability. The cross walls were cut back from the perimeter by 3 metres, central openings increased and a lightwell created in the centre. Bricks and timber arising were used to effect all necessary repairs. A replica floor was constructed in the burnt out half. Raised service floors with fire protection enable timber soffits to be exposed. Vertical circulation is accommodated outside the blank gable walls in glazed 'bookends'. The structural glass interpreting the internal cross walls.

A: Ian Simpson Architects

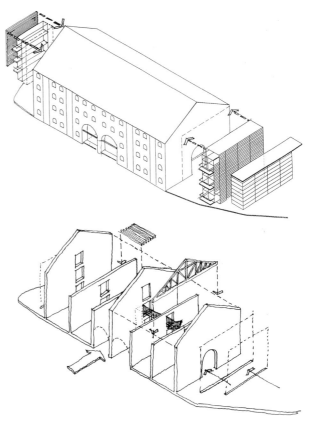

Design philosophy of glazed stair tower 'bookends'. Clarification of access and structural elements.

Buildings must be seen in the context of both the people and the society that uses them. The proposed use may need to be, and look, different than in the past for the visitor to identify the activity within, and the user to occupy it practically, efficiently and economically. The installation of heating and ventilation, sanitation, cleanliness and information technology will affect the character of any alterations. The scale of spaces required in addition to the existing building may point the way to the character of the design required. A large new assembly space added to a small cellular building may best be achieved by emphasising the contrast rather than trying to make them similar.

Current conventions must be considered. A classical Victorian art gallery with its walls covered in paintings has a lively character in contrast to a modern gallery presenting a single painting on a blank wall. So significant changes are required to convert old art galleries into new ones in order to satisfy the requirements for display, conservation and security of today.

Sometimes a building survives but its original setting has been radically redeveloped, compromising the originally perceived relationship between built form and open space. The character of any proposed extension should take account of the

Before.

After from the basin.

End view showing clarity of new addition.

Example   8.3

USE: Warehouse, Sloane Avenue, London
1911, Stevens and Munt. Two interlocking L-shaped blocks one two-storey, one five-storey with a slot in between. Neo-classical terracotta.

TO: High specification offices, shops and a large restaurant
Externally, the building retains partial existing terracotta elevations and combines them with new glass, metal and stone façade elements. Internally, it is conceived as two interlocking L-shaped forms: one solid in appearance, the other glazed and transparent.

A: YRM and Stanton Williams[2]

Before.

After. (*Chris Gascoigne*)

Interior. (*Peter Cook*)

date and scale of such changes to its surroundings. It is important to think about the character of the new extension and how it should best reflect that which it extends.

If neighbouring buildings are plain or nondescript, they may allow a similarly designed extension to blend in with the background and not compete with its earlier and more elaborate precedent. It could represent its own monument in time either with humble architecture of simple proportions in sympathetic materials, or make an identifiable statement using the most modern techniques and materials with ingenuity and skill to celebrate the addition as equal to, yet respectful of, the original.

Once the new fabric for the re-use has been decided upon, decisions about the process and extent of repair to the existing fabric must be made. William Morris's (SPAB), philosophy of 'repair not restore' can be then incorporated.

■ REPAIR TECHNIQUES

Use techniques of repair rather than restoration. Instruct the minimum rather than the maximum repair work necessary.[3]

This is more than simply replacing worn elements with new ones. It will have to be decided exactly how much needs to be replaced, and whether the new fabric should look worn or distressed, or bright and new in contrast.

At Enquiry, planning authorities and amenity bodies commonly present cases to retain a building that the owner argues is too costly to repair. Sometimes the owner has an ulterior motive because the land value will be higher if the building is demolished, but more often they have simply been ill-advised by professionals who do not understand the fabric of old buildings.

It is possible to walk around a building in need of repair, list everything that might need doing, cost it all, add a contingency, total it and realise that the cost exceeds the value of the building. Too many professionals simply assume the worst and allow approximate sums, which can be grossly misleading. A typical example is when they assess a building with settlement cracks. They may allow for underpinning a difficult and expensive operation whereas stitching of the fabric may suffice.

After one Enquiry where I represented the objections of an amenity body, the solicitor acting for the owner who wished to demolish, approached me to see if it really would be in his client's interests to repair the building. Once he learnt that it would, he persuaded his client to withdraw the appeal, and the building was repaired at low cost. It has now been happily occupied for fifteen years and during that time not only has that solicitor similarly advised many other clients, but also undertaken substantial but sensitive repair programmes on a couple of small country houses himself.

Essentially, we must identify in detail what repairs are really necessary, although this is no easy matter to determine. Surveyors may easily be tempted to advise excessive repair or replacement as a safe option.

Funding institutions may well insist for mortgage purposes that a property be given a 30-year or even 60-year life. To comply with this, roofs, windows and walls are often replaced to procure a 'professional guarantee' of longevity, when repairs would have sufficed. It sometimes becomes apparent that repairs assumed to be desirable have not increased in importance ten years later. Older buildings do not necessarily require more repairs than new buildings. New buildings constructed to government standards for a sixty year life have required major repairs after only thirty.

It is far better to predict a cycle of continuing expenditure, which can be undertaken at the same time as other changes to the use, or fabric of the building. That approach has been taken with cathedrals for years.

■ WHEN RESTORATION IS NECESSARY

Ensure that restoration, when it appears appropriate, is thoroughly researched and subject to the agreement of a second opinion before proceeding.[4]

It is not always appropriate simply to repair. Vandalism, war, fire, insensitive alteration, partial demolition, severe settlement or just excessive weathering may have disfigured a building. Some types of old building can accommodate such distortion and retain their historic interest and architectural value. We are used to seeing ancient monuments in ruins and reconstructing the missing elements in our mind's eye. We even appreciate buildings that had strong symmetry, order and form such as Rievaulx or Fountains Abbey, and accept their ruined state as sufficient representation of their previous form. Later vernacular buildings are also often accepted in a much truncated or altered form. But the essence of most renaissance architecture was the completeness of the design, the proportion, balance and symmetry that achieved firmness, commodity and delight. Such buildings may accommodate minor deficiencies such as shrapnel scars or smoke scarring or sensitive additions such as an extra floor, wings or portico: these develop its character. But insensitive new openings or window replacements, loss of cornice or significant mouldings can convert a previously attractive building into an ugly one.

A building's entire history cannot be read simply by looking at it. The more recently it has been altered, and the better maintained it is, the more it is necessary to make a detailed analysis of the building before attempting to restore it. The architect will need to study local methods of construction and the dates on which different materials were used in that area which may require archival research.

Specialist handbooks can be invaluable. For example *Conservation of Clay and Chalk Buildings* by Gordon Pearson[5] is essential reading for the architect needing to repair a cob (mud-built) construction. It is also worthwhile consulting experts for their advice in some aspects. For instance, when a timber frame structure has been much altered, an expert who understands jointing techniques, can identify carpenters' marks and evaluate how previous generations of intervention affects structural integrity, can be invaluable. The cost of such an opinion can save the architect work, and reduce the costs of any subsequent alteration or repair.

Inspection of the building can reveal how it was constructed, particularly in those areas that require repair. Methods can then be devised for repair, closely recreating the methodology and appearance of the original. Many buildings have been repaired so often that a new phase appears to make little difference. It is not always prudent to copy earlier repairs as they may be ill-conceived, and their long-term effects as yet unknown. A repair itself may need repairing, or an area could be deteriorating due to an earlier repair. For example, a common cause of structural cracking is underpinning, performed without understanding the cyclical movements of buildings and their continuing settlement patterns. Tie bars rarely work effectively. Simple removal, after identifying they are taking no strain, may result in no remedial work other than making good the holes. If the tie bars are strained, joists and internal walls can be retied to the outer wall, achieving a more effective restraint with less visual impact.

Sometimes, existing repairs can have historical interest in their own right. If reasons of cosmetic appeal or restoration force you to remove them from sight, it is worth keeping a record of them, both written and photographic, to assist future custodians in their analysis of the building's fabric. The larger the missing section of fabric, the more important it is to establish what it was like previously. Old photographs, drawings, and in some cases, items removed and relocated, can give us clues, although supporting evidence must always be sought. We must avoid following the example of Victorian ecclesiologists who thought they knew how medieval architecture should look but only imposed solutions unrelated to the original.

The critical process used with new design concepts is no less applicable to restoration work. Consult the planning authority and amenity bodies informally at an early date. Once a project reaches presentation stage discussion tends to lose objectivity, as some parties' arguments can become defensive or even emotive.

Likewise, the development of the user brief, and related design proposals need to be progressed alongside this historical analysis. Synergy can be created by applying the new design philosophy together with learning from the analysis of existing fabric. Thus a unique identity of the re-use project will be created.

REFERENCES

1. cf Appendix in this volume, page 215, Principles for Re-use.
2. Evans, B., 'Integrating Old with New', *Architects Journal*, Vol 198, No 284, 1993, pp 41–9 and Architects Stanton Williams.
3. cf Appendix in this volume, page 215, Principles for Re-use.
4. Ibid.
5. Pearson, G., *Conservation of Clay and Chalk Buildings*, Donhead, London, 1992.

CASE STUDIES

Wirksworth: a town and its buildings

Small towns as well as cities can benefit from creative re-use. Wirksworth, during the late Middle Ages, was the second largest town in Derbyshire, renowned for lead mining, and prominent in the development of mining law. The demise of the lead industry in the seventeenth century was followed by a decline in the stone quarrying industry in the twentieth century due to mechanisation. In 1980 a small terrace house could be purchased unimproved for £1,500 or improved for £3,000, when the equivalent in Derby was £5,000 and £8,000 respectively. Many older properties lay derelict, as it was uneconomic to repair them. The Civic Trust, sponsored by the Monument Trust undertook a pilot project to rejuvenate the old town. This was achieved by:

1. Appointing a skilled project officer, Gordon Michele, who lived in the town.
2. Appraising the potential through research and feasibility studies.
3. Awakening public opinion through meetings, newsletters and projects with schoolchildren.
4. Bringing the councils, amenity bodies and grant-aiding agencies into a partnership focused towards a primary objective.
5. Funding feasibility studies to demonstrate possibilities (8.4).
6. Use of a revolving trust fund (DHBT) to act as a catalyst by tackling the worst building (8.5).
7. Reviving traditions (e.g. well dressing to encourage a sense of community and develop self-help).
8. Promoting the town as an attractive place to work and live.

Originally a three year plan, it actually took six years to achieve the critical part of recovery – the second three years being sponsored by the County Council. Still far from robust, Wirksworth completed its convalescence with a part-time project officer employed by the Town Council for a further three years. A total of nine years. The re-use process for a town takes considerably longer than a single building. Despite its duration the project was an unqualified success having since been copied, or repeated, in Ilfracombe, Calne, Bourne and other small English towns.

The project involved many buildings the re-use of which was undertaken in a variety of ways. Perhaps the most crucial was 1–3 Greenhill.

1–3 Greenhill
A realistic feasibility?

The Civic Trust commissioned a feasibility study to identify a way of repairing this derelict building to remove the debilitating psychological impact the dereliction was having upon the centre of the town.

1–3 Greenhill had been a prominent pair of lead merchant's houses built just behind the Market Place on one of the main routes out towards the lead rakes. It remained so for about 60 years and then the property became subdivided and multi-occupied. At first, changes were taken with some care architecturally, but later, less so. Along with the fortunes of Wirksworth, the property had already become partly derelict between the wars. By the early 1950s three-quarters of the roof had fallen into the shell, reducing the inside to a pile of rubble. The property was acquired by the solicitor in the adjacent house facing the Market Place who altered part of the shell with bits of asbestos and plywood to form a garage for his house – an ignominious end for a building that had started with high aspirations.

The property was simply the shell, there being no grounds or curtilage other than the perimeter of the building. It faced directly onto a narrow street but had windows in the rear and one gable, with rights of light that still enabled its use. There were effectively four bays. A decision had to be made whether it was most suitable to divide the property up vertically into these four bays, or to maximise its use horizontally uniting the floors along its whole length, despite changes in floor level due to the way the property stepped up the hill.

Depressed prices for houses in the historic core of Wirksworth reflected economic reality. Industrial use was considered inappropriate, without any form of proper access, so use for offices was considered.

The office market in Wirksworth was non-existent. There was one solicitor who lived next door, a doctor's surgery in the town and a similar merchant's house that was used by the local health authority. There were offices in the Town Hall but these had never been

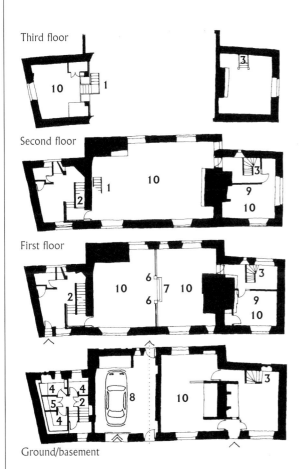

Third floor

Second floor

First floor

Ground/basement

Plans as proposed.

Key

1. New timber stair to attic
2. New concrete stair
3. Original stair restored
4. WCs
5. Boiler
6. Steel frame
7. Steps between levels
8. Garage to adjacent property
9. New fire partition
10. Office

Greenhill before.

After, showing how the new gables match the original stonework though with more regular coursing.

Interior showing how the internal blockwork faces of the new walls are clearly different from the original masonry of the ruin.

commercially valued. Agents advised that there was no demand for office space in Wirksworth. Employment in the quarrying industry was declining and apart from one recently completed small industrial estate on the edge of town, there was little employment, forcing residents to seek work outside of town. The team was determined that the refurbishment of 1–3 Greenhill should provide employment for the town, however little.

The refurbishment of the shell was costed and even with a minimal approach the prospects were not good. Project costs would result in nearly twice its perceived value as office space. Monies had to be sought elsewhere.

The Council for Small Industries in Rural Areas (Cosira), a branch of the Development Commission, had funded the industrial estate on the edge of town. When approached they said their remit was to fund only industry. A policy that assumed people in rural areas should be provided with industrial jobs and not office work appeared outdated. A presentation was therefore made to a senior civil servant in the Development Commission in London. Using models and drawings, this explained the unique proposition to provide workspace in a town with high unemployment, and why it was so important for Wirksworth. This elicited a positive response, and even though the Development

Commission normally restricted itself to funding new rather than converted buildings, they agreed to a trial. They offered a 50 per cent grant-payable to the County Council. But the client was the Civic Trust and the property was privately owned.

Derbyshire County Council was then approached. The proposals clearly met their economic development objectives. A 50 per cent grant was available from the Development Commission if the County Council could purchase the property and provide the other half. At first they declined, estimating the costs of refurbishment at twice that indicated in the feasibility study. It was argued, in the end convincingly, that the Derbyshire Historic Buildings Trust (DHBT), by using a philosophy of 'repair not restore' could undertake this work within the cost plan. In a special meeting the Chief Executive and Committee Chairman decided to authorise a grant equal to half the costs in the feasibility. This was on the basis that it was a 'once and for only' grant given to the Trust, who would act as agents for the County Council and the Development commission in undertaking the work. Under no circumstances would further monies be given due to inflation, unforeseen problems or any costing errors. The County Council then acquired the property for a nominal sum and appointed DHBT as agents.

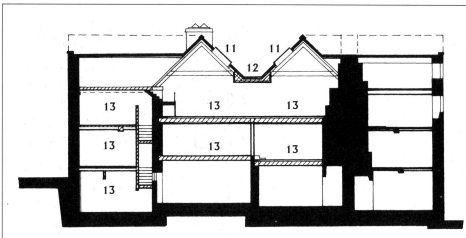

11. Roof windows
12. Structural gutter spanning front to back
13. New floors at original levels

Key
11. Roof windows
12. Structural gutter spanning front to back
13. New floors at original levels

Long Section (parallel to road)

In this way the feasibility study identified a possible use for commercial purposes that had a clear, viable implementation plan. 1–3 Greenhill was developed and upon completion handed to the DHBT to manage into perpetuity. The space was let to a variety of users some of whom have subsequently moved on to convert other premises in the town for their own use. In this way the premises have attracted new small businesses to the town. Rents have since increased to more realistic levels so that the property now represents a good investment. Most significantly, the completion of this project acted as a symbol of optimism for the town's people, demonstrating that even their most prominent derelict building could be given a fresh start. This acted as the catalyst from which the success of the Wirksworth project began to flourish.

| Case Study | 8.5 |

1–3 Greenhill
Re-using a ruin (for offices)

It was the stability of the walls and openings in the structure that caused alarm. It seemed miraculous that stonework, acting as a corbelled arch, was still supported on beams which had been so infested with beetle and woodworm they had turned to powder internally, whilst their outer face remained as a cracked but characterful crust. One option was clearly to remove these and replace them with a new lintel, and yet in their twisted, cracked and deformed state they were an essential part of the patina of the building. Any replacement would have to be either second-hand or green oak. Working old oak is like working iron – it is certainly solid, but the result always looks different from the original. Green oak is more acceptable in that it will

Before, the rubble in the ruin, including staircase newel post.

move and turn and twist, not in an identical way, but similar to that of the original. This does, however, take some time, which can be a problem.

■ Concrete beams

As the aim was to maintain the structure's integrity it was necessary to find the best way to tie it together to create one coherent mass. It was decided to replace the timber beams with reinforced concrete. To maintain its appearance, the existing beams were either retained, in whole or part, with new beams behind (see Figure 8.5d) or replicated by shuttering with a solution of plaster of Paris poured in between the shuttering and the existing beam. The decayed beam was then removed, reinforcement inserted, and concrete placed. Once set, the shuttering and plaster could then be removed to show a concrete beam with a surface texture like that of the original timber beam, with cracks, twisting and deformity still visible though apparently painted in grey matt.

■ Restraining the walls

The wall on the street frontage was considerably out of plumb. This was most obvious at the centre. The central cross wall had been constructed in timber and supported a valley gutter which, due to neglect had leaked, causing the rotten timber to eventually collapse in the early 1950s. The most important principle for the maintenance of any historic building – that of cleaning out the gutters – had not been followed. Lack of any restraint for the following 25 years had allowed the front wall to bow out up to 300 mm and the inner and outer faces to part company. There were no buttresses, nor room for them, as the property fronted directly on to the narrow street. Movement had been uneven and it was not possible to jack the structure back into place. So the whole structure was stabilised by removing the central core of the rubble walling and inserting a reinforced cage to form a concrete ring-beam at eaves level, acting in tension, to resist the outward thrust of the roof. This was tied in to the gables at each end, and centrally by two steel tie beams spanning between wallplates across the width of the building to support a new valley gutter. Where the existing wall was bowed so was the ringbeam, to allow the deformed structure to remain whilst rendering it structurally stable. The gables on the street and rear elevations were then reconstructed above the new eaves level ring beam.

■ Reconstructed gables

These gables, being reconstructed on top of the original façade, use the original stone rescued from the rubble that fell into the ruined structure. The pointing of the stonework was undertaken in the same manner

After, the 'repaired' stair (including newel).

Reinforced ring beam holds the top of the walls of the ruin in place (note how beam follows the bulging line of the wall).

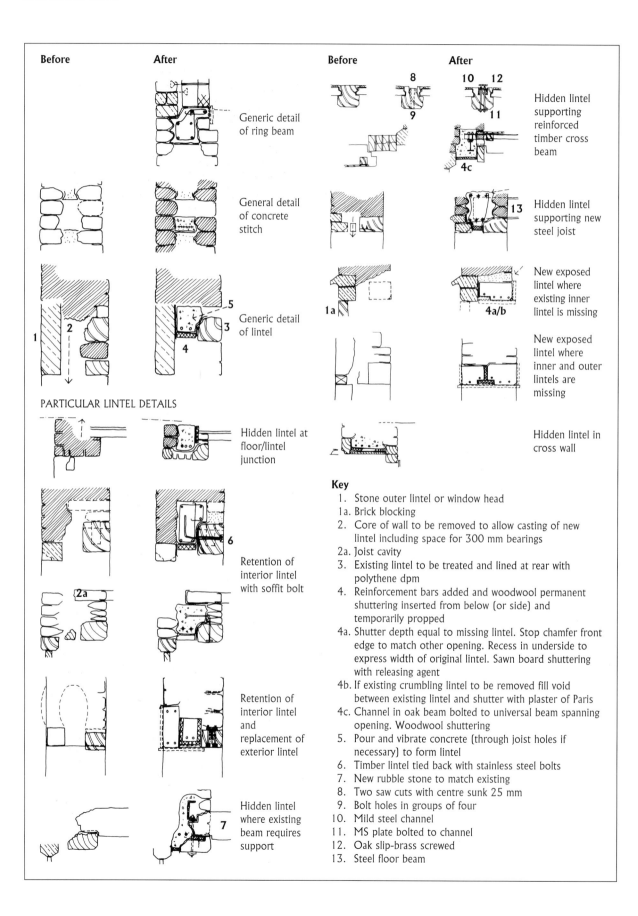

Generic detail of ring beam

General detail of concrete stitch

Generic detail of lintel

Hidden lintel supporting reinforced timber cross beam

Hidden lintel supporting new steel joist

New exposed lintel where existing inner lintel is missing

New exposed lintel where inner and outer lintels are missing

Hidden lintel in cross wall

PARTICULAR LINTEL DETAILS

Hidden lintel at floor/lintel junction

Retention of interior lintel with soffit bolt

Retention of interior lintel and replacement of exterior lintel

Hidden lintel where existing beam requires support

Key

1. Stone outer lintel or window head
1a. Brick blocking
2. Core of wall to be removed to allow casting of new lintel including space for 300 mm bearings
2a. Joist cavity
3. Existing lintel to be treated and lined at rear with polythene dpm
4. Reinforcement bars added and woodwool permanent shuttering inserted from below (or side) and temporarily propped
4a. Shutter depth equal to missing lintel. Stop chamfer front edge to match other opening. Recess in underside to express width of original lintel. Sawn board shuttering with releasing agent
4b. If existing crumbling lintel to be removed fill void between existing lintel and shutter with plaster of Paris
4c. Channel in oak beam bolted to universal beam spanning opening. Woodwool shuttering
5. Pour and vibrate concrete (through joist holes if necessary) to form lintel
6. Timber lintel tied back with stainless steel bolts
7. New rubble stone to match existing
8. Two saw cuts with centre sunk 25 mm
9. Bolt holes in groups of four
10. Mild steel channel
11. MS plate bolted to channel
12. Oak slip-brass screwed
13. Steel floor beam

Internal concrete lintel matching original timber.

New routes for rainwater disposal have greater capacity.

Reconstructed chimney stack (no attempt has been made to reconstruct a conjectural detail). (*Ron Jones*)

between both the new and the original structure. Yet a building historian can still identify that the gables have been rebuilt. The secret is in the bonding of the stone. The original stonework has an additional randomness to its bonding of random coursed rubble, which includes the odd diminishing course and the occasional break-line between depths of courses. This is particularly difficult to imitate and has therefore not been repeated in the gables. It would be difficult for any but the trained observer to notice this.

■ Floors

To support the floors a new steel structure was inserted in the centre of the building (where the structural timber partition lies). This carries greater loads than hitherto, enabling the building's use for offices. The pressure created by the new foundations for the steel columns

Original 'window' retained with relieving lintel over, new glass louvre window behind and lead dressed drainage channels under sill beam. (*Ron Jones*)

New window, no attempt at conjectural restoration. (*Ron Jones*)

Landing at top of concrete stair.

being placed centrally, has no effect upon the existing perimeter walls (which have no foundations). The steel beams they support were designed not only to rest in the original locations where the oak beams had been, but also to load the masonry to the same extent. Other floor joists were then inserted into the holes where earlier joists had been – and to the same sizes. The over-sizing of the original oak joists meant that the new joists could be in softwood with sufficient sacrificial timber, in the event of a fire, to allow them to remain exposed.

The remnants of the original steep spiral stairs were retained and 'repaired' back to their working condition. (Repairs do not fall within the jurisdiction of Building Control.) However a new concrete stair was erected at the other end of the building within a fire safe enclosure, providing an alternative means of escape.

New work internally is not disguised (new blockwork walls are left fair-faced) so that the extent of the original ruin, and the new building work to bring it into use, can be clearly differentiated.[a] The implications of re-using ruins are examined further in Chapter 16, Volume Two.

■ **References**

a. Project Architect: Anthony Rossi, Latham Architects.

Case Study	**8.6**

From: No. 1 The Dale: empty and unsafe
To: Shop and residential (Grade II Conservation Area)

No. 1 The Dale was a three-storey seventeenth-century merchant's house opposite 1–3 Greenhill. It had been converted in the late nineteenth century to a shop with a large window in the ground floor of the gable end, and enlarged windows above to light the upper storage floors. The exterior was rendered.

Movement of the gable towards the street caused alarm and the property was vacated. Proposals to strengthen with a new internal steel frame, or even to take down and rebuild, cost more than the ultimate value. Careful analysis indicated that the outer face of the wall had moved further than the inner face. Removal of the render revealed the problem. The insertion of the shop window had, during the installation of the lintel, caused a collapse of the outer skin of the stone rubble wall, which had been refaced in brick with new windows (without mullions) but not tied back into the inner rubble wall behind. The solution included removing the brick and rebuilding a stone outer face, bonding into the innerskin, and tying the elevation back into the corners with concrete elbows within the core. This still allowed the removal of all the render and exposure of the original stone on other elevations. Stone mullions were reinstated as they formed part of the structural integrity of the whole.

Before – the bulging front wall was declared unsafe and the upper floors vacant. (*Peter Newton*)

After – the outer face of stonework between the windows has been rebuilt and stone mullions re-introduced to improve structural integrity.

An extension at the rear in the small yard was just large enough for a separate entrance lobby and stair, accessed off Greenhill, enabling conversion of the upper floors into a maisonette. Though upgrading of the fire protection under the first floor allowed the shop to be occupied separately from the maisonette, they were in fact purchased as a whole. Nevertheless, the separation enabled a mortgage to be taken on the maisonette with a separate bank loan on the shop and business.[a]

■ **References**
a. Project Architect: Anthony Rossi, Latham Architects.

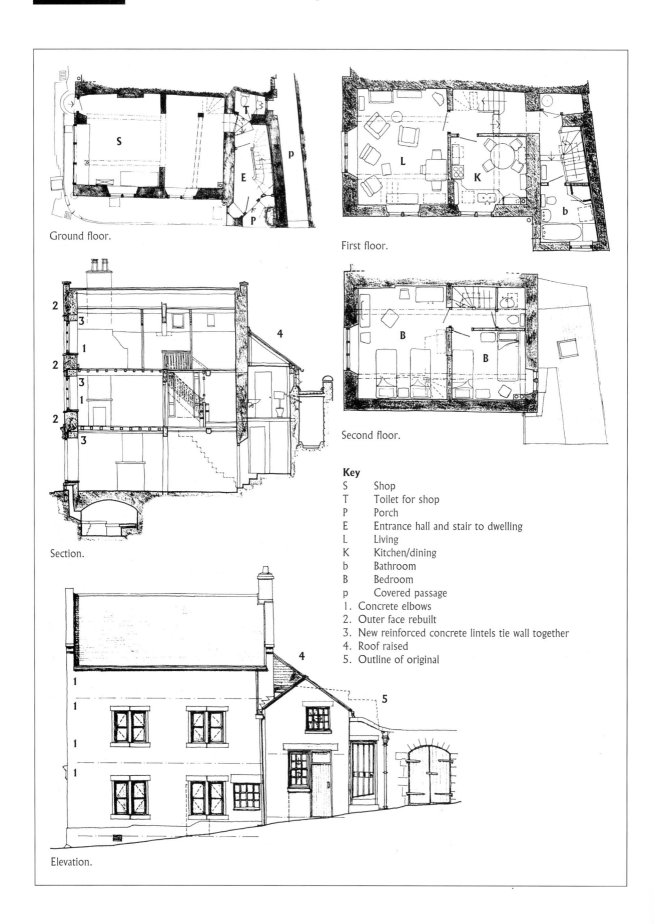

Ground floor.

First floor.

Section.

Second floor.

Key
S   Shop
T   Toilet for shop
P   Porch
E   Entrance hall and stair to dwelling
L   Living
K   Kitchen/dining
b   Bathroom
B   Bedroom
p   Covered passage
1. Concrete elbows
2. Outer face rebuilt
3. New reinforced concrete lintels tie wall together
4. Roof raised
5. Outline of original

Elevation.

Before – derelict.

Case Study	8.7

From: The silk mill
To: Heritage centre: the role of non-conformity

Following the early initiatives of the Wirksworth project in Derbyshire by the Civic Trust, the local townspeople banded together to form a civic society. One of their priorities was to convert a derelict building for use as a heritage centre. The building they chose was an old derelict silk mill built into the hillside. A small, corrugated, asbestos-roofed transport garage, built in the 1930s, was attached to it. Apart from a small rubble

After – new roof and glazed screen to garage. Hard landscape of gritstone slabs and setts with raised area for impromptu performances. (*Gordon Michele*)

Top floor before.

forecourt, and a minuscule garden there was no other land. The only access was through an archway, beside the greengrocer's in the market place, and up a steep alleyway. It seemed unlikely that a vehicle, let alone a pre-war lorry, had used the alleyway!

The brief was to provide a place with a distinct identity and to create a memorable experience for the visitor.

An exhibition was to be created inside the building. This progressed from an audio-visual programme and illuminated displays at the basement level, through re-created room displays on the middle floor, to a gallery on the top floor with views across the rooftops of Wirksworth through the frame knitters' windows facing the town. This meant the greatest change to the historic building was in the basement previously used for storing oil drums and machinery, which had little character. The least change was on the top floor where, with the walls consolidated and the roof and windows repaired and restored, most of the original character remains.

A restaurant or café still had to be accommodated. The building's identity also needed to be established. The existing building, having been restored, was much like its neighbour's in character – except for the old transport garage. For this reason it was decided to emphasise the element of non-conformity and replace the asbestos roof of the garage with another lightweight roof of insulated profiled steel. At the front, where previously there had been just wooden doors and some brickwork, a characterful, glazed timber screen was introduced to facilitate exit and entry, to light the interior, and enable people to look through it from

After – a panorama of Wirksworth is viewed through the windows. (*Stuart Blackwood*)

Café on the ground floor.

inside or outside. A rusty red colour was chosen for the roof, rather than a safe grey, thus creating a building with presence and character. Approaching visitors are pleasantly surprised to see what they realise is now the heritage centre.[a]

■ **References**

a. Project architect: Martin Sutcliffe, Latham Architects.

Ground floor.

Key

1. Entry
2. Reception
3. Exhibition
4. Escape
5. Toilet
6. Café
7. Kitchen
8. Store
9. Craft workshop

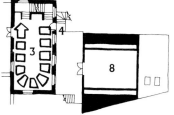

First floor.

Second floor.

CHAPTER 9

Presenting the Project

After the project team has developed their approach to re-use, they may have to present their proposals to a number of other bodies. These could include banks, investment institutions, agencies, charities, English Heritage, amenity bodies, The Commission for Architecture and the Built Environment (CABE) (formerly the Royal Fine Arts Commission (RFAC)), planning authority, building control, fire prevention, owners and lessees. They will either represent the source of funds, or the means to obtain necessary consents.

■ TAKING A TEAM APPROACH

The role of the funding or consenting bodies is crucial and the best way to involve them is by encouraging them to become extended team members. At first, the agenda of these bodies may not embrace the concept of creative re-use, having been either conditioned to the needs of new building plans, or preserving existing uses in older buildings. They may treat a creative re-use project in the same way, without recognising differences such as townscape or landscape, using existing fabric, or infrastructure.

The architect, the quantity surveyor and the client have to tackle these prevailing attitudes. The team has to decide which grants and funding to apply for or reject. Grants can be a mixed blessing if the attached restrictions are too onerous, but the team can at least select the most suitable funding body to approach. They have little choice when seeking statutory approvals, although there may be some flexibility in negotiation.

■ PRESENTATION TECHNIQUES

Before approaching a funding body, your presentation must be carefully prepared, anticipating any particular requirements or attitudes likely to be encountered.

Presentations must be tailored to suit each target audience (e.g. listed building consent, works eligible for historic building grant and VAT exemption, will all differ). Emphasise preservation and status quo to planners, English Heritage and Heritage Lottery Fund. The Regional Development Agency or the Arts Lottery Fund will respond to emphasis on innovation, activity and investment.

■ Show the project at its best advantage

Not everyone is adept at interpreting plans. Plans showing people may aid understanding (9.1). To make the proposal accessible to all, a CAD (Computer Aided Design) visualisation is invaluable (9.4). Once plans and elevations are logged into the computer, full colour representations can be created quickly and accurately as a 3-dimensional model. These can be as detailed as required. Most software also

| Example | 9.1 |

Presentation of re-use at Repton Music School

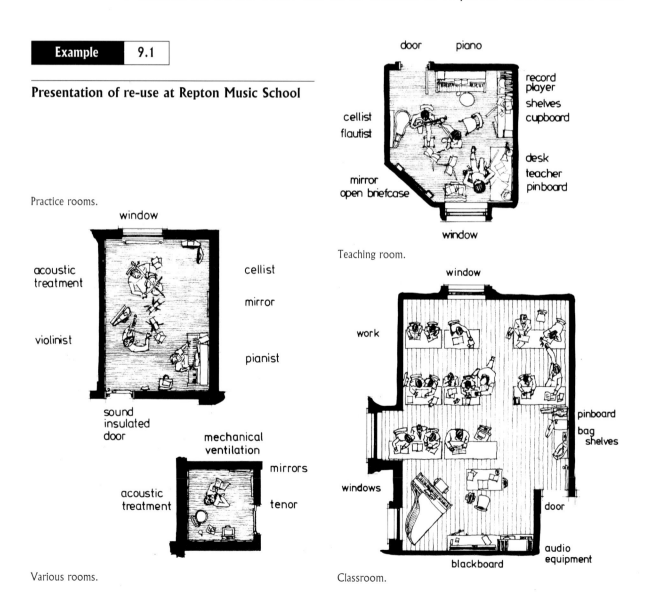

Practice rooms.

Teaching room.

Various rooms.

Classroom.

Main rehearsal room – full orchestra.

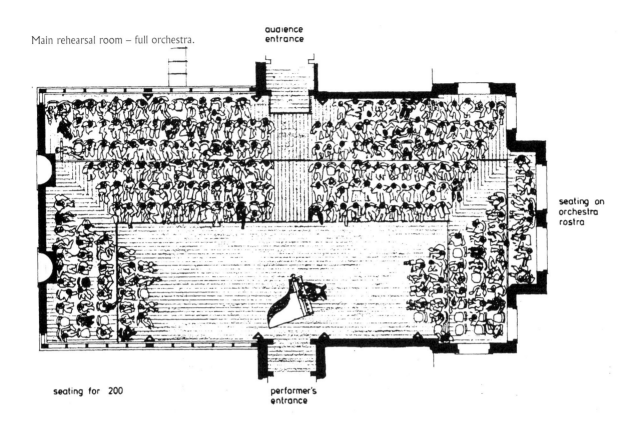

audience entrance

seating on orchestra rostra

seating for 200

performer's entrance

Main rehearsal room – recital.

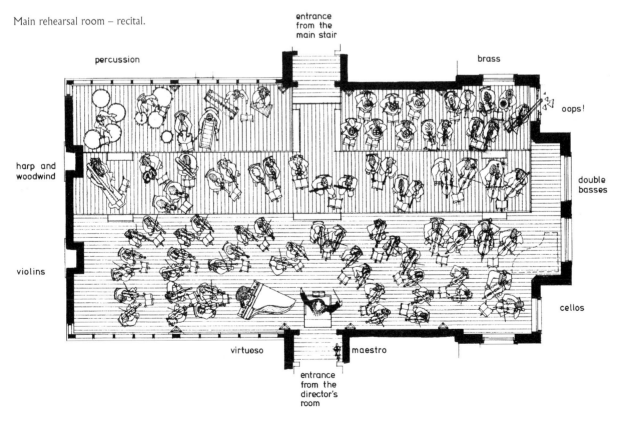

entrance from the main stair

percussion

brass

oops!

harp and woodwind

double basses

violins

cellos

virtuoso

maestro

entrance from the director's room

Comparison of activities.

enables the visual to be seen as in daylight or artificial light. Virtual Reality Fly-Throughs are expensive in software and input time. The presentation should demonstrate the sensitivity of the site and the effectiveness of the proposal. Aim to show what the building will look like to the ordinary viewer. Avoid confusing graphic techniques such as 'Worm's Eye View'.

Aerial views may be acceptable if they explain the configuration or layout of a proposal better than a plan. Axonometrics (with a viewing angle of 45°) provide a useful method of combining a scale plan with a visual representation (9.2).

Example   9.2

USE: Mill: Barnwell, Oundle

Seventeenth century, three-storey, narrow span water mill, stone and slate with projecting lucam, located on a narrow isthmus between river and canal.

TO: Hotel and restaurant

First conversion to a restaurant required only a small single-storey kitchen extension. Expansion to a hotel required a large extension back along the isthmus. Higher floor to ceiling levels are disguised by elevations of proportions to the mill, and a 'double pile' section maintains the scale whilst accommodating double the width. The plan form, and elevations, open out to accommodate swimming pool and entrance away from the existing wall.

A: Latham Architects

Barnwell Mill.

Model.

Detail of model.

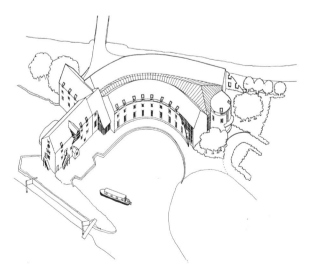

Axonometric of proposal.

Colour schemes can be displayed by tracing from a photograph of an existing building and then colouring the result. Comparisons can quickly be made with the original by comparing with the photograph or by using a photographic collage comprising the painting and the photo of the existing building. This may be done on a computer using Adobe PhotoShop software.

Dramatic changes to a building's exterior are often best displayed by scale models (9.2, 9.3). They should be realistically painted, and include people, plants and cars.

Example   **9.3**

Presentation of proposals for the Kings Fund

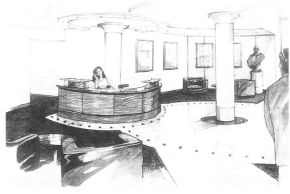

Perspective of proposed entrance hall.

Model of 11-13 Cavendish Square before conversion/rebuilding.

Model.

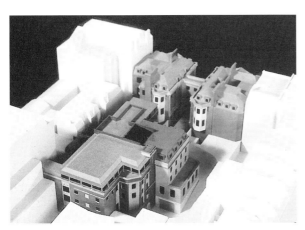

After, showing relationship of new structure with surrounding buildings.

As built.

These can show the scale, compatibility, even texture, and help people see the re-use prospect in a positive light.

■ APPROACHING THE PLANNING AUTHORITY

■ Understand policy

The town and country planning legislation supports the concept of re-use (PPG 15/EH Advisory Notes) subject to retaining items of architectural or historic value. The interpretation of policy varies. Staffs in local planning authorities and English Heritage interpret guidelines according to their employers' objectives. They sometimes appear narrow-minded, possibly influenced by working with insensitive builders or property owners.

Both planning and listed building issues should be addressed in terms of the latest national legislation and regional policy guidelines, as well as the relevant development plans of the local authority (UDP or local plan). Locally produced non-statutory documents may also help you to appreciate local concerns and sensitivities. These issues should be discussed with the appropriate officers, even though it may be necessary to consider an appeal. Seek the views of other agencies and amenity groups, and, where relevant, those of the public to prepare for negotiation.

■ Include as part of the master plan

It sometimes helps the client to present proposals as part of a master plan. Minor deviations from policy may be overlooked when viewed as part of the grand scale. Showing the building in context may make it easier for anyone to understand how a change of character or identity might be necessary.

There are other times, however, when a 'softly, softly' approach is more appropriate. Where stages are revealed to an authority over a number of years, they can see the benefit of early phases and feel more politically able to support later phases.

■ Timing is crucial

The timing of a presentation is vital to its success. Clients have to avoid both anxiously consulting the planning authority before proceeding, and conducting covert operations before releasing approved designs to the public as a fait accompli.

Remember that when a planning authority is approached for an opinion, you will only receive an individual's interpretation. It is better to prepare methodically in the first place. The presentation should incorporate all the issues the authority has to consider. It may include site surveys, analysis of context, study of policy documents, consideration of traffic and parking management, and dialogue with neighbours. Any disadvantages of the proposal should not be swept aside but contained as part of a balanced assessment. The advantages can, however, be highlighted.

In this way the project team can take the Council systematically through the analytical and decision-making process, and be able to prompt persuasively when they are open to suggestion.

■ Allow scope for suggestion

Any presentation should be about possibilities; in no way should a fully detailed design be presented to the authority, as this leaves no room for negotiation. It is better to present a coherent proposal that allows some scope for the planning authority to make suggestions and feel involved in the project. Once the planning officers become part of the extended team their particular expertise about council policies and politics can be invaluable to the project.

While planning and listed building regulations have some flexibility they apply mainly to new buildings, requiring older buildings to be converted to the same standard. To adhere to these regulations 'to the letter' may damage the harmony of the conversion. Try to understand what the basic intention is, and prepare strategies for each, and avoid the building control officers' 'check-list' mentality.

Where a building must be stabilised, don't employ engineers to calculate how to bring it up to new build standard as you will incur over design and unnecessary cost. A better solution is to ask what is needed to keep the building stable and fulfil statutory regulations, and ask the client, or user, how much restriction to the use would be acceptable. The building may not need to be changed.

When complying with accessibility requirements, rather than simply altering accesses to accommodate the disabled, look at the whole picture of access for everyone – the walking disabled, the blind, the deaf, and parents laden with push chairs or bags. It may be that one solution can improve access for all. (See Cavendish Square, 12.4.)

■ Fire prevention

The best fire prevention is to stop it at source. The three main sources are heat emitters (including cooking), electrical faults and people smoking.

Central heating can be made even safer by adopting low surface radiators, which are safer for children and kinder to existing buildings by reducing overall temperature variations. If open fires are still used in existing buildings, ventilating the structure requires specialist safety advice.

Old electric wire can be a hidden source of danger. Check existing wiring systems with a qualified electrician and replace older fuse boxes with more sensitive contact breakers.

The public now accepts smoking prohibition in most historic interiors, but in buildings such as hotels, smoking areas have to be allocated. Reduce fire risks by using incombustible materials with minimum flame spread, and a good detection system. Existing materials that are combustible such as textile or timber can be treated with flame retardant or a fire barrier such as intumescent varnish. Fire escape regulations are essentially the same for all buildings, but some alternative methods of reducing fire spread may be required to avoid destroying the character of historic buildings.

■ Space and ventilation

Since slum dwellers were huddled together like 'maggots in carrion flesh, or mites in cheese'[i] in notorious 'back-to-back' rooms, eleven feet square facing onto narrow three-storey courts, ravaged by cholera, the Victorian health engineers assumed that light and air were the perfect antidote. Legislation resulted in established minimum distances between dwellings that still apply to modern housing. Window sizes one-tenth and ventilation one-twentieth of the room area were required for all habitable rooms.

The modern movement introduced sunlight and overshadowing factors for public housing design, adding aspect and orientation criteria that encouraged larger windows. However, prospect and privacy also became issues, as did defensible space. More recent energy consciousness has reduced window sizes except on south-facing elevations. Miserly owners retaining every watt of heat now condone ventilation only in puffs and leaks. Recirculation of air is now permitted and bedrooms lit only with small rooflights are, once again, acceptable.

Cottages were once condemned as unfit for human habitation because their windows were near floor level (only window area over 900 mm above the floor could count towards two-tenths of floor area – an impossible target for large serviceable rooms with low eaves). They are now fashionable again, and sought after by the upwardly mobile. Toilets were, originally, only allowed at the bottom of the garden because of possible infection; later they could be attached to the house, but only accessible internally; then they were allowed internally (but not in bathrooms), and with openable windows and ventilated lobbies between toilet and habitable room; now they are permitted, unventilated, directly off a bedroom, as long as high humidity levels can be avoided.

We no longer stick to rigid rules of thumb when designing light and air source, but take a flexible look at the options. If ceiling levels are too low for the average person, improvements will usually have to be made, except that in some circumstances, a low arch or beam might be seen as desirable, and so remain with a suitable warning.

■ Services

Similarly, we use different criteria with regard to water supply and sewerage. Drains that had to be external are now internal. Overflows which previously discharged outside can now discharge into a WC pan; drain pipes which had to be vented to fresh air can now have one-way valves. With biodegradation of waste and pumping of sewerage, there are fewer locational restrictions on toilets. Even a decade ago, there was not this freedom of layout, the potential options for re-use are now significantly increased.

■ Refuse

Refuse disposal needs have changed. Whereas previously hoppers, chutes and ducting in high rise buildings were used to keep refuse separate, the advent of the bin liner and increase of packing in ratio to putrescent waste has changed our attitudes. People are now prepared to carry their own rubbish down passenger lifts, and contractors can be asked to collect twice daily where necessary. We no longer need to allow for large, smelly, refuse containers.

■ Energy conservation

Increasing insulation requirements of walls, floors and roofs present problems. Blind adherence to particular construction methods with predetermined materials simply to meet U-value[2] requirements simply leads to problems of interstitial condensation[3] leaks and cold bridges.[4] Not only would the character of the building be lost, but also its interior quality would be reduced and money wasted. Buildings that have always breathed should continue to do so; structures that were cool or warm should remain the same. Building control officers must be made aware of the special demands of older buildings in order to establish how improvements can be made without causing damage.

■ Strategies to deal with approving bodies

Several strategies are possible to deal with these stringent stipulations. It may be possible to comply with most requirements, but request relaxation of certain minor ones. Or if a larger issue is in contention, it may be preferable to prepare a comprehensive alternative strategy, going back to first principles. In some cases, a better strategy may be to avoid confrontation completely. Repair does not come within the jurisdiction of the regulations, so structure and staircases may be repaired without compliance.

Fire Regulations are laid down in the same way as Building Regulations. However, as Fire Prevention Officers realise that the characteristics of serious fires are not totally predictable, they take a pragmatic approach when assessing a building's fire risks. When inspecting a finished project they often require fixtures and equipment in addition to, or instead of, those on the approved plans. It may therefore be wise to either work with the Fire Prevention Officer from the beginning or, if necessary, consult a specialist who can work with the design team on fire prevention issues (Victoria Quarter, 7.3).

■ Obtaining funding

The aim is to secure the necessary funding for the project without incurring excessive conditions such as high specification for loading levels on office floors. Preliminary research should confirm the availability of grants or funding, and what criteria need to be satisfied to obtain this. Once a suitable source has been identified, a presentation must be carefully planned. This should persuade the funding body to invest or make the grant, by appraising them of the vision and at the same time demonstrating awareness of their standpoint and culture.

Part of the presentation could include the Feasibility Study, or for major projects, the Interim Report – Survey and Analysis, possibly including options. The final report's conclusions and recommendations must include both input and output costs, suggest the steps for implementation, and identify who needs to take responsibility for whatever role they play. Then give them time to think about the proposal.

Price is an important factor, but may be inextricably linked to other value considerations. For example, when applying for Lottery funding, support may depend upon benefits given to the community. Therefore identify shortfalls in the area's facilities and match the project's aspirations to this. Gain community support before bidding.

■ CONCLUSION

Whether presenting to an approving or funding body there are seven key aspects that can be brought into play:

1. Knowledge of the project and the implications this might have for approving and funding bodies.
2. An understanding not only of the requirements but the culture of the funding/approving body.
3. The development of a strategy to address the issue at stake.
4. The possible shift of perception from established views into a new paradigm.
5. The presentation of the case in stages to enable others to feel involved in both the problem and a potential solution.
6. Concentration upon outcomes, value rather than price, effectiveness rather than compliance to the letter.
7. Ensure the ultimate presentation of your case is appropriate for the audience. After extensive research and thorough planning, one recipient may only require an informal chat, whereas another may require a full audio-visual extravaganza.

At this stage it is important to network. If appropriate, publicity can be generated about the project. Be prepared to respond to comment or criticism.

REFERENCES

1. Chambers, J.D., 'Modern Nottingham in the Making' (Ph.D. dissertation, Nottingham University), p 7, quoting from Sir Richard Phillips, writing of Broad Marsh, Nottingham, 1829.
2. The degree of heat loss through a wall, roof or floor.
3. Water condensing within the wall structure.
4. Material acting as conductors for escaping heat.

Case Study	9.4

Midland House, Derby
Victorian heritage provides high-tech image

A spectacular new structure of glass and steel links two giant redbrick buildings in Derby and reduces them to a more human scale.

Key issues involved in re-use were:

- Removing later accretions.
- Resolving circulation within and between buildings (including glazing the steel fire escape).
- Convincing the client that the old buildings could present a modern go-ahead image with a new entrance.
- Convincing the conservation committee that the new image would enhance the historic value of the existing building.

Key
1. 2nd floor bridge is only link between Blocks A and B
2. Later sub-divisions of office space clash with fenestration
3. Long 'dead-leg' corridors with institutional image
4. Internal corridor due to sub-division
5. Fire escape corridor and stair: not general circulation
6. Fire escape tacked on – replace with internal at end of corridor
7. Provide new physical link between Blocks A and B
8. Single-storey unit: does not link blocks
9. Two principal staircases, each with single lift adjacent
10. Remove existing lifts and replace with new lift in new central reception
11. Hatched areas: proposed demolition

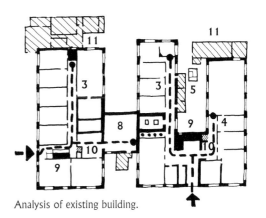

Analysis of existing building.

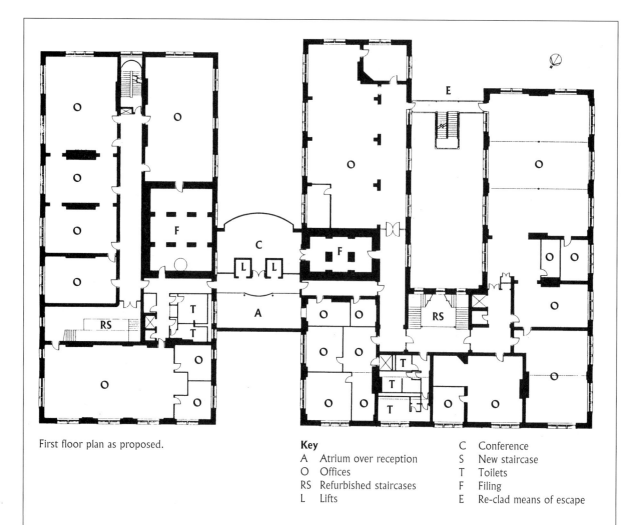

First floor plan as proposed.

Key

A	Atrium over reception	C	Conference
O	Offices	S	New staircase
RS	Refurbished staircases	T	Toilets
L	Lifts	F	Filing
		E	Re-clad means of escape

- Conserving, restoring and enhancing the best original features internally.
- Cleaning and repairing externally to re-present the property.
- Using high ceilings to reduce air changes per hour enabling natural ventilation (with some solar control).
- Lowering the perceived ceiling height using lighting grids and colour schemes.
- A discrete services installation.

The following article by Sarah Hardcastle published in *Building* (26 February 1993) describes the project.

A giant of a man must have designed Derby's Midland House, now British Rail's Intercity regional headquarters. Everything about this mid-nineteenth century three-storey property is over-scaled and larger than life. There are rooms 4.5 m high, vast sash windows reaching to the ceiling, an over-proportion of glazing to solid wall, and corridors of such generous dimensions you could drive a train down them.

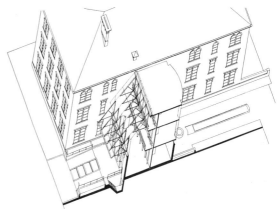

Axonometric of new link.

Its scale says much about the aspirations and ambitions of the Midland Railway Company, for whom the property was built in 1865 to serve as administration and wages offices. Adjacent to Derby

Link block before.

Station, it had been used by British Rail until 1987 when it became redundant. Following the restructuring of Intercity, BR decided to refurbish the property to accommodate 450 staff at a cost of £4.8m.

British Rail's brief called for exterior restoration and upgrading of the 7,600 sq m floor area 'with minimal alteration to existing internal structural layout'.[a] A property of such huge scale and large features does not readily lend itself to modern requirements that call for a number of small, individual offices, a good 'traffic flow' to ease person-to-person communication, plus extensive computer and telecommunications services.

Link block after as the main entrance.

Rear of link block after showing conference rooms (*Stuart Blackwood*)

View from the conference room between the existing blocks. (*Stuart Blackwood*)

Compounding these difficulties was the property's layout. It comprises two blocks, rectangular and 'U'-shaped, which had been unsatisfactorily connected at ground and second floor level by a brick 'link'. Little more than a covered walkway, the link hindered circulation between the two blocks, and was therefore demolished.

The link has now been replaced by a spectacular three-storey contemporary structure of frameless Planar glass and delicate steel trusses. It accommodates the entrance, reception, lifts and conference and meeting rooms, and is the pivot for horizontal and vertical circulation between the two office blocks. A large glass canopy stretches towards the street, flagging the entrance.

Set in a modern context, the steel and glass structure would not seem exceptional. Squeezed between two hefty Victorian blocks, it is a sparkling, dramatic foil to their massiveness. At night, brilliantly illuminated, it brings a touch of theatre to the surrounding railway landscape. 'British Rail was strongly committed to a thoroughly modern idiom for this thinking structure. After long consultation, the planners agreed that the contrast would be a good idea.'

Although unlisted, Midland House is in a conservation area. The structure's interior has been kept white and light deliberately, with glass as the predominant decorative material. The solid walls at the rear of the reception are clad with glass blocks and illuminated from behind, 'so they give the appearance of being transparent'.

Upper storey internal balconies overlooking the reception well are of Planar glazing, while doors to the conference and meeting rooms are glass with frosted panels. In these south-facing rooms, external louvres on the Planar glazing walls provide protection from the sun, supplemented by electronically controlled internal blinds.

Left and right of the structure, the architects have positioned new doors on all levels with lintels matching the existing ones on the exterior. Attempts to retain the existing plaster and lath ceilings proved counter-productive, so suspended ceilings were installed as high as possible to avoid clashing with the heads of the sash windows.

We addressed the disproportionate height of the office space by suspending rectangular lighting rigs approximately 3 m from the floor, and complemented this with picture rails on the walls at a similar height, with dark wall fabric applied below, and light, reflective surfaces above. The rooms now have a perceived 3 m height, while retaining the full height sash windows.

Some walls were knocked through, as BR's office style is open plan. Where small meeting rooms and individual offices were required, these have been created with glazed partitions with horizontal slatted blinds to provide privacy.

Sympathetically installing mechanical and electrical services into the buildings formed a major portion of

Corridor before.

Corridor after. (*Stuart Blackwood*)

the contract value. Midland House accommodates a regional BR telephone enquiry bureau, and a large amount of computer equipment. A high priority was also placed on security and monitoring services.

The solution was to run a perimeter heating system, incorporating cable trays that can be tapped into at any position. It is supplemented in the larger open offices by power sockets set into the timber floors on a 5 m grid. As there are basements throughout 70 per cent of the building plan, this enabled horizontal distribution from the main switchgear rooms and gas fired boilers. But vertical distribution and the need for service runs to be accessible involved considerable adaptation of the structure.

External work included re-roofing, the redesign of two courtyards and encasement of a visually-dominant fire escape with Planar glazing, plus hard and soft landscaping. The brick façade was cleaned and repaired and the huge sash windows refitted with 'broad' sheet glass imported from Eastern Europe. Resembling original Victorian cylinder glass, it has a soft glint and avoids the flat appearance of modern float glass.

Having pushed the contract along 'at a cracking pace', BR moved its Intercity staff into the revitalised offices in the autumn. British Rail was delighted with the refurbishment. Head of architecture and design, Alan Hurst said 'we have ended up with an economic solution that meets our requirements and preserves two very handsome nineteenth century buildings. The glass/steel link is a tremendous success, acting as a twentieth century bridge to the nineteenth century buildings.'

■ **Reference**

a. Project Architect: Stephen Buckman, Latham Architects.

Office before.

Office CAD illustration.

Office after. (*Stuart Blackwood*)
Also see colour plates 7 a–c.

CHAPTER 10

Techniques: Material and Craftsmanship

Use proven techniques, natural materials and traditional craftsmanship in preference to high-tech solutions.[1]

To get the best results when undertaking repair or restoration work, always select high quality natural materials, and traditional artisans to implement the work, researching what and who will be appropriate for that particular building. There are a number of repair techniques that have proved effective for specific activities. These include:

* Repairing stonework with new stone from a similar bed in the same quarry, or the nearest match, or second-hand stone of similar character, dressed to suit.
* Repairing brickwork with similar second-hand bricks or having new bricks specially made to match the existing in character and colour.
* Removing worn or eroded stones and bricks that can be turned around, cleaned (or re-dressed if applicable) before re-inserting them in their original position.
* Avoiding substitute materials for external repair work, e.g. artificial stone concrete, or fibreglass mouldings, as weathering is likely to highlight and exacerbate any change rather than allowing it to blend in.
* Using green oak rather than second-hand matured oak for major structural work, but allow for shrinkage so that as joints tighten they do not cause failure to older joints elsewhere.

■ FINDING A GOOD ARTISAN

In spite of there being a lot of shoddy building work around, it is possible to find a good craftsperson. You need to be persistent, and willing to pay a fair price.

Directories of artisans can form a useful starting point, although a personal recommendation would be better.

Good craftsmanship is not dying out. There are many young people who have obtained diplomas and gained practical experience as masons (often on cathedrals), bricklayers, roofers, thatchers, plumbers, carpenters, joiners and plasterers. They are committed to high standards of application and have a scholarly background.

It is worth employing these craftspeople rather than accepting standard contract techniques. To get the best out of these individuals, incorporate them into a team with the scope to make observations and suggestions. The architect, in return, must be able to talk knowledgeably about the artisan's trade, whether this involves selecting stone from a quarry, masonry pointing, stone slate roofs, thatching, sand lime cement plaster finishes, running plaster moulding, leadwork, joinery, electrical cabling, or, most frequently, preparation work for painting and decorating.

■ USING MODERN TECHNOLOGY

Where traditional methods would be destructive, use modern technology as a hidden means to preserve fabric in situ.[2]

Some building work cannot be done using traditional methods. There comes a point in most traditional masonry and simple beam construction that, due to building decay or movement, a whole structure has to be rebuilt and the patina of age and the historical validity is lost. To avoid this and save the original fabric, various methods can be adopted to reinforce the structure and retain it in situ.

The choice of method depends upon the problem. Firstly, carefully analyse the movement of the structure by identifying and measuring the cracks; then record their movement with calibrated telltales or sophisticated surveying equipment, plotting this on plan and elevation or even a Perspex model. Thus you can make a clear visual assessment of the relationship of cracks inside and outside – the symptoms that betray the unseen stresses within the structure. At this stage, consult a specialist structural engineer who can identify the cause, nature and severity of the structural movement over the time span.

There are two types of effective solution. We can illustrate this in the case of simple foundation settlement.

The first addresses the original cause of the problem. The solution would be to underpin the property. The underpinning removes the inadequate sub-soil, or at least penetrates through it to form a satisfactory load-bearing foundation.

The second addresses the current symptoms. The solution would be to reinforce the fabric or tie it back in some way to present its further movement. Tying the fabric back increases the integrity of the structure, thereby spreading the load back onto other under-stressed foundations, and relieving the over-stressed foundation and the ground under it.

GROUTING TECHNIQUES

Grouting is an essential technique of consolidation where masonry has lost its bond and structural integrity.

If due to instability external shores are unavoidable, steps can be taken to counteract the settlement of the shore under its own weight once erected and so maintain the façade of the building in a constant position. By placing the shore upon hydraulic flat jacks on specially prepared foundations with instrumentation to monitor increased stresses, the flat jack can be inflated to take up the differential in foundation settlement and counteract potential movement of the façade to create temporary stability.

If this is not possible, consider rebuilding or consolidating unstable sections. Otherwise consolidation of masonry invariably involves grouting either on its own or with other measures to fill the interstices that have arisen within the wall, and bond the stones together to recreate homogenous masonry.

There are four methods of grouting: hand, gravity, vacuum and pressure grouting.

First, clean out the old mortar by the irrigation of open joints, pouring in water from a high level; the outer face of the joints is sealed with tow – a tarred hemp. For hand grout a birds-mouth is then formed with clay around a gap in the pointing and the grout is poured into the cavities via the birds-mouth. To fill by gravity, the height of the receptacle is raised and a hose and nozzle used (see 10.1). Smaller fragile elements may be grouted in polythene after air has been evacuated by a powerful vacuum pump.

The grout usually comprises fine sand, pulverised fuel ash (pfa) and lime in the proportions 2:1:2. The fly ash allows the setting of the mortar within the depth of the wall where lack of air prevents the normal carbonisation of lime. Ensure the ash has a low soluble salt content. Where fine joints are to be grouted use a more easily flowing mix of Dentonite clay additive, pfa and lime in the proportions 1:2:2. Use Epoxy resin grout when high structural properties are required in specified locations. Once set, the tow is then removed and the joints pointed in the normal manner with a matching mortar mix for the first 30–50 mm of the building structure. Ensure that strength and porosity match that of the adjacent stonework, and cut back the final finish behind the worn arises of the masonry, unless some special effect is required to match existing pointing elsewhere. The best method, if done purposefully and progressively, is from the base of the structure upwards working in lifts of approximately 2–3 ft (600–900 mm) at a time leaving tell-tale holes to check the progress of the grout fill.

If the structure is inaccessible, it may be necessary to adopt a mechanical grouting technique injecting grout under pressure or by vacuum. If the area to be grouted is not large a hand pump can be used, but otherwise high pressure equipment is normally adopted. Take care that designed pressure is not exceeded and grout does not break through internal finishes causing damage, especially to such items as wall paintings; or creating a seal under pressure at the back of such items as window frames restricting future thermal movement. Also, protect furniture, fittings and other masonry from grout spray and spillage.

It is impossible to predict exactly where the pressured grout will go. When consolidating the outer wall at Bolsover Castle, the amount of grout accepted indicated extensive cavities within the wall, until an adjacent property complained of a dirty grey liquid seeping into their basement. If grout extends into unknown areas it may restrict natural movement of parts of the structure or, by penetrating beyond the normal foundation create a different bearing pattern. This can be avoided by analysing the structure using a thermal imager.

A thermal imager is a video camera which records different temperatures in the structure indicating where there are voids with warmer air within the cooler masonry; these show up in a coloured pattern. This image can then be translated either into stills for visual inspection or recorded on disk for analysis by computer.

If these voids extend into areas where the grout is not required, the masonry can be opened up, the void blocked off and resealed so the ultimate extent of grout can be controlled. Sometimes cracks have to be retained within an old structure to act as an informal expansion joint. Such cracks should be cleaned out and filled with a weak, flexible filler sufficient merely to keep the water at bay.

Vacuum grouting must be undertaken by specialists, usually using a resin polymer mix, and is best used for artefacts that can be sealed.

Grouting is a method of consolidation but whilst it can act as a bond to allow a wall to act in unison under compression, only epoxy resin grout has any significant strength in tension. To enable a wall to act in tension it is necessary to add some form of reinforcement. This can be a stainless steel rod or cable, which can be post-tensioned and set in a grout to seal it into the structure. This requires sophisticated engineering techniques but can be effective over large areas, and is commonly used in the major reinforcement of foundations. The technique involves precision drilling, often of many holes, to create a complete matrix to tie an existing foundation into new foundations constructed on either side.

At a simpler level, smaller holes can be drilled in the masonry at angles through the structure, and the holes filled with epoxy resin to form resin rods as reinforcement to stitch the structure together. This usually happens after the remainder of the structure has been consolidated so that there is a contiguity of structure to bond to the resin rods.

The same techniques can be applied even when merely trying to retain the decorative facing of a structure. At the Victoria Quarter in Leeds (7.3), 2,600 terracotta tiles were drilled and fixed with small stainless steel pins set in resin to bond the terracotta back to the masonry. This avoided the complete replacement of terracotta on the building which would have meant loss of patina, and allowed the retention of terracotta even where cracked or crazed. The drilling location of every one of these terracotta pieces was identified on drawings detailing work to be undertaken.

The overall objective is to undertake the minimum amount of work necessary to secure the building's future, to use traditional methods whenever effective, but to adopt innovative solutions when they are needed (The Abbey, 10.2).

■ THE CONSERVATION ARCHITECT'S PERSPECTIVE

Use subtle repair techniques ensuring that the building appears in good repair rather than newly repaired.[3]

The architect is driven throughout his career by the dual desire to create something meaningful, and to provide a service. He tends to develop quite an ego as a defence against the abuse of the building trade and the public. To be an architect conservator you need something beyond that – a perfectionist drive to painstakingly analyse, specify and supervise the repairs to a historic building.

Surface areas of a historic building which are significantly eroded or damaged or contain old repairs or replacement are known as *lacunae*. In the past, before conservation philosophy was developed, damaged or unstable areas were either replaced with some material thought to match the original, or with whatever came to hand. Considerable rebuilding often occurred, a process exemplified to excess by the Victorian restorers.

SPAB then responded by promoting repair methods that were deliberately contrary to the fabric. This approach regarded the building as the object of an academic exercise, often disregarding the aesthetic harmony of form and texture.

There is no single method of treating lacunae. In stonework the replacement of worn stone to its original profile can leave masonry projecting from the worn surroundings of its neighbours. But if this stone is artificially made to look worn, it can cause confusion when deciding upon later repairs.

Bernard Feilden, in *Conservation of Historic Buildings*, states:

> The treatment of lacunae should reduce neither the artistic wholeness nor the message of the historic site or building or any element therein, and must not aim at deception of trained observers. The general principle is that lacunae should seem to recede visually behind the original material, yet be so harmonious as not to detract but rather add to the whole.[4]

Example 10.1

Hand and Gravity Grouting

Grouting can often obviate the need for extensive underpinning such as this.

Brickwork requiring consolidation by grouting together with new lintel.

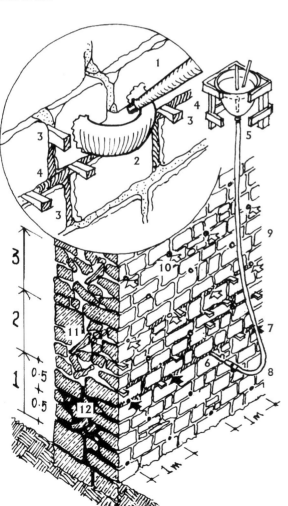

Pointing up masonry at 1 Greenhill.
New or consolidated masonry is pointed up from the top down. The lowest section shows the wall raked out with the mortar, or grout, set back ready for pointing. The middle section has been pointed and is left to dry for a couple of hours. The surface is then brushed back to expose the coarse aggregate in the pointing mix and set the face of the mortarslightly behind that of the stone (or brick) to become 'visually recessive'. This can be seen in the upper section.

Hand grouting[5]
1. Grout poured from can
2. Clay grout cup
3. Oak wedges
4. Tow stopping in open joints

Gravity grouting
5. Grout pan raised 4 m above nozzle on scaffold
6. Nozzle with stopcock connected by hose
7. Grout introduced in 1 m high lifts
8. Plugging and wedges removed ready for repointing joints
9. Loose mortar raked out of joints
10. Grout points and intermediate holes drilled where pointing is sound at 1.0 m horizontal, 0.5 m vertical centres
11. Voids in wall
12. Voids filled with grout

The application of this philosophy is illustrated by the approach to reconstructing the gables at 1 Greenhill (see 10.1, also 8.4).

Buildings do not weather evenly, which makes it almost impossible to re-create the original appearance with rebuilding; the material that is weathered gets mixed up and does not follow its original pattern, and the original patina of age that remains on the individual stones is lost. And even when some remains, it is not possible to make it look exactly as before. The only way to achieve a reasonably similar replica is to disassemble a wall after first numbering the elements and then reassemble them using measured and photographic records to achieve the closest copy. In the Jewellery Business Centre, Birmingham (6.4), a technique was used whereby reclaimed bricks from both internal and external walls with some faces of soot and whitewash were laid at random. They were used on new structures built of reclaimed brick, and also in the reconstructed rear wall of the factory building. This is not a replica of something that was there before but, with its original cast iron windows surrounded by traditional brick detail, now looks authentic to the untrained eye.

Architects may well appreciate using such techniques which, when skilfully applied, achieve the purpose of protecting the building's appearance, yet can be detected and understood by the expert or academic observer.

I have written in detail about some of the techniques used to retain the essence of historic buildings. This may seem surprising as such level of detail would not usually be considered at this stage of a new build project. Yet it is only by working with the building and appraising the potential alternatives in detail at an early stage that the full scope for re-use, and its cost, can be realised.

REFERENCES

1. cf Appendix in this volume, page 215, Principles for Re-use.
2. Ibid.
3. Ibid.
4. Feilden, B., *Conservation of Historic Buildings*, Butterworth Heinemann, Oxford, 1982.
5. Ashurst, J. & N., *Practical Building Conservation*, English Heritage Technical Handbook, Gower Technical Press, Aldershot, 1988.

Case Study **10.2**

From: 'The Abbey', Darley Abbey
To: Pub: dramatic repairs now unseen (Ancient Monument, Conservation Area)

The Old Abbey building constructed between the thirteenth and fifteenth centuries, although with some later alterations, belonged for many years to the Derbyshire Archaeological Society. Roofed following a bequest in the 1920s a stone buttress was added, but movement continued and the side walls were shored up with heavy timber shores in the 1950s. The monument was unused and the Society had insufficient funds to maintain it in a proper state. This was followed by the installation of a main sewer down the centre of the road resulting in a sideways movement of the ground adjacent to the building under pressure from the shores – the outer wall to the street having settled against the shores to over 400 mm out of plumb. The shores blocked half the road but it was clear that their removal would precipitate the collapse of the wall which was leaning out beyond its point of equilibrium, yet also had to contain

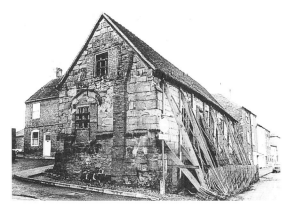

Before as ruin. (*Derby Evening Telegraph*)

the sideward thrust of the roof between the roof trusses, a momentum which further exacerbated its condition.

The property was a liability to the Society. The solution was to find a use which would fund the building's repair. Research was required. Sometime after the dissolution of the Abbey the village was developed by the Evans, mill owners who, as strict methodists, had put covenants on all their land preventing the sale of

After as a pub. (*Stuart Blackwood*)

Interior first floor after. (*Derby Evening Telegraph*)

alcohol. The only land they had not bought was the small piece containing the only remaining section of the Abbey building. This led to its re-use as a pub, still the only one in the village. This required:

1. Thorough research to discover the unique absence of covenant.
2. Economic rectification of 'the lean' by temporarily jacking up the roof, inserting flat jacks into the buttresses and jacking the wall back 250 mm, lowering back the roof and tying in the wallplate.
3. Re-tiling.
4. Inserting a spiral stair to gain internal access to the first floor (only previously accessible by external stair).
5. Laying a stone floor in the undercroft (tiles at one end for the toilets).
6. Two oak bars – first floor and undercroft.
7. Oak and plaster partitions for the toilets.
8. Cellarage in the basement of an adjacent house.
9. Simple lighting power and furniture.

Michael Wood purchased the building from the Archaeological Society to convert it into the public house, now known appropriately as 'The Abbey'.[a] Initially he was advised that the only way he would be able to remove the shores would be to prop up the roof, take down the outer wall and rebuild it. But this would have rendered the structure virtually valueless as an historic artefact. The decision was made to prop up the roof, as suggested, but to raise it very slightly so that it was freed from the wall plate, a stone was then removed from each of the three buttresses, and certain sections of the wall, to allow the insertion of flat jacks. The flat jacks were inflated very slowly, under controlled co-ordinated conditions, to jack the wall back to only 200 mm out of plumb. The joints which had been opened up at the end of each elevation, prior to the operation, were then regrouted to allow the re-integration of the structure. The flat jacks were replaced with stones and wedges to maintain the new position and the whole structure grouted to fill the newly created voids. The outer face was then repointed to provide a matching finish. By straightening the structure the load now fell upon the original foundations rather than upon the buttresses, thereby finding an equilibrium which prevented progressive settlement continuing. Finally the roof was lowered back onto the wall plate, the oak trusses repaired by traditional methods, pegs replaced to ensure the joints were effectively in tension, and two additional ties added to the wall plate at mid span between the trusses to reduce the outward thrust of the roof at mid span. (These now form supports for light fittings in the upper bar.)

The original external steps to first floor level were retained, with new railings, giving access directly into the upper bar. The upper bar comprises the full volume of the original hall with the restored roof uplighted from eaves level. A new stone spiral stair gives access down to the ground floor which has been divided into a lower bar, entrance hall and toilets. The new floor is finished in second-hand stone, except for the toilets in quarry and encaustic tiles. Doors and bar fittings were made on site from green oak.

A previously inaccessible, derelict relic is now a popular community focus for young and old alike. All the original fabric can still be seen – a low cost solution benefiting building and user alike.

■ **Reference**

a. Project Architect: Michael Wood, Partner Wood Latham Newton Partnership.

Front wall after reducing lean by 250 mm.

The jack still remains hidden in the buttress behind the stonework.

From: Conversion of Mill
To: Houses in a difficult property market

An old derelict corn mill and miller's cottage at Wither-slack in the Lake District.

■ Viability

This started with application and approval to convert the main mill into only four cottages which proved to be uneconomic.

Keith Scott, the architect, decided to purchase and act as his own developer. He explained how he could make a profit and control his cash flow.

> First, I would write off my own fee. Second, I would be the contractor employing my own labour and buying a large proportion of second-hand materials. Third, and most important, I would not sell after the conversion, but let one bit at a time to swell the fund to enable payment of labour and buying a large proportion of second-hand materials for the next bit.

Building work proceeded on the approved plans until the large spaces were framed up. When the planning officer was invited to the site, he was shown how excessive the rooms were and how readily the plan could be split into two units (five in all). With his support, a revised planning application was made and approved; the project became much more viable.

■ Low cost gutters

As the second mill unit neared completion, a groundsman was taken on to look after an earlier development eight miles away in Beetham as well as the evolving Witherslack site. He had been foreman of a glass fibre factory and was highly skilled in all forms of in situ applications. He said he could line valley gutters, make flashings and cut working time by half, and he could charge low costs by using glass fibre rather than lead. He had no idea about differential expansion and stresses in materials to which the glass fibre was stuck, but said that as long as the plywood formwork was securely screwed to the bearers he would guarantee the result. He was proved right; from the third house onwards no lead was used. The grey resin looks identical to the lead; no technical problems have surfaced; and no complex lead detailing was required. This is

Large framed dormers open up the interior to views and light.

Windows are deeply recessed or projected as oriels, enhancing the sculptural quality of the stone walls.

Galleries within the roof allow internal volumes to be expressed.

another illustration of how much the building industry could learn from other fields.

■ Rooflights for sunlight

The rooflight was used extensively to get sunlight into the main living accommodation. Two techniques were used. One in the second cottage included a tall, V-shaped glazed structure which lets light and sunshine into the kitchen from the east face glass and into the living room from the west face side.

In the third cottage the second device is another tall, wedge shape, but here the eastern face is vertical and solid, and only the western slope of the rooflight was glazed. To bounce the sunlight down into the room, however, the internal vertical face was mirrored so that the room could be sunny in late afternoon.

All windows were made specially on site, from second-hand pitch pine scantlings stained brown. Glazing throughout is in hermetically sealed double units.

Details of the front doors developed as the project proceeded, but were derived from Keith Scott's visit to Japan. The grey resin used provides a close resemblance to lead.

■ Low ceilings

One of the main problems of the conversion was the floor-to-ceiling height of only 1.9 m, which was resolved by removing parts of floors and creating split levels, while leaving the window pattern untouched.

CHAPTER 11

Implementation: Time and Quality

The quality of the final product is determined by the choice of procurement route, the time devoted to design detail and the preparation of good contract documents.[1]

Many clients believe that after the necessary funding and planning consents have been obtained, the project can start at full speed. In fact, there is quite a long list of things to be checked and implemented. These include:

* Checking the building is in a fit state.
* Deciding upon the method of procurement.
* Making detailed design decisions.
* Preparing production drawings.
* Writing specifications.
* Shortlisting and interviewing contractors.
* Assembling, sending out, and upon their return, scrutinising and reporting on tender documents.

Fast track projects will require different objectives and methods, and may alter the order of activities. They require a more experienced and better co-ordinated team, but create higher risks and costs. The success of creative re-use projects, however, usually depends upon keeping costs down and minimising risks, so the entire implementation process must be managed creatively.

■ THE BUILDING

When undertaking the initial survey, it is not always possible to gain access to record enough detail. The building operatives' instructions must be relevant, so it is vital that the survey is completed in detail and updated just before work on site begins. The objective now is not to analyse the past but to communicate clearly the action required.

■ Occupied or vacant

If the property is occupied there is no need to record any fittings that will be removed by the existing tenant or owner. If it is vacant, the survey should differentiate between the items to be removed immediately and the fabric that will remain, intact, as the basis for conservation and rehabilitation.

■ Protect the building

If the property is neglected or derelict, it needs to be protected from further damage by weather or vandalism. If it is to become vacant, an inventory will need to be prepared promptly and the building secured as the possibility of theft is a real one. These are some real cases that occurred:

- A stone slate roof taken in the night from an occupied farmhouse in the Pennines.
- Whilst the Peak Park Trust were converting a previously derelict cruck barn to a dwelling on remote moors near Sheffield, the stone slates were twice taken from the roof before it was possible to install alarms.
- Lead repairs of the towers at Swarkestone Stand were undone twice by lead thieves. A third repair using a lead substitute was also damaged. The problem was resolved by a sign saying, 'To deter thieves: the roofing of this building has been undertaken with a simulated lead material which has no resale value.'
- Prior to the restoration of 11–13 Cavendish Square, London the client installed 24-hour security staff. However, as the building work was about to begin, and a few hours before the contractors' security staff arrived, three valuable fireplaces were stolen.

What lessons can we learn from these?

- Unless materials are available for re-use within the site buy new ones rather than second-hand from elsewhere. This will help to reduce the trade in stolen used materials. In special circumstances second-hand materials from certified architectural salvage suppliers can be used for sensitive piecing-in repairs.
- If there is a high risk of theft of valuable materials such as in remote areas, consider using appropriate substitutes.
- If there is a need for security, ensure that continuous cover is arranged.

■ PROCUREMENT METHODS

Decide upon the method of procurement before proceeding beyond the Scheme Design as it will influence the preparation of detailed design and documentation.

■ Design and build

Design Build comprises an offer by a builder to prepare drawings and convert a building to a client's specification. If the brief is not well researched and the specification too simple, the client should appoint an adviser to act on their behalf.

■ Develop and construct (detail and build)

An architect is engaged up to Stage 'D' Scheme Design obtaining planning permission and then prepares a typical set of detailed design drawings which indicate standards of finish and construction, but leave the method to the builder. This suits simple buildings with a number of repetitive elements, where the condition is predictable, such as when re-suiting a 1900s office building or hotel.

■ Management contracting (contractor led)

A series of subcontracts, the exact nature of which may not be known at the time of appointment, are managed for a fixed fee. Useful for large fast track projects where access cannot be gained prior to start on site.

■ Contract management (professional led)

Professionals paid on a fixed percentage or time fee, tender or negotiate subcontracts, direct trades contracts, or directly employ skilled operatives on a time and materials basis – a range particularly suited to re-use involving both conservation and conversion work.

Some of the techniques used in contract management are applicable to simple applications where the objectives are clear and singular.

■ Trade contracts

Appropriate for a single operation such as recovering a roof or repairing plasterwork where one team can provide all the skills without resorting to subcontractors. Thus experience and familiarity can be harnessed and overheads reduced.

■ Time and materials

When subcontractors and craftspeople can be trusted, personal contact and control between client, professional and builder can reduce time and costs by eliminating overheads retaining flexibility and encouraging innovative on-site solutions.

■ Rates (via partnering) and re-measurement

The cost per unit is known – but the number of units is not. Cost is controllable but the outcome may be unpredictable. Useful for complex fast track projects where access has not been available, it requires teamwork and trust. Avoidance of confrontation, reduced duplication and increased flexibility create a virtuous circle of increasing quality and reduced costs.

Partnering agreements harness the desire of both client and contractor to develop a good working relationship where the client is in a position to commission a number of projects (e.g. a chain of pub or restaurant conversions).

■ Approximate quantities

Provides an estimate of the outcome where the nature of work is predictable but the quantity variable because time for survey and preparing drawings is limited. Also relies upon a schedule of rates for cost control.

■ Fixed price

Potentially still offers the most certainty as long as the work to be undertaken is designed and carefully measured before the contract is let.

There are various contracts, the most common being the Joint Contracts Tribunal (JCT 80) for large and complex projects; a Minor Building Works contract which is appropriate for projects up to £150,000 and Intermediate Form (IFC 84) for projects between £100,000 and £1 million. The IFC 84 limits the number of nominated sub-contractors so if specialist contractors are required use the JCT 80.

■ Variations

Although called 'Fixed Price', there are a series of clauses under which the contractor can be reimbursed by additional payment or time extensions.

Avoid arguments over lack of information by engaging a good architect, allowing enough time for design, and choosing builders who work well as a team and are non-litigious.

Allow for minor changes, but ensure the client is fully aware of the proposal before the building starts so they can let the team get on with the job, without variations.

The certainty of the more traditional forms of contract has to be weighed against the extra time taken to prepare them and the inherent costs of an essentially confrontational relationship where the contractor seeks increased income by finding flaws in the contract documentation. The better the documentation the higher the contract sum (tender price) but the lower the final account.

Whilst competitive tendering is appropriate for commonplace elements, it is not essential for specialist work. The choice of contract form should depend on how much specialist trades, traditional or innovative, are involved. The architect can organise specification and contract documentation accordingly. Use the building as a reference document. It helps to know the specialists and their capabilities; their knowledge and experience may be worth a higher price.

■ DESIGN AND DOCUMENTATION

The RIBA sets out the stages for managing a project following scheme design (D); detail design (E); production information – drawings, schedules and specifications (F and G) up to tendering, planning and operations on site (H, J, K and L).[2]

These stages need to be addressed, but they can be varied as appropriate when dealing with refurbishment and conversion. For instance, when preparing inspection reports, undertake a full survey itemising and describing the work to be done in a specification form, which can be used to obtain prices and act as a schedule of work – thereby combining the survey and production information stages. Photocopies of photographs can be effective in describing location and extent of work, especially if access for inspection was gained by special means such as a scaffolding tower, cherry picker or helicopter.

■ Detailed design

Detailed design should enable building and fire regulations approval to be complied with, along with calculations for ventilation, lighting standards, fire spread, structural support and personnel safety. All components will need to be identified and described. Choices of materials and technical solutions may still be innovative (11.1).

■ Co-ordination: structure and services

This is the stage that all the team professionals' information can be co-ordinated. When agreeing on changes, it is worth checking whether some of the work can be combined. For example, if you need to open up the fabric in key locations to allow the insertion of a new structure, consider whether this route can also be used for

Example 11.1

USE: Prison (previously converted to flats)
Burlington Lodge Studios, Fulham
Victorian, brick, adjacent to courtyard.

TO: Office
Conversion restricted to dry trades, black
and white colour scheme and utilises glazed
screens, spiral stair and mezzanines to create
dramatic spatial form. Using mdf, good
ironmongery and expensive chairs combines
both parsimony and luxury. Purpose
designed lightshade/sunscreens protect the
conservatory.

A: Weston Williamson[3]

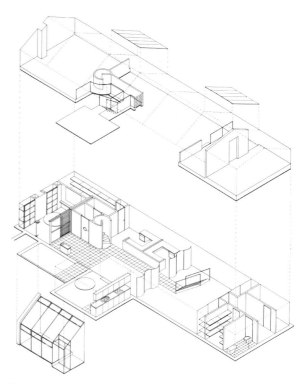

Early axonometric of the scheme for presentation to the client in order to explain the relationship between spaces.

Sunscreen/lighting in the conservatory.

Reflection of the studio.

services. Or perhaps the services route can double up for the new structure. Costs can be compared. If, for instance, you were thinking of channelling out masonry to provide conduits for alarm cables, it may cost less to install new remote control alarms.

Some elements may surface that dictate the method used around them. For example, in St Mary's Church, Nottingham, a pair of large bore heating pipes run either side of the knave, just below clerestory level, highly visible, but creating a heat curtain to reduce down-draughts from the windows. These can be replaced by electric panel heaters only 30 mm thick placed upon the sloping sill of each clerestory window and painted to match the stone, barely discernible by the naked eye, allowing the removal of the unsightly pipework.

■ Communication

One professional can prepare a simple master drawing to which others can refer – either physically, on CAD or via the Internet. Using these forms of communication can challenge the team members to come up with innovative solutions. Nicholas Grimshaw and partners have achieved a good example at the new baths in Bath. Here, a structural engineer, architect, and services engineer have devised a double-glazed wall filled with warm spa water. Their construction achieves light translucency, minimal condensation, no down-draughts, privacy by obscurity, and a visible expression of the movement of water.

Once the architect and his team have firm detailed designs and decided upon methods of communication, they can start to prepare the drawings, specification and schedules. These will describe every detail from the first element to be demolished, to the cleaning of the last room. They will then form a legal document to be measured by the quantity surveyor and costed down to the last nut and bolt. They will need several weeks to work to this end.

■ Drawings and schedules

Good contract documents should be comprehensible and unambiguous. When dealing with existing buildings, the intended arrangements can be related to a centre line, or an equal rhythm and need not be dimensioned. Consider scheduling work in the context of the various trades and operatives and not simply as a list of contract procedures. Matching an existing detail by description rather than drawing it may make it more comprehensible.

A National Building Specification (NBS) is available in both a full and small works version. However, where creative re-use involves conservation work, strict adherence to Co-ordinated Production Information (CPI) within the NBS can sometimes involve extended additions and alterations to the basic copy.

A flexible contract arrangement can enable a more flexible method of specifying. Thus an item of work described in a schedule using the QS/Estimator's language of standard clauses for measurement and pricing can be also written as a clear, specific instruction to the on-site craftsperson. Informal time plus material contracts, cutting down paperwork can save time and money. An instruction can even be a spoken one accompanying a detail diagram on the wall.

■ THE CONTRACTOR

Before appointing a contractor, visit the ones on the shortlist first. An inspection of their premises can tell you more than a lengthy presentation. Always try to meet the team who would actually work on the project and assess their track record.

Only consider the contractors you think would be right for the job. If there are only three on the tender list, the tenders may be keener and more constructive. If you know that one contractor is particularly well suited, you could decide to negotiate directly, instead of inviting tenders. It is often better value to select on quality rather than price.

■ ON SITE

At this stage, proposals should be implemented according to the design and specifications. The project team should be prepared to reconsider decisions but only within the parameters of the brief and constraints of the contract. Momentum and focus must be maintained.

Nevertheless, expect the unexpected. The following are just a few possibilities:

- Unsuspected constructional techniques causing a review of structural strengthening methods.
- Unknown voids in the structure requiring sealing, ventilating or filling.
- Hidden attacks of rot or beetle requiring removal or treatment.
- Drains which interconnect when they shouldn't.
- Poorly detailed materials such as metal roofing, which require refixing to enable expansion or contraction.
- Conflicting materials that have deteriorated due to acid attack or electrolysis.
- The discovery of archaeological remains.

■ Archaeological remains

Archaeological remains may take the form of early buildings covered over by later generations (often re-using some of the original materials which may give an early clue); or parts of early timber frames or windows encapsulated within the walls (11.2); or wall paintings under layers of distemper or paint, requiring conservation and protection.

Archaeological discoveries need additional expertise to evaluate them. They may only require recording before loss; they may be capable of removal to a more appropriate location, secure stable and suitably displayed and away from conflict; or they may be regarded as so important that they must remain in situ. Developers often view

Example   11.2

USE: Farm/hall, Derbyshire
c1480, Grade II, two-storey with 1620 stone front and nineteenth century brick rear disguising original timber frame hall house with parlour, solar and cross wing. Deteriorated into near dereliction.

TO: Home
Refurbishment exposed the previously uninspected timber frame. Simple no-interventionist improvements and eco-friendly living style with lime washed walls, sisal mat floors and open fires provide a perfectly sustainable environment.

A: Latham Architects

Timber frame revealed.

Original hidden fireplace revealed.

them as an unwanted disruption, yet they can be seized upon as opportunities. When put on display as part of the new re-use, they can add historic value to the building: a particular bonus if the public will see it in say, a pub, hotel or restaurant. If the relic cannot be displayed, or even threatens the re-use project, radical rethinking may be needed, as well as diplomacy and decisive action.

■ Finding artefacts

When first taking over a disused building, be aware that among the rubbish of recent occupation might lie some valuable or interesting artefacts. If you should come across them, find out what relevance and use they once had. It may be possible to incorporate them into the final project. I am not suggesting this inspection is treated as an archaeological dig, but nevertheless look carefully for interesting items. By doing this I have discovered: a Minton tile floor and pulpit rail in an abandoned church; newel posts, handrails, parapet pinnacles and other key stones on the floor of a ruined building; an original jeweller's bench in converted housing; 1820s newspapers in the flimsy partition wall of a folly, and a sundry collection of books, instruments, equipment and furniture. Sometimes the more obvious artefacts need rescuing. At first sight a set of railway buffers within a building may appear entirely inappropriate for the new use proposed, but if retained, this same set of buffers may well indicate the building's original use. (See St Mary's Goods Warehouse, 17.3, Volume Two.)

■ Team spirit

In order to foster a team spirit, the professional team must develop individual working relationships with specialists in the building team, listening and encouraging them to contribute their knowledge and demonstrate their skills.

The site team may have unsuspected abilities and experience, and provide some invaluable suggestions for overcoming problems. It could be that with a little extra time, a lead drip, metal railing, turned newel or paint finish can be lifted to the extra-ordinary, adding delight and interest without seriously affecting overall cost or timetable.

Professionals may wish to achieve special effects of repair or restoration especially textures with such materials as plaster finishing. Being prepared to get hands dirty by trying to demonstrate the effect may teach the operative a new technique, or at least show the professional's intent.

It is not unusual for the client to suddenly ask for changes. This may be for a number of reasons: family relationships, company take-over, financial hardship or changes of policy, or because the client has become aware of the full potential of the refurbished building. As long as the client understands the consequences of making irreversible changes at this stage, and the effect on costs, this may be an opportunity for the client and architect to realise an even better vision. To retain financial control the scope of the original contract could be reduced and a separate contract negotiated or even tendered.

Good project management requires not only compliance with production drawings and specification, but an ability to respond quickly to possible threats and recognise opportunities to provide a sensitive human touch.

REFERENCES

1. cf Appendix in this Volume, page 215, Principles for Re-use.
2. *Architect's Appointment*, RIBA Publications Ltd, 1990.
3. Owens, R., 'New Life for Buildings 5: Studio Workspace', *Architects Journal*, Vol 187, No. 33, 1988, pp 47–52.

**Empress brewery, Manchester: 'fermenting
businesses'**

A sympathetic conversion has transformed the derelict
and tatty Victorian Empress Brewery in Manchester into
managed business space with a timeless quality.

Key issues involved in re-use were:

- Demolition of a long brick lean-to enabling road
  widening which improved access.
- Introduction of new floors including mezzanines, and
  reorganisation of others, with inconspicuous alterations to windows.
- Additional support structure, where necessary,
  respecting existing structural rhythm.
- Basement opened up with ramped access.
- Extension, in character presented a respectable face
  to passing traffic on the main road.
- New buildings of robust character, extending the
  range of space available and creating a sense of place.

The following article by Sarah Hardcastle published in
Building (26 February 1993) describes the project.

Compared with its more illustrious neighbour – a
former life assurance office of towering Victorian
splendour – the Empress Brewery is a straightforward, no-frills, factory building in typical late
nineteenth century style. Pruned, extended and refurbished, it is now the focal point of the Empress
Business Centre, which includes new-build
factory/workshop blocks in complementary style
arranged to form a quadrangle.

Situated a mile west of Manchester's city centre,
the completed £4m development offers 1,858 sq m

of managed office accommodation and 3,121 sq m
of workshop space in a variety of unit sizes geared to
the needs of small business ventures. Grosvenor
Laing Urban Enterprise was the developer – a
partnership formed in 1988 between John Laing and
Grosvenor Estates to handle inner city projects.

Like many Victorian industrial buildings, the
brewery rises straight from the pavement and originally comprised four sections ranging from single to
seven-storeys high, plus a tower. When conversion
work began in 1991, 'it was derelict and the rear yard
had a series of desperately tatty buildings'.[a]

Grosvenor Laing's brief was to turn the whole site
'into usable space in as hard-headed a way as possible. However, they accepted that our philosophy is to
respect the pattern and history of a building and that
we would strive to achieve a compromise between
that and the most commercial answer. What they did
was to set financial targets and left us to resolve the
architectural and heritage problems'.

Only Mancunians familiar with the site will be able
to put a finger on Latham's subtle changes to the

Section before.

Typical plan after.

The completed business park creating its own urban square.

Section after.

Elevation after showing adjustments to window opening.

exterior of the brewery buildings. On the street elevation a single-storey, brick lean-to was demolished to enable road widening, and six window lintels were lowered to squeeze in a floor level. As the new brick lintel infill matches existing decorative panels elsewhere on the facade, the change is unnoticeable.

A two-storey extension in matching brick with an octagonal end and hipped roof replaces a tatty single-storey section. Brick ramps were excavated to provide a route to the previously inaccessible basement. Its former hopper chute openings were turned into windows, with arched brick lintels added to match the rest of the building.

Windows have been added elsewhere. The third storey now has a new horizontal run of eight windows with arched lintels, while wooden louvres in the former brewery's vents on the fourth storey have been replaced with clerestory lights. The building's original 'warehouse'-style windows with wide arched brick lintels have been retained. The new frames are standard units in colour-coated steel with single glazing, from Metal Casements.

The toughest challenge internally, was accommodating the building's list. Like a tanker in a storm, it has a fall and cross-fall, 225 mm out over the length, with a 125 mm difference front to rear. It is also out of plumb.

This means the windows sills aren't level and slope across the building. You would notice this inside, but we've masked it to a great extent by keeping a distance between floors and sills. There's also differential settlement between the new and old elements of the building that we've tackled by making internal elements – such as floors and beams – structurally independent of the exterior walls. The basement was also difficult, as we had to excavate to insert a lift shaft and new column bases, which then led to temporary flooding.[b]

Floors were another challenge. Existing levels varied across the building's four sections, so these were realigned where possible, and new floors positioned to create generously high rooms with beautifully balanced windows. Half- and three-quarter size-mezzanine levels, supported on coated steel columns, have been 'dropped' into some storeys where full-width floors would have impeded the windows or distorted the relationship of window to room height. They also add to the interior's charm.

Latham has made the most of the original features, leaving exposed areas of brick wall, timber trusses and beams. Graceful cast-iron structural columns have been kept, and steel replicas made where additional support was needed.

Most atmospheric are the basement, with its low, brick, triple-vaulted ceiling supported by cast-iron columns, and the fourth-storey open-sided mezzanine set beneath a pine-clad pitched roof inset with clerestory lights. Equally dramatic is the new two-storey

Bay after, showing old and new brickwork. (*Stuart Blackwood*)

octagonal-end extension, which also has a mezzanine floor reached by a spiral staircase and a pine-clad roof.

The offices are of varying sizes – from two-person upwards. Cream walls, green carpet and paintwork, coupled with blond timber doors with glazed inserts; create a light, natural environment. Electrical, heating and telecommunications services are trunked around the perimeter walls. Creating an appealing environment has paid off, as less than a year after it was opened the main building has 92 per cent occupancy [1993].

Latham's 'sense of place' is fully realised with three new-build terraced factory/workshop blocks that lie at the rear of the Empress Building. Instead of lining the blocks in a row, to maximise space they are pleasingly arranged to form a courtyard.

A far cry from 'crinkly tin', Latham has given the two-storey, pitched roof blocks a 'large-scale rugged look', which cleverly ties in with the Empress's architecture but avoids Victorian pastiche. The brick elevations are topped with corbelled, coped brick parapets, while the relief panels are in common brickwork 'to reflect industrial detail on the original buildings'.

To create a sense of 'massiveness', first floor windows and glazed entrance doors are arranged in pairs along the elevations. Window and door frames are standard colour-coated steel Crittall units arranged in a pattern that relates to the brewery's glazing. 'We wanted a timeless quality. I don't think people will look at these units and be able to put a date on them. It is achieved by avoiding fashionable elements.'

Latham's approach is undoubtedly effective. 'By picking up character and taking it through, you present the building not as it was, but as it might have been if sympathetic extensions and alterations had been made to it over a period of time.'

■ **References**
a. Derek Latham.
b. Project Architect: Raphael Waksberg.

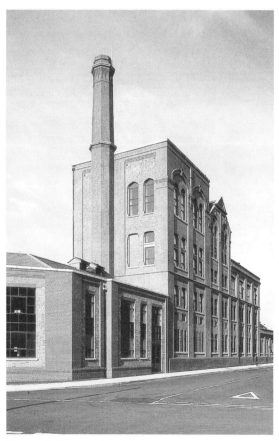

The new 'B1' terraced workshop units connect to the converted brewery. (*Stuart Blackwood*)

'B1' units with inexpensive brick and window detailing in empathy with that on the brewery. (*Stuart Blackwood*)

PART THREE

POST COMPLETION

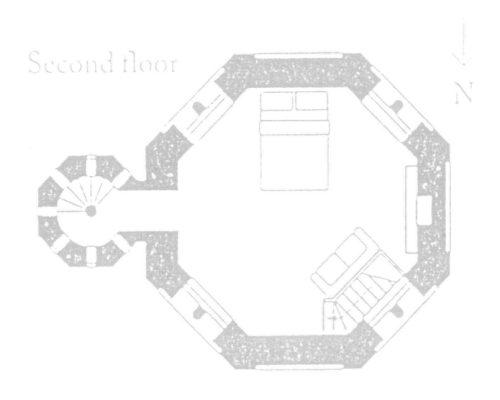

Second floor

N

CHAPTER 12

Management in Use

It is not always feasible to complete a project and then hand it over to the client. If it is speculative, the property may be developed to a certain stage at which the building is marketed, and the eventual tenant or purchaser will complete the process (ideally instructing the original project team to continue to completion). If bespoke, then commissioning and occupation become an integral part of the process enabling the client to harmonise with the building more easily.

Completion of a re-use project marks its rebirth. The building will need good management and care to reach its optimum lifespan. The management will need to maintain the building in good condition, respect the building's history as well as understand the needs of the users.

■ CARE OF THE BUILDING

■ Long life

Apart from routine maintenance there will certainly be special requirements to retain the building's character and preserve its original quality. Even when a purchaser hopes to get by with minimal maintenance costs, they will normally have to provide for specialist cleaning and redecoration due to factors such as extra high walls and ceilings; light fittings that are expensive to replace; the need to conserve delicate elements such as mouldings on plaster and joinery, or original ironmongery; or compliance with regulations such as remote control fire detection and alarm systems, and relaxation of 'Deemed to Satisfy' procedures in favour of a strategic plan of operations.

Aiming for a low maintenance or low energy consuming building can involve the installation of complex and sophisticated systems. When they go wrong they are very expensive to repair. The wise designer will have ensured that cableways and equipment remain discreetly accessible, despite conservation considerations requiring them to be covered. An overall balanced approach needs to be decided upon, having weighed up the possible costs of a fully automated system against the convenience of individual user control with more ongoing active maintenance.

■ Limited life

The elements of a building will vary in lifespan, either due to choice of materials or prevailing conditions. Where rehabilitation assumed a more limited life, the facilities manager will have to make crucial decisions about when and how to repair. A slate roof may start to fail because the nails rust through, but simple replacement of slipped slates by tingling may be a cost-effective remedy that could work for years. If passers-by were in jeopardy, or the roof was exposed to high winds, more radical measures may be necessary. The cost of replacing remote elements weighs against their assumed longevity. It is cheaper to replace loose slates, one at a time, on a single-storey than a church steeple.

Similar considerations will apply to eroding masonry, glazing and worn floorboards, rusting steel and creeping leadwork. No one's safety should ever be put at risk, but after that, cost considerations need to be made. A property that is well maintained, however, will require less (or later) large scale replacements.

■ Continuing repair

Repairs are not always undertaken, even though needed in normal circumstances. This may occur in the care and occasional restoration of ancient monuments. Occupied, if at all, by a custodian, with office, store, exhibition, shop or café, they are really visitor attractions and may require repairs to be managed over many years, to reduce the attendant disruption.

Sometimes repairs are delayed in order to understand the problem better. Monitoring a building over seven years, in all seasons, may lead to a greater understanding of the long-term pattern of cyclical movement. More effective and appropriate repairs could then be made. Some minor repairs may still be made during that time, to keep the building habitable, but radical work would be put off until later. This may require low key use in affected areas, removable partitions or different service distribution with appropriate isolated points.

■ Monitoring

Monitoring a structure does not always end in action. Say, for instance, some valuable panelling has been affected by dry rot. At one time this would have been radically removed, and the surrounding area heavily treated with chemicals. Current technology allows us to retain the panelling, but remove the humidity in the voids behind the panelling which causes the rot to develop. Then monitoring is very important to ensure correct climatic conditions are being maintained. Such techniques imply a pact between the creative re-use team and the facilities manager, though the two may never meet.

■ RESPECTING THE BUILDING'S HISTORY

Consider the interpretation of the building in the most innovative and attractive way for the user and the public.[1]

Many people may be interested in the re-use of buildings. The occupiers will undoubtedly be keen to learn about it, but in many cases it will have a wider public appeal. (Occasional public access is sometimes a requirement of grant aid.) This interest can only lead to a greater general respect of historic buildings, and less vandalism. Birmingham Workhouse, now converted to a hotel, is a good example (12.1).

Example	**12.1**

USE: Workhouse, Rowton House, Birmingham
1903, Grade II, Harry Measures, five-storey Ruabon and terracotta, Gothic, with entrance hall, dining room, library and games room.

TO: Hotel, Chamberlain
Retaining the interior of the tiled dining room and colombian pine panelling of the library a modern conference hotel has been created whilst eight of the former bedrooms are replicated for historic interest.

D: Rose Project Services[2]

Rowston House (poor house) converted to The Chamberlain Hotel. (*Simon Livinsgtone*)

The dining room with the original glazed bricks still on the walls. (*Simon Livinsgtone*)

A building can interest people in various ways. Some will want to know about its construction; others will be more interested in previous occupants, or in its related social history. They should all be able to appreciate and understand the building. The scholar may be able to add to his own extensive knowledge, but the curious layman should also be given the means to understand and interpret the building. Both should enjoy a sense of personal discovery. Richard Attenborough once said of the remarkable films he directed:

> My objective is to present the truth, but not in such a wholly accurate way that it is limited merely to the epicentre of the film buff, but to allow more generalised understanding of the truth that is open to and appeals to everyone, for generalised truth that is received by millions is a far more successful message than an exact one that is only received by hundreds.

Example **12.2**

USE: Prison, Alcatraz – The Silent Sentence
The island of Alcatraz in the Bay of San Francisco, USA, is no longer used as a prison. The fabric is hardly historic by European standards and there are no special technical forms of construction to be observed. One cell looks much like another and larger rooms look like – just larger rooms.

TO: Visitor experience
However, when the visitor dons a set of earphones to guide them around the complex, explaining as they walk through different doors, what each of the wings was used for, recording the sounds of the prison when in use, re-enacting the riot and personalising the experiences of some of the inmates in different cells, then the building comes alive and the empty rooms need no 'reproduction artefacts' to furnish them, for reality is in the mind. It is not until the headphones are removed and, in the ensuing silence, one witnesses person after person silently walking through, and turn by turn looking first to this side and then to the other, and then sitting in a cell and gently closing the door, looking around them in wonderment, clearly participating with their own headphones in their own private interpretation independent of everyone else, that the brilliance of this reality can be fully understood.

The Alcatraz experience.

Example   12.3

USE: Ancient monument: Tutbury Castle
Twelfth century summertime seat of King
John and Court. Stone curtain wall with
towers plus motte and bailey.

TO: Interpreted visitor attraction
Although open to visitors the castle seemed a
well kept secret. Study of old documents
showed the hill had been kept free of trees
until the nineteenth century. Removal of the
sycamores surrounding the tower remnant
exposed it to the skyline, advertising its
presence, attracting visitors and presenting
its defensive role more clearly.

In preparing an interpretative study for the
Castle, consideration was given to restoring
floors and ceilings to better enable people to
interpret the structure. Not only would this
solution be expensive but the degree of
conjectural intervention necessary to achieve
it would have seriously eroded the value of
the structure. Interpretation was therefore
proposed by means of a model and
modelscope in a visitor centre prior to seeing
the castle. Any conjectural elements of
reconstruction in the model would then have
no deleterious effect upon the structure. Such
a method can be further extended with a sort
of model *son et lumière* as used at Hampton
Court to explain the use of kitchen rooms,
social habits and even anecdotes of the time.

The trees on the motte.

The bailey without trees.

■ **Let others interpret the building**

In practice, interpretation aids can take the form of written explanations and or photographs and paintings. Unless the management understands that education about the building is part of their duty, there is a danger of it being neglected. Fitted carpets may cover valuable floors, new surfaces replace worn ones, and partitions could be installed. Sometimes these may be done to protect precious artefacts, but the main hope is that these actions can be reversed. They can even have more serious consequences for the building. There have been instances where suspended ceilings have been fitted to allow partitions to be fitted. Then, when IT operatives arrived to install cables, they drilled through mouldings which they thought were unimportant as they were hidden away.

A good starting point is for the creative re-use team to explain and emphasise the need for careful management to the first user. Hopefully, the message will then be passed on to subsequent users and a climate of care and respect for their historic building will be engendered and unwitting or institutionalised damage avoided.

■ USE OF THE BUILDING

Balance the need for public access against the maintenance requirements of the property.[3]

To gain the maximum benefits from the building, its future management should be considered as an integral part of the proposals for its re-use.

There is an intrinsic conflict between maintenance of historic fabric and user access in all buildings, whether managed by English Heritage, the National Trust or private owners. Many of our national monuments are now measured by the number of visitors they can attract rather than for their intrinsic architectural or historical qualities. The floor to a pretty country house can receive more wear in one year of public access than in its entire life previously. The public can actually wear away the artefact they have come to see.

One effective way of limiting the numbers is by setting up a booking system. This allows anyone seriously interested to visit the property, yet precludes the curious hordes too idle to book who would otherwise damage it. A most appropriate method is that employed by some private houses who open their doors for booked dinner parties – the house being used for the purpose it was intended – a perfect form of interpretation.

■ **Managing for sale or to let**

Only buildings of exceptional historic interest will rely on visitors for their re-use. The management of others may simply involve preparing the property for marketing.

In this case the building needs to retain a strong image whilst offering as many re-use possibilities as it can. Marketing agents often refer to industrial space as sheds, retail space is called shell only, and offices are shell and core. The more the portfolio has to be managed because it is to be let or sold to a number of tenants or occupiers, such as in a shopping centre, the greater impact that management will have upon the brief. But within each unit options will be left open for the tenant to meet his individual needs.

■ Residential use

Developing properties on a speculative basis, and offering them as shells for residential use is becoming increasingly popular. This follows an American trend, and is illustrated by the number of loft conversion companies. They buy a redundant building, and resell the space with enough flexibility for the purchaser to fit it out to their own taste. The developers tend to acquire buildings with large floor to ceiling heights, capable of accommodating mezzanine floors, so they can sell volume rather than area. The purchaser than has the choice of leaving it as a single lofty space, or turning it into two-floor accommodation. This last option is not so effective, and can restrict daylight, but it is their choice to do so.

These residential units will be sold using show houses demonstrating their potential to live a different lifestyle. So much creativity has been applied to this concept, that it has actually changed people's attitudes towards housing in general. Whereas in the 1980s, housing purchase was investment led, in the 1990s after the housing market crashed, younger people started to consider living style as a higher priority. This is evidence of the role creative re-use plays in the market place.

■ Involving the commercial user

With all uses, it is best to have the end user involved in the re-use process, preferably having commissioned it in the first place. The user can be involved at the beginning before work starts on site. They can assist in developing a maintenance and management strategy, influence the design, and clarify decisions on site. On larger projects, it is advantageous to appoint the management team from the start, so they can put their points forward about the way the services will operate. They can remind the designers about their need for such things as practical cleaning methods, easily replaceable lamps, integrated alarm systems, adequate provision for IT, small recesses for drinks machines, signage, and any other requirements. User groups may also be involved at this time. A change in accommodation may be associated with a change in culture and working practices, but bear in mind they may not be able to visualise the completed picture.

■ Managing change

Some decisions about the fitting of a property are best left until after the users have moved in. Sometimes the move will cause different work patterns. For example, lavish staff accommodation and a canteen could be provided and yet found to be under-used as the new building is in an area full of restaurants and shops. Or a change in commuter patterns may create pressure for flexitime or hot-desking. These ideas could well occur during the design process, but have to be tested in reality first.

It is a good idea to arrange an induction meeting for all the incoming staff, to help them work within the building, and give them an opportunity to make suggestions for improvements – useful feedback to the design team too.

■ Fine tuning

The Design and Production Team will usually be involved for a year or so follow-ing contract completion to monitor the building during the Defects Liability period and agree the Final Account. The wise client will have set aside a budget for fine-tuning of user facilities with which the architect can assist. This could actually continue indefinitely, say, on an annual basis, until all the adjustments are made.

To avoid misunderstanding and unnecessary adjustments, the project teams must explain to the management team exactly what maintenance is required. Even in a small-scale property, it helps if the owner is committed to keeping the property up to scratch.

■ Maintenance manual

A maintenance manual should be supplied to the owner. This should give informa-tion on the following:

- Why certain materials were used.
- What is old or authentic and what is a replica.
- Information about cleaning, repairing and replacing any items.
- Location of service entries and the on/off position for stop taps.
- How to work the heating system and mechanical extractor fans.
- The location of ring mains and their capacity.
- Advice on wearing soft shoes if walking along lead gutters.
- Instructions to use a crawling ladder to reach over slate roofs.
- What not to put down the toilet or waste disposal.
- How frequently to paint the outside.
- What to do in the case of fire.

- Procedures for potential or optional additions or alterations.
- External requirements – who owns and has responsibility for maintaining which walls; where and when parking is allowed.
- Advice on over-hanging trees and any tree preservation orders.

The maintenance manual can be provided in a loose-leaf format in a ring binder to enable additions by owner or tenant regarding maintenance of white goods, telecommunication or other electrical equipment and guarantees for items purchased. In 1999, owners of Railways Cottages refurbished in 1981 were still using the maintenance manuals provided at the time. New owners were still contacting the architect to check out guarantees for woodworm treatment and damp proof course insertion long after the installing companies had ceased trading. The manuals should include concise, sensitive, jargon- free information for the general user, or the companies' staff that can form part of the induction process.

■ Building management systems

Larger properties need more complex and responsive management systems, run by a facilities manager who can monitor the impact of use.

Restrictions will have to be imposed on some buildings. This could be the number of visitors – necessitating queue management, or user capacity in public assembly buildings due to limited fire escape provisions, or a limit on loadings at mid-span in old structures. Any such restrictions too should be set out in a loose-leaf manual. When the Empress Brewery, Manchester was converted into a managed business centre, three large lever-arch files, including as built drawings, formed its mainte-nance manual.

It helps if the facilities manager is involved throughout the development process, and can contribute to the maintenance manual. This may not be possible as he may be contracted or employed later, and the manual must be robust enough to enable this.

Management of the building must be regarded as an integral part of the creative re-use process. Good communication between the project team and owner or manager is essential. Involvement of the users in the care of the building and the appreciation of its historic context represents a good prescription for the building's continued health.

REFERENCES

1. cf Appendix in this Volume, page 215, Principles for Re-use.
2. Owner.
3. cf Appendix in this Volume, page 215, Principles for Re-use.

From: **Theological College**
To: **Office Headquarters**
        11–13 Cavendish Square, London W1: a
        multi-professional approach

The King's Fund brief required an increase in net useable floor area of 20 per cent on existing. A successful mixture of conservation, rehabilitation and redevelopment resulting in a structured and accessible environment. This was achieved in the face of planning restrictions, the constraints of a tight inner city site, embracing a variety of built form with little cohesive layout or levels. They key factors enabling re-use were:

■ **Historical research to understand the building's incremental development**

Two pairs of houses with a fine, five bay, Paladian style façade of Portland stone, were built around 1770 by G F Tufnel. Between the houses was an opening – Deans Mews – aligned on the axis of Cavendish and Hanover Square, and retained as one of London's important site lines. However the space only ever led to a mews yard which housed laundries, a split-level coach house, and a small walled crescent for turning coaches.

Acquired by the Convent of the Holy Child of Jesus in the early 1890s, substantial changes were made to the rear, followed in 1912 by a three-storey teaching building constructed behind Nos 11 and 12. The Convent acquired No. 13 and constructed a large new building (c 1930 E W Banfield, ARIBA) adjacent to the 1912 building at the rear. The south façade of this is on the key site line from Hanover Square, as viewed down the length of Deans Mews. In the early 1950s architect Louis Osman undertook alterations and constructed a bridge link between Tufnel's two original houses. Osman adorned this with a lead sculpture of the Madonna and Child by Jacob Epstein. By 1960 a chapel, lecture room and a residential block were built to the north end of the site; designed by architects Walworth, Hill and Brown who in 1963 also added a fourth-storey to the 1912 building.

Front to Cavendish Square.

Stair hall in No. 11 restored. (*Stuart Blackwood*)

■ Evaluating and utilising the relative significance of different areas

One of the attractions of the buildings was the way in which the diversity of interiors could benefit the variety of functions. The listed interiors of the buildings fronting the Square lent themselves to boardroom and small conference use, while the 1912/1930 buildings in the centre of the site yielded a mix of open-plan and cellular offices. Reconstruction at the north of the site catered for specialist spaces requiring large clear spans. This mix of volumes, combined with the ancillary basement spaces and under pavement vaults, suited the King's Fund brief.

Mews entrance before.

Mews/Main entrance after (also note raised mansard roof). (*Stuart Blackwood*)

■ **Rationalising floor levels to facilitate disabled access**

Intermittent development of the site over 300 years had resulted in a disparate collection of structures and spaces with numerous changes of level. The 1960s chapel and the multi-level residential buildings on the north of the site were demolished to allow for a new construction which would tie in with the principal levels of the 1912/1930 building. The mansard roof of the 1930s block was removed and a new floor and roof inserted 1.2 m higher. This achieved disability access direct to all five floors of accommodation from the new entrance and reduced the by product of circulation space.

■ **Locating a new lift in a part of the 1770s building altered in the 1950s**

At the front, No. 13 Cavendish Square was linked to No. 12 by Osman's bridge and the tunnel under Deans Mews, so a new lift was inserted within the area already altered in the 1950s (in preference to that with original interiors) to enable wheelchair access at each level.

■ **Relocating the secondary entrance as the main entrance centred on the mews access**

The entrance to the former Heythrop College that was tucked into the corner of the 1930s elevation was moved by one bay to centre on the critical axis through the Square and create the new main entrance. Visual impact was further increased by the construction of a stone portico and stone architrave to the window above.

■ **Removing twentieth-century additions from the courtyard and opening up the original lightwells to the basement**

The courtyard provides valuable, protected, external space to the east of the site. This runs from the back of the listed buildings, past the 1912 block, to the new construction at the north of the site. A single London plane tree dominates the space, its root system finding ways through the wall construction of the basement accommodation directly below.

■ **Utilising the basement level to connect the three sets of buildings**

The only link between the more recent buildings at the rear, and the listed buildings was by way of a single-storey toilet block lit with a lantern rooflight. This link became pivotal in the smooth operation of the King's Fund Headquarters, once it had been converted into a garden room overlooking the courtyard. The basement area was opened up to create a corridor link connecting all buildings with ramps to accommodate changes of level.

Lightwell before.

Lightwell/new staircase hall after.

Replacement building at the rear. (*Stuart Blackwood*)

Garden court with replacement building behind tree, conservatory behind arches. (*Stuart Blackwood*)

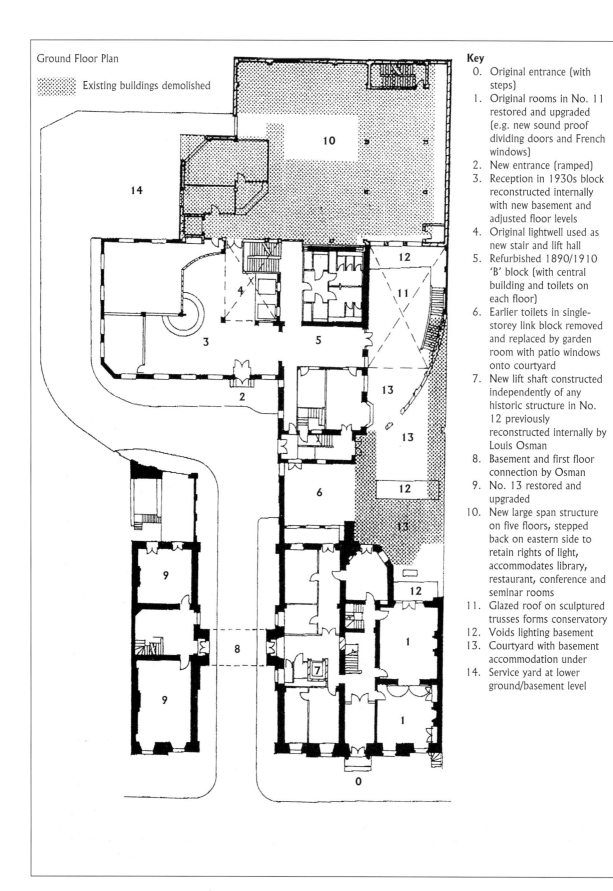

Ground Floor Plan

░░░░ Existing buildings demolished

Key

0. Original entrance (with steps)
1. Original rooms in No. 11 restored and upgraded (e.g. new sound proof dividing doors and French windows)
2. New entrance (ramped)
3. Reception in 1930s block reconstructed internally with new basement and adjusted floor levels
4. Original lightwell used as new stair and lift hall
5. Refurbished 1890/1910 'B' block (with central building and toilets on each floor)
6. Earlier toilets in single-storey link block removed and replaced by garden room with patio windows onto courtyard
7. New lift shaft constructed independently of any historic structure in No. 12 previously reconstructed internally by Louis Osman
8. Basement and first floor connection by Osman
9. No. 13 restored and upgraded
10. New large span structure on five floors, stepped back on eastern side to retain rights of light, accommodates library, restaurant, conference and seminar rooms
11. Glazed roof on sculptured trusses forms conservatory
12. Voids lighting basement
13. Courtyard with basement accommodation under
14. Service yard at lower ground/basement level

■ **Replace the 1950s residential and amenity blocks with a large, open span building**

The full volume available at the rear northern end of the site was used on five levels for specialist spaces: library, bookstore, restaurant, two conference suites with lecture room, seminar rooms, crush foyer, and offices on the top floor.

■ **Glazing over a lightwell to form a lift and staircase hall**

The 1912/1930 buildings had developed around an external well which acted as a vertical service shaft with a toilet block at its base. This uninviting space became an internal atrium, by the new entrance. It houses the principal staircase and scenic lifts, enabling an efficient use of circulation at each floor level, and it still boosts internal daylight where needed.

■ **Modern conservatory provides social space and allows daylight down to basement**

Planning policy prevented an additional top floor, so a conservatory was constructed at the north end of the courtyard, uniting a variety of disparate spaces and providing an information meeting room, also accessible from the lower ground conference spaces. A bar was developed within the vaults directly below.

■ **Reconstruction of arcaded walling to separate the new from the conserved**

The former curved, arcaded wall which bounded the carriage route down to stabling in the early eighteenth century was reconstructed to act as a visual foil between the contemporary conservatory structure, and the listed houses on Cavendish Square.

■ **Material character**

The restoration of the listed buildings required specialist trades and skills: fibrous plaster works, running of cornices, gilding, fireplace restoration, and the upgrading of panelled doors and claddings to meet the fire safety requirements. Where possible, crown glass was specified for refurbishment. Internal decoration was based upon specialist historical paint analysis to achieve colours contemporary to late eighteenth-century interiors. The exterior avoided large-scale restoration and underwent local repair where water penetration was a risk. Bomb damage to the Cavendish Square elevations was deliberately left as part of the surface patina. Similarly, brick repointing was selective, with lime tuck pointing deployed. Joinery in the new and refurbished areas is maple for solid sections, with sycamore veneer for facings. The reception floor is of slate and limestone. For daylight to penetrate down to the base of the atrium, toughened glass is used in the balustrading.

■ **Fire strategy**

Extensive negotiations with the authorities resulted in a successful, non-intrusive fire strategy. Compartmentation within the listed buildings was achieved by upgrading to existing fabric: increase of door stops, intumescent strips and paint, fireproof board within panelled walls, etc. In the refurbished and new build areas there are now more occupants than when the buildings were last used as a Theological College, but the strategy has resulted in fewer staircases without compromising safety. The use of large glass screens (Pyrostop) designed to withstand fire for one hour, give a deceptively open and accessible feel to compartmented spaces.

■ **Non-intrusive services**

The steep downward slope of Dean's Mews results in basement spaces to the rear of the site actually being at road level. This justified excavation under the ground floor of the 1930s block to form a delivery bay and plant rooms. Radiators running off gas boilers heat office and administrative spaces. From roof plant, tempered, ducted air systems feed low velocity air into the larger specialised spaces. The floor mounted displacement units have a large surface area to minimise air-flow noise. The listed buildings demanded sympathetic methods of incorporating modern services. Radiators are indistinguishable from wall panels below dado rails, control valves are set behind hinged panels in skirtings, fan convectors are floor mounted under brass grilles and any conditioning plant is encased in furniture designed to be contemporary with the late eighteenth-century interiors. The numerous flues and chimneys are utilised where possible for ducting and mechanical ventilation. Distribution of wiring for power, IT and AV is achieved through raised floors in the new-build block, raised and existing floor voids in the refurbished block, and existing floor and ceiling voids in the listed buildings. The listed building installation took ingenuity to deliver the level of power and IT demanded in a non-intrusive manner. Considerable design effort was directed at floor boxes and concealed, but accessible, vertical service runs in alcoves alongside chimney breasts.

■ **Fast track**

A Management Contract route was chosen to gain the advantages of early input from the contractor together with a staged sequence of elemental package contract tenders. The earliest possible start could then be made on-site with the demolition and enabling works. The high number of package contracts – 30 in all – reflected the distinctions between, for example, utility joinery, specialist joinery in the listed buildings, and shopfitting. The sequencing of trades within the restoration works as opposed to the refurbishment and new-build works, also justified separate packages for certain trades.

■ Facilities management

Working with the Client's Facilities Manager through the design process enabled a tight 'fit' to user requirements. High screens between work spaces for staff unfamiliar with open plan were reduced or removed within the first year as working practices changed. A maintenance manual remains to communicate both the design intentions and detailed decisions taken by the team, to the current and subsequent facilities managers. Also, see 9.3.

Also see colour plates 8 a and b.

CHAPTER 13

Application

The concept of re-use can be re-applied again and again. If the original concept is clear, displaying the value of the original and the elements introduced for conversion, and the interpretation and management of the building has maintained an understanding of the concept then, when a new use is required, the building can be re-evaluated and the process completed. Once building stock is understood to be a re-useable resource with creative potential, rather than a consumer product with inevitable obsolescence, many of our buildings, or at least elements of them, may remain to add to the cultural value of many future generations.

The concept is timeless, outliving fashions and particularly styles. It is available for reinterpretation generation by generation. As current new buildings get older, most will become available for re-use, increasing the available stock every decade.

This process will stabilise our townscape and city structure, directing investment towards the improvement of what exists. More money can be spent on less, and more time taken to considering detail with a clearer perception of the end result. Wholesale renewal and replacement can stretch budgets so that only large areas of repetitive elements void of variety or even quality are afforded. Reinvestment in fabric that already has value is likely to achieve more overall value than clearance and new investment.

There will always be exceptions – buildings so poorly constructed they become a liability, or so badly conceived that they are unusable. However, we must avoid preconceptions in this regard. Many 1960s tower blocks thought to be beyond redemption are now being successfully rehabilitated with weatherproofing and insulation improved by new cladding, and upgraded common areas proactively managed and secured by a concierge system. They now form the flagships for the renewal of their areas, with appropriate tenants enjoying the open prospects they provide.

There may be circumstances where high quality new buildings, constructed for a specific client for a specialised purpose, may have advantages over re-use because no existing structure can accommodate the scale and location required (e.g. large trading floors for the stock exchange – though Billingsgate Market proved one exception to this – and perhaps Spitalfields could have proved another). Yet even before these buildings have accumulated their first patina of age, further changes in technology herald their demise. However, most uses with average funding can be economically accommodated within the existing fabric of city, town or village.

The process of creative re-use must be seen as one element of a healthy, balanced, thriving community. It needs to be a continuing process with each building (or group of buildings) responding to the particular needs of each user. In this way each building will have its own cycle of re-use, dependent upon its location, use, economic climate, structure, servicing and the creativity of its original conversion. A healthy community is represented by buildings in differing stages of this cycle. An unstable community will have all the buildings in the same area being in the same cycle as was the case with large areas of council-owned housing stock. In the inner city this often replaced earlier large-scale construction of housing for company workers reliant upon an identical investment cycle.

The advantages of fragmented ownership and differing investment cycles can now be seen following the introduction of General Improvement Areas and Gradual Renewal in Victorian terrace housing, and private house ownership in two storey council housing estates. The investment decisions of each individual reinvigorate and uplift the adjacent properties, thereby encouraging them to reinvest. This series of individual decisions, provides a continual backcloth of investment maintaining not just a vibrant appearance but a small scale local economy of renewal. This example can be compared to a healthy High Street where at least one shop front is changing at any point in time, or a healthy industrial estate where individual businesses grow or decline, then move allowing another to take their place. Where such reinvestment is not apparent, whether residential or business or both, it may indicate ill health.

The extreme condition of ill health may be represented by a ruin (see 1–3 Greenhill, Wirksworth, 8.4). In such cases re-use may be out of the question due to particular factors such as: the length of time it has been a ruin, the extent of remaining structure, condition, location, historic importance, etc. A table for evaluating ruins is set out in Chapter 16.

Less extreme is a derelict building – still mostly intact but partially open to the elements, and at risk of vandalism. With much of its inherent value lost it may be considered a liability, and dramatic intervention may be necessary to realise the value that remains. To a certain extent the better the condition of the building, the less the intervention is needed, and possibly, the more restricted the apparent range of uses.

A diagrammatic analysis of the cyclical nature of re-use is illustrated in Figure 13.1. This indicates the value of periodical reinvestment. It illustrates how designing or converting a building without considering its future capacity for re-use can end up requiring greater investment. Of course this diagram illustrates a cycle led by the normal obsolescence and deterioration of building elements rather than user requirements. A user's requirements may change at any stage due to economic forces or other circumstances outwith the building's natural investment cycle; its residual value will depend on how much change is necessary. Yet anyone buying a building in good condition may still alter it to suit their own requirements. The key is that investment is being made into their own requirements, not into recovering value lost by lack of past investment. If extensive alterations are needed it may prove more viable for an owner to sell their current building and invest in another at a different stage in its cycle. If a whole commercial sector undergoes operational change, it may be necessary to sell the building onto another sector (e.g. the purpose-built Times printworks at Wapping now converted to a Leisure Centre).

Such cyclical changes of use are not new. Witness numerous examples in this book that illustrate past conversion cycles, e.g. multi-storey mills and warehouses to offices or flats, or churches to community centres, offices or housing. Current examples include banks to public houses and older, smaller in-town supermarkets to night-clubs. Empty properties over shops in town and district centres are still a wasted asset, despite government LOTS (living over the shop) schemes and grant incentives, that represent a continuing challenge for creative re-use.

If the trend for removing cars from city centres in favour of public transport continues then future examples might include car parks to housing and in-town petrol stations to taxi or bus depots. One thing is certain, changes in society and its lifestyle will continue to require the creative re-use of buildings ancient and modern.

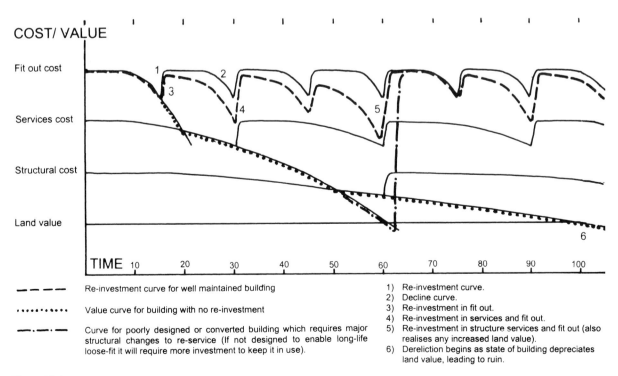

— — — — Re-investment curve for well maintained building	1) Re-investment curve.
	2) Decline curve.
• • • • • • • • • • Value curve for building with no re-investment	3) Re-investment in fit out.
	4) Re-investment in services and fit out.
— · — · — Curve for poorly designed or converted building which requires major structural changes to re-service (If not designed to enable long-life loose-fit it will require more investment to keep it in use).	5) Re-investment in structure services and fit out (also realises any increased land value).
	6) Dereliction begins as state of building depreciates land value, leading to ruin.

Figure 13.1

Creative re-use is to be encouraged; combining innovation with tradition it can truly represent a balanced civilised society at peace with its past, present and future. There is a growing awareness that evolution is more productive than revolution; it is better to retain what is good rather than destroy the lot and start again afresh. Hence the principles set out for the creative re-use of buildings can also be applied to whole areas in the urban design of our cities.

Appendix

■ PRINCIPLES FOR RE-USE REFERRED TO IN THIS BOOK

- Identify solutions that work 'with' the building and not 'against' it.
- Think laterally about the uses to which the building is to be put.
- Treat the elements of a building that need to be conserved as 'long-life' elements.
- Use sympathetic material where new additions are to be made, either as an extension of past techniques, or in contrast to them (dependent upon the nature of the brief, context, setting, etc.).
- Use techniques of repair rather than restoration (and instruct the minimum rather than the maximum repair work necessary).
- Ensure that restoration, when it appears appropriate, is thoroughly researched and subject to the agreement of a second opinion before work proceeds.
- Maintain proven techniques, natural materials and traditional craftsmanship, in preference to 'hi-tech' solutions.
- Adopt modern technology as a hidden means to preserve fabric in-situ, where traditional methods would (might) be destructive.
- Leave work apparently just in good repair rather than newly repaired (or restored).
- The quality of the final product is determined by the choice of procurement route, the time devoted to detail design and the preparation of good contract documents.
- Consider the scope for interpretation of the building by the public and the user using the most innovative and appealing means.
- Balance the demands of the user, and/or public access, with the maintenance requirements of the property.

Further Reading

Ashurst, J. & N., *Practical Building Conservation*, English Heritage Technical Handbook, Gower Press, Aldershot, 1988.

Ashurst, N., *Cleaning Historic Buildings, Volume One, Substrates, Soiling and Investigation*, Donhead, 1994.

Binney, M., *Chatham Historic Dockyard: Alive or Mothballed*, SAVE Britain's Heritage, London, 1984.

Binney, M. and Martin, K., *The Country House: To Be or Not To Be*, SAVE Britain's Heritage, London, 1982.

Cantacuzino, S., and Brandt, S., *Saving Old Buildings*, Architectural Press, London, 1980.

Cantacuzino, S., *New Uses for Old Buildings*, Architectural Press, London, 1975.

Cantacuzino, S., *Re/Architecture: Old Buildings/New Uses*, Thames and Hudson, London, 1989.

Cantacuzino, S., *Old Buildings, New Uses*, Thames and Hudson, Spain, 1990.

Circular 8/87 *Historic Buildings and Conservation Areas*, Policy and Procedures, DoE.

Cunnington, P., *Change of Use: The Conversion of Old Buildings*, Alpha Books (A & C Black), London, 1988.

Darley, G., *A Future for Farm Buildings*, SAVE Britain's Heritage, London 1988.

Day, C., *Place of the Soul: Architecture and Environmental Design as a Healing Art*, Aquarian Press.

DoE, *New Life for Historic Places*, HMSO, London, 1972.

Feilden, B. M., *Conservation of Historic Buildings*, Butterworth's Scientific, London, 1994 Revised Edition.

Foster, L., *Access to the Historic Environment, Meeting the Needs of Disabled People*, Donhead, 1997.

Historic Farm Building Group; *Old Farm Buildings in a New Countryside: Redundancy, Conversion and Conservation*, Pamphlet, Reading, 1991.

HMSO, *New Users for Older Buildings in Scotland – A Manual of Practical Encouragement*, Edinburgh, 1981.

Irsall, D. W., *The Care of Old Buildings Today – A Practical Guide*, Architectural Press/SPAB, London, 1972.

James, N., *The Conversion of Agricultural Buildings: An Analysis of Variable Pressures*, Department of Agricultural Economics, Newcastle upon Tyne, 1992.

Johnson, A., *Converting Old Buildings*, David and Charles, London, 1988.

Markus, T. A., *Building Conservation and Rehabilitation*, Butterworth, London, 1979.

Markus, T. A., *Old Buildings – New Opportunities: A Guide to the Possibilities of Converting*, second edition, COSIRA, Salisbury, 1988.

Morris, W., *Manifesto* for SPAB, 37 Spital Square, London E1 6DY.

O'Farrell, F., *Farm House Conversion: A Handbook on Renovating the Farm Home*, Dublin, 1977.

Pearce, D., *Conservation Today*, Routledge, London, 1989.

Pearson, G., *Conservation of Clay and Chalk Buildings*, Donhead, 1992.

Powell, K. and de la Hay, C., *Churches: A Question of Conversion*, SAVE Britain's Heritage, London, 1987.

Powell, K., *Architecture Reborn – The Conversion and Reconstruction of Old Buildings*, Laurence King Publishing, London, 1999.

Richards, Sir J. M., *An Introduction to Modern Architecture*, London, Baltimore, 1953.

Rose, V., *Catalytic Conversion: REVIVE Historic Buildings to Regenerate Communities*, SAVE, AHF, IHBC, and UKABPT, London, 1998.

Scottish Civic Trust, *New Uses for Old Buildings in Scotland*, HMSO, Edinburgh, 1981.

Strike, J., *Architecture in Conservation – Managing Development at Historic Sites*, Routledge, London, 1994.

Talbot, M., *Reviving Old Buildings and Communities*, David and Charles, Newton Abbot, 1986.

Wines, J., *De Architecture*, Rizzoli International Publications Inc., 1987.

Index